ERIK DORN

CHICAGO IN FICTION
SAUL BELLOW
ADVISORY EDITOR

ERIK DORN

A NOVEL BY BEN HECHT

Introduction by NELSON ALGREN

THE UNIVERSITY OF CHICAGO PRESS
CHICAGO AND LONDON

ERIK DORN
was first published in 1921 by G. P. Putnam's Sons, New York

THE UNIVERSITY OF CHICAGO PRESS, CHICAGO & LONDON
The University of Toronto Press, Toronto 5, Canada

Introduction © *1963 by The University of Chicago. Erik Dorn © 1921 by Ben Hecht;* © *renewed 1949 by Ben Hecht. All rights reserved. Published 1963. Printed in the United States of America.*

To Marie

ERIK DORN

A THOUSAND AND ONE AFTERNOONS IN NADA

"We don't even know what living means now, what it is and what it is called," one of Dostoevski's isolated pellets of humanity warns us. "Leave us alone without books and we shall be lost and in confusion at once. We shall not know what to join onto, what to cling to, what to love and what to hate, what to respect and what to despise. We are oppressed at being men—men with a real individual body and blood, we are ashamed of it, we think it a disgrace and try to contrive some sort of an impossible generalized man. We are stillborn and for generations past have been begotten, not by living fathers, and that suits us better and better. We are developing a taste for it. Soon we shall contrive to be born from an idea."

So Hemingway's Hollow Man, a Spanish waiter trying to reassure himself as he closes a café in Madrid for the night, is foreshadowed:

"You do not want music. Certainly you do not want music. Nor can you stand before a bar with dignity although that is all that is provided for these hours. What did he fear? It was not fear or dread. It was a nothing that he knew too well. It was all a nothing and a man was nothing too. It was only that and light was all it needed and a certain cleanness and order. Some lived in it and never felt it but he knew it was nada y pues nada y nada y pues nada. Our nada who art in nada, nada be thy name thy kingdom nada thy will be nada in nada as it is in nada. Give us this nada our daily nada and nada us our nada as we nada our nadas and nada us not into nada but deliver us from nada; pues nada. Hail nothing full of nothing, nothing is with thee. He smiled and stood before a bar with a shining steam pressure coffee machine.

" 'What's yours?' asked the barman.

" 'Nada.' "

Erik Dorn is a man who seems, to himself, to be a perfect translation of his country and his day: one who has lived since boyhood in a changeless vacuum waiting for something to happen, a contact to overtake him or reality to seize him. But nothing has happened at all.

"What the hell am I talking about?" he finally asks himself at thirty: "I'm like men will all be years later, when their emotions are finally absorbed by the ingenious surfaces they've surrounded themselves with, and life lies forever buried behind the inventions of engineers, scientists, and businessmen. This business of being empty is all there is to life."

Could it be that somebody is kidding us? Could it be that Dorn's changeless vacuum is only a hideout from the winds of passion? Could it be that his claim to emptiness is a boasting made of fear?

What did Dorn fear? It was not fear or dread.

". . . the elastic distortion of crowds winding and unwinding under the tumult of windows gave him the feeling of a geometrical emptiness. . . . No drawn picture stirred him to the extent that did the tapestry of a city street. No music aroused the elation in him that did the curious beat upon his eyes of window rows, of vari-shaped building walls whose oblongs and squares translated themselves in his thought into a species of unmelodious but perfect sound. . . ." Dorn had achieved almost complete indifference to literature and especially toward painting.

" 'Nothing' was a word his thought tripped on. He was used to mumbling it to himself as he walked alone in the streets. And at his desk it often came to him and repeated itself . . . his thought murmured 'nothing, nothing,' and a sadness drew itself into his heart."

Yet excepting Charles Louis-Philippe, in *Bubu de Montparnasse*, no other writer of modern times has caught the beat of a great city with such simplicity:

"In the evening when women stand washing dishes in the kitchens of the city, men light their tobacco and open newspapers. Later, the women gather up the crumpled sheets and read. . . . Tick, say the words and tock say the juries. Tick-tock, the cell door and the scaffold drop. Streets and windows, paintings of the Virgin Mary, beds of the fifty-cent prostitutes, cannon at Verdun and police whistles on crossings; the Pope in Rome, the President in Washington, the man hunting the alleys for a handout, the langorous women breeding in ornamental beds—all say a tick-tock."

As in no other American novel is the relationship between the book's hero and the novelist revealed so lucidly.

For as Erik Dorn had once held an appreciation of all things in life and art "which filled him with the emotion of symmetry" and had seen streets and crowds "pleasantly blurred and in motion," yet now saw all things as "an arrested cinematograph; grotesquely detailed and with the meaning of motion out of it," so everyone who has witnessed those scenarios revealing life as an arrested film, under Hecht's name, may perceive the relationship readily. *Erik Dorn* is a demonstration of this relationship.

For no American yet has written a novel this good yet this bad. This is the one work of serious literature we have that by the same token stands as a literary hoax. *Erik Dorn* is so true that nobody but his creator could have made him so spurious. No other writer has written a novel anything like it—and yet it resembles many novels.

This underground American whose nature is a shallows, who claims that in himself life does not live, that life is something he would like to experience but cannot because he has contrived to be born from an idea, this hybrid of Hecht and Dorn, walks smiling through the aimless din and multiplicity of crowds, "oblivious of the lesser destinations" of faces, pleased to dream of his life and the lives of others as a mere bobbing of heads and a movement of legs. Yet, when "a glow of excitement brightens the dusk" of Rachel Laskin's face, it does not seem to Dorn that this face is one with a lesser destination at all. Indeed, we begin to perceive here that Dorn is passionate and romantic, a man who has merely assumed the posture of aloofness toward the world in order not to be bruised by it. It is not, indeed, so much that no contact has overtaken him but that he is in hiding from any such contact.

" 'You remind me,' " he assures Rachel lightly, " 'of a nymph among dowagers and frightened to death. There's really nothing to be frightened of, unless you prefer fear to other more tangible emotions.' "

" 'I know,' " Rachel replies, " 'you talk because you have nothing to say. And I like to listen to you because I understand.'

" 'I speak out of a most complete emptiness of emotion or idea' "—Dorn is still boasting— " 'and my words seem to take body in your silence—and actually give me a character.'

" 'I always think of you as someone hiding from himself,' " the girl cuts in more closely than she knows.

" 'There's no place of concealment in me,' " Dorn assures her, " 'but perhaps I hide in others.' "

Now we begin to see that Dorn's insistence upon the nothingness of everything is actually a fear that death is real: that he is not in a changeless vacuum, but is crouching behind some obstacle.

What is this curious obstacle equally dividing Dostoevski's underground man and Erik Dorn from the world? Again it is Hemingway who provides a clue:

> *It was a frightfully hot day. We'd jammed an absolutely perfect barricade across the bridge. It was simply priceless. A big old wrought-iron grating from the front of a house. Too heavy to lift and you could shoot through it and they would have to climb over it. It was absolutely topping. They tried to get over it, and we*

potted them from forty yards. They rushed it, and officers came out alone and worked on it. It was an absolutely perfect obstacle.*

And explains why Hecht's people come alive only when he looks at the city through *their* eyes. Back in her room after a long walk with Dorn, Rachel becomes both vivid and veiled:

"Beyond the scratch of houses and the slant of home lights she watched the darkness lift against the sky. The city had dwindled into a huddle of streets. Noise had become silence. The great crowds were packed away in little rooms. Sitting before the window, unconscious of herself, she laughed softly. Her black hair felt tight and heavy. She shook her head till its loose coils dropped across her cheeks. She had felt confused when she entered the room, as if she had grown strange to herself.

" 'Who am I?' she whispered suddenly. . . . She stood up quickly and turned on a light. Her dexterous hands twisted her hair back into loose coils on her head. Strange, she did not know herself. . . . Loneliness caressed her heart and drew dim fingers across her thought."

Yet it is with a woman whose intimacy with Dorn had left her, after seven years of marriage, "hollowed out as by some tenaciously devouring insect" that the novel is more immediately concerned. For to Anna nothing was either good or bad any longer. Her mind had borrowed from her heart and become wholly occupied with her love for Dorn. More than lover and more than husband,

* *In Our Time,* by Ernest Hemingway.

he had become an obsession that had replaced the world for her.

And her smile shone upon him in a strangely Hebraic light. "Like the light cast by lilies and candles from a sad, quiet altar."

Yet the man Anna's smile shines so sadly upon, himself has no smile for the world. Even as Dorn seems foreshadowed by Dostoevski, so does Dorn adumbrate those organization men of nihilism, the beatniks. For, like them, he keeps protesting so much that there is nothing square about *him*, we at last get suspicious.

Our suspicion deepens when Hecht presents us with the first, and really fine, portrait of The All-American Square. (Some years before Mencken devised the inclusive term *Booboisie*.) For though George Hazlitt is diametrically opposed, as a man, to Dorn, yet at moments they seem to be opposites of the same personality:

"In the tick-tock of life Hazlitt saw a perfection—the hanging of a man for the crime of murder was a reward paid to Hazlitt for his abstinence from bloodshed. The jailing of a seducer offered a tangible recompense for the self-denial which he, as a non-seducer, practiced.

"The punishment of lawbreakers vindicated his own virtue. But his rage against dreamers was such that their punishing offered him no sense of satisfactory vindication . . . left him with no fine feeling of the victorious sufficiency of himself.

" 'Yes, I'm a reactionary,' he would say, 'I'm for the good old things of life. Things that mean something.' And even this definition of faith would leave him unsatisfied.

"For the paradox of Hazlitt was not that he was a thinker, but a dreamer. His puritanism had put an end to his brain. He had bartered his intelligence for a thing he proudly called Americanism, and thought for him had become a placid agitation of platitudes. . . . His emotions avenged his stupidity."

And no one but Ben Hecht could have juxtaposed two men as distinct as Dorn and Hazlitt, two women as distinct as Rachel and Anna, from these four creating a first act so captivating in its fidelity that nobody but Ben Hecht could rewrite all four during intermission; so that all that has been so tightly wound becomes so loosely raveled:

"'Anna, for God's sake, Anna, hate me,'" the man, of whose invulnerability to passion we have just been convinced, cries out—"'hate me. Loathe me the rest of your life. I've lied and lied to you—nothing but lies. . . . No, that's not true. But now it is. Think of me as vile when I go away. . . . Otherwise . . . I'll die thinking of you. Don't look at me that way. Yell at me. . . . You've known it. I can't help it.' . . .

"Tears blubbered out of him."

Indeed, in his relationships to women, Dorn begins to come on more as we would have expected Hazlitt to act. In a meeting with a Negro prostitute, Dorn carries on in a passage so overwritten that one feels he is overwhelmed by fear of the woman.

"'She's not a woman,'" he assures his friend Lockwood. "'She's a lust. No brain. No heart. A stark unhuman piece of flesh with a shark's hunger inside it.'"

Erik Dorn

Yet all the woman is doing is sitting waiting to see if she can make five dollars.

" 'You remember the thing in Rabelais about women —insatiable, devouring, hungering in their satieties,' " Dorn goes on. " 'The prowling animal. Well, here it is. Alive. Not in print. She's alive with something deeper than life. Wheels of flesh grinding her blood into a hunger for ecstasies. She's a mate for me. Come on, little one.' "

Yet all the woman is alive with is something deeper than print: Dorn really has slipped into Hazlitt's clothes during intermission.

This deterioration of a naturalistic novel into a Grade B scenario is concluded by Hazlitt intent upon revenge:

"Hazlitt stood breathing heavily. This was Erik Dorn —the man who had had Rachel. Wine swept a flame through his thought. God! this was the man. She was gone, but this was the man. Shoot him down like a dog! Shoot him down! Kill the grin of him. He'd pay. He'd killed something. Shoot him down! There was a gun under his coat—army revolver. Better than shooting Germans. This was the man.

" 'You're going to pay for it,' he spoke, 'Go on, say something.'

"Dorn's rage hesitated. A mistake. What the devil was up?

" 'Oh, you've forgotten her,' Hazlitt whispered. Shoot him! Voices inside demanded wildly that he shoot. Not talk, but kill.

" 'Rachel,' he cried suddenly. His eyes stopped seeing.

"Dorn jumped for the gun that had appeared and

Erik Dorn xv

caught his arm in time. Rachel—then this was something about Rachel?"

It's something about Rachel all right, but mostly it's something about Ben Hecht. For *Erik Dorn* is not one of those works of a many-splendored beginning whose creator simply runs out of splendor. Hecht was a young man full of gas and brass making his first big try, a west side boy on his way up whose warmth and wit were fascinating an older hand who had already arrived: Sherwood Anderson appears as Dorn's friend Lockwood.

" 'If I only had this man's simplicity,' " Dorn sighs. " 'If on top of my ability to unravel mysteries into words I could feel those mysteries as he does, I might do something.' "

What Anderson was feeling at the time was that he'd been sleeping with the Bitch Goddess too long—

> ... thinking of money and success as a bitch, and my fellow Americans having gotten wind of her long since, they trotting at her heels, that peculiar look in the eyes, the look of humiliation not real, pride not real, hope not real. . . . The Bitch was trotting the South now. She had long since invaded my own Middle West, turning men from the cornfields and the forests to the factories and the factory towns.

And can it be, Anderson pressed his questioning of his country farther, "that the instinct, on the part of our industrial leaders, to draw away from towns and cities, to set up separate towns, unincorporated, to build high steel fences about the mills, is an unconscious part of a program to make mill workers beings quite separate from the rest of American life?"

That was it, and that is what happened: except that the high fences were not always of steel, and what they ultimately inclosed was not only the mill towns, but the office buildings of the great cities as well. So that we came at last to the time foreshadowed by Dostoevski's isolated Russian who feels he had not been born, but contrived.

We came to a time adumbrated by Hecht's isolated American, even now haunting Erik Dorn's old haunts wearing a tin key with a rabbit's ears engraved upon it to symbolize his status as a Playboy, officially.

Poor Dorn. He had the hundred dollars to purchase the key—but there was no key club then at which he could, for that sum, purchase a personality to replace his emptiness.

For it wasn't splendor that was lacking in Hecht, it wasn't gas he ran out of, and it surely wasn't brass. It was belief. For he came, too young, to a time when, like Dorn, he had to ask himself, "What the hell am I talking about?"

And heard no answer at all.

"What is literature?" Jean-Paul Sartre once inquired. One might reply—"*Erik Dorn*."

And if someone then asked—"What is *not* literature?" the answer might also be—"*Erik Dorn*."

For the value that is derived from the novel today is not within the novel itself, but from the curiously prophetic shadow that a book, written half a century ago, now casts across our own strange times.

NELSON ALGREN

Contents

PART ONE	*SLEEP*	PAGE 1
PART TWO	*DREAM*	PAGE 75
PART THREE	*WINGS*	PAGE 173
PART FOUR	*ADVENTURE*	PAGE 277
PART FIVE	*SILENCE*	PAGE 369

PART ONE

SLEEP

Chapter One

AN old man sat in the shadows of the summer night. From a veranda chair he looked at the stars. He wore a white beard, and his eyes, grown small with age, watered continually as if he were weeping. Half-hidden under his beard his emaciated lips kept the monotonous grimace of a smile on his face.

He sat in the dark, a patient, trembling figure waiting for bedtime. His feet, though he rested them all day, grew heavy at night. Of late this weariness had increased. It reached like a caress into his mind. Thoughts no longer formed themselves in the silences of his hours. Instead, a gentle sleep, dreamless and dark, came upon him and left him sitting with his little eyes, open and moist, fastened without sight upon familiar objects.

As he sat, the withered body of this old man seemed to grow always more motionless, except for his hands. Resting on his thighs, his twig-like hands remained forever awake, their thin contorted fingers crawling vaguely about like the legs of 8 long-impaled spiders.

The sound of a piano from the room behind him dropped into the old man's sleep, and he found himself once more looking out of his eyes and occupying his clothes. His attitude remained unchanged except for a quickened movement of his fingers. Life returned to him as gently as it had left. The stars were still high over his head and the night, cool and murmuring, waited for him.

He lowered his eyes toward the street beyond the lawn. People were straying by, seeming to drift under the dark trees. He could not see them distinctly, but he stared at their flowing outlines and at moments was rewarded by a glimpse of a face—a featureless little glint of white in the shadows: dark shadows moving within a motionless darkness with little dying candle-flame faces. "Men and women," he thought, "men and women, mixed up in the night . . . mixed up."

As he stared, thoughts as dim and fluid as the people in the street moved in his head. But he remembered things best not in words. His memories were little warmths that dropped into his heart. His cold thin fingers continued their fluttering. "Mixed up, mixed up," said the night. "Dark," said the shadows. And the years spoke their memories. "We have been; we are no more." Memories that had lost the bloom of words. The emaciated lips of the old man held a smile beneath the white beard.

This was Isaac Dorn, still alive after eighty years.

The music from the house ended and a woman's voice called through an open window.

Erik Dorn

"I'm afraid it's chilly outside, father."

He offered no answer. Then he heard Erik, his son, speak in an amused voice.

"Leave the old man be. He's making love to the stars."

"I'll get him a blanket," said Erik's wife. "I can't bear to think of him catching cold."

Isaac Dorn arose from his chair, shaking his head. He did not fancy being covered with a blanket and feeling Anna's kindly hands tucking its edges around his feet. They were too kindly, too solicitous. Their little pats and caressings presumed too much. One grew sad under their ministrations and murmured to oneself, "Poor child, poor child." Better a half-hour under the cold, amused eyes of his son, Erik. There was something between Erik and him, something like an unspoken argument. To Anna he was a pathetic little old man to be nursed, coddled, defended against chills and indigestions, "poor child, poor child." But Erik looked at him with cold, amused eyes that offered no quarter to age and asked for nothing. Good Erik, who asked for nothing, whose eyes smiled because they were too polite to sneer. Erik knew about the stars and the mixed-up things, the dim things old senses could feel in the night though he chose to laugh at them.

But one thing Erik didn't know, and the old man, turning from his chair, grew sad. What was that? What? His thought mumbled a question. Sitting motionless in a corner of the room he could smile at Erik and his smile under the white beard seemed to give an answer to the mumble—an answer that irritated his son. The answer said, "Wait, wait! it is too early for you to say you have lived." What a son, what a son! whose eyes made fun of his father's white hair.

The old man moved slowly as if his infirmities were no more than meditations, and entered the house.

Chapter Two

THE crowds moving through the streets gave Erik Dorn a picture. It was morning. Above the heads of the people the great spatula-topped buildings spread a zigzag of windows, a scribble of rooftops against the sky. A din as monotonous as a silence tumbled through the streets—an unvarying noise of which the towering rectangles of buildings tilted like great reeds out of a narrow bowl, seemed an audible part.

The city alive with signs, smoke, posters, windows; falling, rising, flinging its chimneys and its streets against the sun, wound itself up into crowds and burst with an endless bang under the far-away sky.

Moving toward his office Erik Dorn watched the swarming of men and women of which he was a part. Faces like a flight of paper scraps scattered about him. Bodies poured suddenly across his eyes as if emptied out of funnels. The ornamental entrances of buildings pumped figures in and out. Vague and blurred like the play of gusty rain, the crowds darkened the pavements.

Dorn saluted the spectacle with smiling eyes. As always, in the aimless din and multiplicity of streets he felt himself most securely at home. The smear of gestures, the elastic distortion of crowds winding and unwinding under the tumult of windows, gave him the feeling of a geometrical emptiness of life.

Here before him the meanings of faces vanished. The greedy little purposes of men and women tangled themselves into a generality. It was thus Dorn was most pleased to look upon the world, to observe it as one observes a pattern—involved but precise. Life as a whole lay in the streets—a little human procession that came toiling out of a yesterday into an interminable to-morrow. It presented itself to him as a picture—legs moving against the walls of buildings, diagonals of bodies, syncopating face lines.

Things that made pictures for his eyes alone diverted Dorn. Beyond this capacity for diversion he remained untouched. He walked smiling into crowds, oblivious of the lesser destinations of faces, pleased to dream of his life and the life of others as a movement of legs, a bobbing of heads.

His appreciation of crowds was typical. In the same manner he held an appreciation of all things in life and art which filled him with the emotion of symmetry. He had given himself freely to his tastes. A creed had resulted. Rhythm that was intricate pleased him more than the metronomic. In art, the latter was predominant. In life, the former. Out of these decisions he achieved almost a complete indifference to literature and especially toward painting. No drawn picture stirred him to the extent that did the tapestry of a city street. No music aroused the elation in him that did the curious beat upon his eyes of window rows, of vari-shaped building walls whose oblongs and squares translated themselves in his thought into a species of unmelodious but perfect sound.

The preoccupation with form had developed in him as complement of his nature. The nature of Erik Dorn was a shallows. Life did not live in him. He saw it as something eternally outside. To himself he seemed at times a perfect translation of his country and his day.

"I'm like men will all be years later," he said to his wife, "when their emotions are finally absorbed by the ingenious surfaces they've surrounded themselves with, and life lies forever buried behind the inventions of engineers, scientists, and business men."

Normal outwardly, a shrewd editor and journalist, functioning daily in his home and work as a cleverly conventional figure, Dorn had lived since boyhood in an unchanging vacuum. He had in his early youth become aware of himself. As a young man he had waited half consciously for something to happen to him. He thought of this something as a species of contact that would suddenly overtake him. He would step into the street and find himself a citizen absorbed by responsibilities, ideas, sympathies, prejudices. But the thing had never happened. At thirty he had explained to himself, "I am complete. This business of being empty is all there is to life. Intelligence is a faculty which enables man to peer through the muddle of ideas and arrive at a nowhere."

Private introspection had become a bore to him. What was the use of thinking if there was nothing to think about? And there was nothing. His violences of temper, his emotions, definite and at times compelling, had always seemed to him as words—pretences to which he loaned himself for diversion. He was aware that neither ideas nor prejudices—the residues of emotion—existed in his mind. His thinking, he knew, had been a shuffle of words which he followed to fantastic and inconsistent conclusions that left him always without convictions for the morrow.

There was a picture in the street for him on this summer morning. He was a part of it. Yet between himself and the rest of the picture he felt no contact.

Into this emptiness of spirit, life had poured its excitements as into a thing bottomless as a mirror. He gave it back an image of words. He was proud of his words. They were his experiences and sophistications. Out of them he achieved his keenest diversion. They were the excuse for his walking, his wearing a hat and embarking daily for his work, returning daily to his home. They enabled him to amuse himself with complexities of thought as one improvising difficult finger exercises on the piano.

At times it seemed to Dorn that he was

even incapable of thinking, that he possessed a plastic vocabulary endowed with a life of its own. He often contemplated with astonishment his own verbal brilliancies, which his friends appeared to accept as irrefutable truths of the moment. Carried away in the heat of some intricate debate he would pause internally, as his voice continued without interruption, and exclaim to himself, "What in hell am I talking about?" And a momentary awe would overcome him—the awe of listening to himself give utterance to fantastic ideas that he knew had no existence in him—a cynical magician watching a white rabbit he had never seen before crawl naively out of his own sleeve. Thus his phrases assembled themselves on his tongue and pirouetted of their own energy about his listeners.

Smiling, garrulous, and impenetrable—garrulous even in his silences, he daily entered his office and proceeded skillfully about his work. He was, as always, delighted with himself. He felt himself a man ideally fitted to enjoy the little spectacle of life his day offered. Emotion in others invariably roused in him a sense of the ludicrous. His eyes seemed to travel through the griefs and torments of his fellows and to fasten helplessly upon their causes. And here lay the ludicrous—the clownish little mainspring of tragedy and drama. He moved through his day with a vivid understanding of its excitements. There was no mystery. One had only to look and see and words fitted themselves. A pattern twisted itself into precisions—precisions of men loving, hating, questing. The understanding swayed him between pity and contempt and left the balance of an amused smile in his eyes.

Intimacy with Erik Dorn had meant different things to different people, but all had derived from his friendship a fascinated feeling of loss. His wife, closest to him, had after seven years found herself drained, hollowed out as by some tenaciously devouring insect. Her mind had emptied itself of its normal furniture. Erik had eaten the ideas out of it. Under the continual impact of his irony her faiths and understandings had slowly deserted her. Her thought had become a shadow cast by his emptiness. Things were no longer good, no longer bad. People had become somehow nonexistent for her since she could no longer think of them as symbols incarnate of ideas that she liked or ideas that she disliked. Thus emptied of its natural furniture, her mind had borrowed from her heart and become filled, wholly occupied with the emotion of her love for Erik Dorn. More than lover and husband, he was an obsession. He had replaced a world for her.

It was of his wife that Dorn was thinking when he arrived this summer morning at his desk in the editorial room. He had remembered suddenly that the day was the anniversary of their marriage. Time had passed rapidly. Seven years! Like seven yesterdays. He seemed able to remember them in their entirety with a single thought, as one can remember a column of figures without recalling either their meaning or their sum.

Chapter Three

THE employees of the editorial room—a loft-like chamber crazily crowded with desks, tables, cabinets, benches, files, typewriters; lighted by a smoke-darkened sun and the dim glow of electric bulbs—were already launched upon the nervous routine of their day. An excited jargon filled the place which, with the air of physical disorder as if the workers were haphazardly improvising their activities, gave the room a vivid though seemingly impermanent life.

On the benches against a peeling wall sleepy-faced boys with precocious eyes kept up a lazy hair-pulling, surreptitious wrestling bout. They rose indifferently in response to furiously repeated bellows for their assistance—a business of carrying typewritten bits of paper between desks a few feet apart; or of sauntering with eleventh-hour orders to the perspiring men in the composing room.

In the forward part of the shop a cluster of men stood about the desk of an editor who in a disinterested voice sat issuing assignments for the day, forecasting to his innumerable assistants the amount of space needed for succeeding editions, the possible development in the local scandals. His eye unconsciously watched the clock over his head, his ear divided itself between a half-dozen conversations and a tireless telephone. With his hands he kept fumbling an assortment of clippings, memoranda, and copy.

Oldish young men and youngish old men gravitated about him, their faces curiously identical. These were the irresponsible-eyed, casual-mannered individuals, seemingly neither at work nor at play, who were to visit the courts, the police, the wrecks, the criminals, conventions, politicians, reformers, lovers, and haters, and bring back the news of the city's day. A common almost racial sophistication stamped their expression. They pawed over telephone books, argued with indifferent, emotionless profanity among themselves on items of amazing import; pounded nonchalantly upon typewriters, lolled with their feet upon desks, their noses buried in the humorous columns of the morning newspapers.

"Make-up" men and their assistants, everlastingly irritable as if the victims of pernicious conspiracies, badgered for information that seemed inevitably nonexistent. They desired to know in what mysterious manner one could get ten columns of type into a page that held only seven and whether anyone thought the paper could go to press at half-past ten when the bulk of the copy for the edition arrived in the composing room at twenty minutes of eleven.

Proof-readers emerged from the bowels of somewhere waving smeared bits of printed paper and triumphantly demanded explanation of ambiguous passages.

Re-write men "helloed" indignantly into telephones, repeating with sudden listlessness the pregnant details of the news pouring in; and scribbling it down on sheets of paper . . . "dead Grant park bullet unknown 26 yrs silk stockings refinement mystery."

Idlers lounged and discussed loudly against the dusty windows hung with torn grimy shades.

Copy-readers, concentrated under green eye-shades, sat isolated in a tiny world of sharpened pencils, paste pots, shears, and emitted sudden embittered oaths.

Editors from other departments, naïvely excited over items of vast indifference to their nervous listeners, came and went.

An occasional printer, face and forearms smeared with ink, sauntered in as if on a vacation, uttering some technical announcement and precipitating a brief panic.

Toward the center of the room, seated at desks jammed against one another in defiance of all convenience, telegraph editors, their hands fumbling cables and despatches from twenty ends of the earth, bellowed items of interest into the air—assassinations in China, probes, quizzes, scandals, accusations in far-away places. They varied their bellows with occasional shrieks of mysterious significance—usually a misplaced paste pot, a borrowed shears, a vanished copy-boy.

These folk and a sprinkling of apparently unemployed and undisturbed strangers spread themselves through the shop. Outside the opened windows in the rear of the room, the elevated trains stuffed with men and women roared into a station and squealed out again. In the streets below, the traffic raised an ear-splitting medley of sound which nobody heard.

Against this eternal and internal disorder, a strange pottering, apparently formless and without beginning or end, was guiding the latest confusions and intrigues of the human tangle into perfunctory groups of words called stories. A curious ritual—the scene, spreading through the four floors of the grimy building with a thousand men and women shrieking, hammering, cursing, writing, squeezing and juggling the monotonous convulsions of life into a scribble of words. Out of the cacophonies of the place issued, sausage fashion, a half-million papers daily, holding up from hour to hour to the city the blurred mirrors of the newspaper columns alive with the almost humorous images of an unending calamity.

"The press," Erik Dorn once remarked, "is a blind old cat yowling on a treadmill."

It was a quarter to nine when Dorn arrived at his desk. He seated himself with a complete unconsciousness of the scene. A litter of correspondence, propaganda, telegrams, and contributions from Constant Reader lay stuffed into the corners and pigeon-holes of his desk. He sat for a moment thinking of his wife. Call her up . . . spend the evening downtown . . . some unusual evidence of affection . . . the vaudeville wouldn't be bad.

The thought left him and his eyes fastened themselves upon a sheaf of proofs. . . . Watch out for libel . . . look for hunches . . . scribble suggestion for changes . . . peer for items of information that might be expanded humorously or pathetically into Human Interest yarns. . . . These were functions he discharged mechanically. A perfect affinity toward his work characterized his attitude. Yet behind the automatic efficiency of his thought lay an ironical appreciation of his tasks. The sterile little chronicles of life still moist from the ink-roller were like smeared windows upon the grimacings of the world. Through these windows Dorn saw with a clarity that flattered him.

A tawdry pantomime was life, a pouring of blood, a grappling with shadows, a digging of graves. "Empty, empty," his intelligence whispered in its depths, "a make-believe of lusts. What else? Nothing, nothing. Laws, ambitions, conventions—froth in an empty glass. Tragedies, comedies—all a swarm of nothings. Dreams in the hearts of men—thin fever outlines to which they clung in hope. Nothing . . . nothing . . ." His intelligence continued a murmur as he read—a murmur unconscious of itself yet coming from the depths of him. Equally unconscious was the amusement he felt, and that flew a fugitive smile in his eyes.

The perfunctory hysterics of the stories of crime, graft, scandal, with their garbled sentences and wooden phrases; the delicious sagacities of the editorial pages like the mumbling of some adenoidal moron in a gulf of high winds; headlines saying a pompous "amen" to asininity and a hopeful "My God!" to confusion—these caressed him, and brought the thought to him, "if there is anything worthy the absurdity of life it's a newspaper—gibbering, whining, strutting, sprawled in attitudes of worship before the nine-and-ninety lies of the moment—a caricature of absurdity itself."

His efficiency aloof from such moralizing moved like a separate consciousness through the day, as it had for the sixteen years of his service. His rise in his profession had been comparatively rapid. Thirty had found him enshrined as an editor. At thirty-four he had acquired the successful air which distinguishes men who have come to the end of their rope. He had become an editor and a fixture. The office observed an intent, gray-eyed man, straight nosed, firm lipped, correctly shaved down to the triangular trim of his mustache, his dark hair evenly parted—a normal-seeming, kindly individual who wore his linen and his features with a certain politely exotic air—the air of an identity.

The day's vacuous items in his life passed

quickly, its frantic routine ebbing into a lull toward mid-afternoon. Returning from a final uproar in the composing room, Dorn looked good-humoredly about him. He was ready to go home. Arguments, reprimands, entreaties were over for a space. He walked leisurely down the length of the shop, pleased as always by its atmosphere. It was something like the streets, this newspaper shop, broken up, a bit intricate, haphazard.

A young man named Cross was painstakingly writing poetry on a typewriter. Another named Gardner was busy on a letter. "My dearest . . ." Dorn read over his shoulder as he passed. Promising young men, both, whose collars would grow slightly soiled as they advanced in their profession. He remembered one of his early observations: "There are two kinds of newspapermen—those who try to write poetry and those who try to drink themselves to death. Fortunately for the world, only one of them succeeds."

In a corner a young woman, dressed with a certain ease, sat partially absorbed in a book and partially in a half-devoured apple. "The Brothers Karamasov," Dorn read as he sauntered by. He thought "an emancipated creature who prides herself on being able to drink cocktails without losing caste. She'll marry the first drunken newspaperman who forgets himself in her presence and spend the rest of her life trying to induce him to go into the advertising business."

Turning down the room he passed the desk of

Crowley, the telegraph editor. A face flabby and red with ancient drinking raised itself from a book and a voice spoke,

"Old Egan gets more of a fool every day." Old Egan was the make-up man. Dorn smiled. "The damned idiot crowded the Nancy story off page one in the Home. Best story of the day." Crowley ended with a vaguely conceived oath.

Dorn glimpsed the title of the book on his desk, *L'Oblat*. Crowley had been educated for the priesthood but emerged from the seminary with a heightened joy of life in his veins. A riotous twenty years in night saloons and bawdy houses had left him a kindly, choleric, and respected newspaper figure. Dorn caught his eye and wondered over his sensitive infatuation of exotic writing. In the pages of Huysmans, De Gourmont, Flaubert, Gautier, Symons, and Pater he seemed to have found a subtle incense for his deadened nerves. Inside the flabby, coarsened body with its red face munching out monosyllables, lived a recluse. "Too much living has driven him from life," Dorn thought, "and killed his lusts. So he sits and reads books—the last debauchery: strange, twisted phrases like idols, like totem poles, like Polynesian masks. He sits contemplating them as he once sat drunkenly watching the obscenities of black, white, and yellow bodied women. Thus, the mania for the rouge of life, for the grimace that lies beyond satiety, passes in him from bestiality to asceticism and esthetics. Yesterday a bacchanal of flesh, to-day a bacchanal of words . . . the posturings of courtezans and the posturings of ornate phrases become the same." He heard Crowley repeating, "Damned idiot, Egan! No sense of human values. Crowded the best story of the day off page one." . . . Some day he'd have a long talk with Crowley. But the man was so carefully hidden behind perfunctories it was hard to get at him. He resented intrusion.

Dorn passed on and looked around for Warren —a humorous and didactic creature who had with considerable effort destroyed his Boston accent and escaped the fact that he had once earned his living as professor of sociology in an eastern university. Dorn caught a memory of him sitting in a congenial saloon before a stein and pouring forth hoarsely oracular comments upon the activities of men known and unknown. The man had a gift for caricature—Rabelaisean exaggerations. Dorn was suddenly glad he had gone for the day. The office oppressed him and the people in it were too familiar. He walked to his desk thinking of the South Seas and new faces.

"I tell you what," a voice drawled behind him, "Nietzsche has it on the whole lot of them." Cochran, the head of the copy desk, was talking —a shriveled little man with a bald face and shoe-button eyes. "You've got to admit people are more dishonest in their virtues than in their vices. Of course, there's a lot of stuff he pulls that's impractical."

Dorn shrugged his shoulders, smiled and lifted his hat out of a locker. He remembered again to telephone his wife, but instead moved out of the office. A refreshing warmth in the street pleased his senses and he turned toward the lake. Walk down Michigan avenue, take a taxi home—what else was there to do? Nothing, unless talk. But to whom? He thought of his father. A tenacious old man. Probably hang on forever. God, the man had been married three times. If it wasn't for his damned infirmities he'd probably marry again. Looking for something. What was it the old man had kept looking for? As if there was in existence a concrete gift to be drawn from life. A blithering, water-eyed optimist to the end, he'd die with a prayer of thankfulness and gratitude.

Thus innocuously abstract, moving in the doldrum which sometimes surrounded him after his day's work, he turned into the boulevard along the lake. The day grew abruptly fresher here. An arc of blue sky rising from the east flung a great curve over the building tops. Dorn paused before the window of a Japanese art shop and stared at a bulbous wooden god stoically contemplating his navel.

During his walks through the streets he sometimes met people he knew. This time a young woman appeared at the window beside him. He recognized her with elation. His thought gave him an index of her . . . Rachel Laskin, curious girl . . . makes me talk well . . . appreciative . . . unusual eyes.

Chapter Four

THEY walked together down the avenue. Dorn felt a return of interest in himself. Introspection bored him. His insincerity made self thought meaningless. Listeners, however, revived him. As they walked he caught occasional glimpses of his companion—vivid eyes, dark lips, a cool, shadow-tinted face that belonged under exotic trees; a morose little girl insanely sensitive and with a dream inside her. She admired him; or at least she admired his words, which amounted to the same thing. Once before she had said, "You are different." As usual he held his cynicism in abeyance before flattery. People who thought him different pleased him. It gave them a certain intellectual status in his eyes.

His thought, as he talked, busied itself with images of her. She gave him a sense of dark waters hidden from the moon—a tenuous fugitive figure in the pretty clamor of the bright street.

"You remind me," he was saying, "of a nymph among dowagers and frightened to death. There's really nothing to be frightened of, unless you prefer fear to other more tangible emotions."

She nodded her head. He recalled that the gesture had puzzled him at first. It gave an eager assent to his words that surprised him. It pretended that she had understood something he had not said, something that lay beneath his words. Dorn pointed at the women moving by them.

"Poems in shoe craft, tragedies in ankles and melodramas in legs," he announced. "Look at their clothes! Priestly caricatures of their sex. You're still drawing?"

"Yes. But you don't like my drawing."

"I saw one of your pictures—an abominable thing—in some needlework magazine. A woman with a spindly nose, picking flowers."

He glanced at her and caught an eager smile in her eyes. She was someone to whom he could talk at random. This pleased him; or perhaps it was the sense of flattery that pleased him. He wondered if she was intelligent. They had met several times, usually by accident. He had found himself able to talk at length to her and had come away feeling an intimacy between them.

"Look at the windows," he continued. "Corsets, stockings, lingerie. Shop windows remind me of neighbors' bathrooms before breakfast. There's something odiously impersonal about them. See, all the way down the street—silks, garments, ruffles, laces. A saturnalia of masks. It's the only art we've developed in America—over-dressing. Clothes are peculiarly American —a sort of underhanded female revenge against the degenerate puritanism of the nation. I've seen them even at revival meetings clothed in the seven tailored sins and denouncing the devil with their bustles. Only they don't wear bustles any more. But what's an anachronism between friends? Why don't you paint pictures of real Americans?—men hunting for bargains in chastity and triumphantly marrying a waistline. If that means anything."

He paused, and wondered vaguely what he was talking about. Vivid eyes and dark lips, a face that belonged elsewhere. He was feeding its poignancy words. And she admired him. Why? He was saying nothing. There was a sexlessness about her that inspired vulgarity.

"You remind me of poetry," she answered without looking at him. "I always can listen to you without thinking, but just understanding. I've remembered nearly everything you've said to me. I don't know why. But they always come back when I'm alone, and they always seem unfinished."

Her words jarred. She was too naive to coquette. Yet it was difficult to believe this. But she was an unusual creature, modestly asleep. A fugitive aloofness. Yes, what she said must be true. There was nothing unreasonable about its being true. She made an impression upon him. He undoubtedly did upon her. He would have preferred her applause, however, somewhat less blatant. But she was a child—an uncanny child who cooed frankly when interested.

"I can imagine the millennium of virtue in America," he went on. "A crowd of painted women; faces green and lavender, moving like a procession of bizarre automatons and chanting in Chinese, 'We are pure. We are chaste and pure.' A parade of psychopathic barbarians dressed in bells, metals, animal skins, astrologer hats and Scandinavian ornaments. A combination of Burmese dancer and Babylonian priest. I ask for nothing more."

He laughed. He had half consciously tried to give words to an image the girl had stirred in him. She interrupted,

"That's me."

He looked at her face in a momentary surprise.

"I hate people, too," she said. "I would like to be like one of those women."

"Or else a huntress riding on a black river in the moon. I was trying to draw a picture of you. And perhaps of myself. You have a faculty of . . . of . . . Funny, things I say are usually only reflections of the people I talk to. You don't mind being a psychopathic barbarian?"

"No," she laughed quietly, "because I understand what you mean."

"I don't mean anything."

"I know. You talk because you have nothing to say. And I like to listen to you because I understand."

This was somewhat less jarring, though still a bit crude. Her admiration would be more pleasant were it more difficult to discover. He became silent and aware of the street. There had been no street for several minutes—merely vivid eyes and dark lips. Now there were people—familiar unknowns to be found always in streets, their faces withholding something, like unfinished sentences. He had lost interest and felt piqued. His loss of interest in his talk was perhaps merely a reflection of her own.

"I remember hearing you were a socialist. That's hard to believe."

There was no relation between them now. He would have to work it up again.

"No, my parents are. I'm not."

"Russians?"

"Yes. Jews."

"I'm curious about your ideals."

"I haven't any."

"Not even art?"

"No."

"A wingless little eagle on a barren tree," he smiled. "I advise you to complicate life with ideals. The more the better. They are more serviceable than a conscience, in which I presume you're likewise lacking, because you don't have to use them. A conscience is an immediate annoyance, whereas ideals are charming procrastinations. They excuse the inanity of the present. Good Lord, what do you think about all day without ideals to guide you?"

Dorn looked at her and felt again delight with himself. It was because her interest had returned.

Her eyes were flatteries. He desired to be amusing, to cover the eager child face beside him with a caress of words.

"I don't think," she answered. "Do people ever think? I always imagine that people have ideas that they look at and that the ideas never move around."

"Yes," he agreed, "moving ideas around is what you might call thinking. And people don't do that. They think only of destinations and for purposes of forgetting something—drugging themselves to uncomfortable facts. I fancy, however, I'm wrong. It's only after telling a number of lies that one gets an idea of what might be true. Thus it occurs to me now that I can't conceive of an intelligent person thinking in silence. Intelligence is a faculty which enables people to boast. And it's difficult boasting in silence. And inasmuch as it's necessary to be intelligent to think, why, that sort of settles it. Ergo, people never think. Do you mind my chatter?"

"Please . . ."

A perfect applause this time. Her sincerity appealed to him as an exquisite mannerism. She said "Please" as if she were breathless.

"You're an entertaining listener," he smiled. "And very clever. Because it's ordinarily rather difficult to flatter me? I'm immensely delighted with your silence, whereas . . ." Dorn stumbled. He felt his speech was degenerating into a compliment.

"Because you tell me things I've known," the girl spoke.

"Yet I tell you nothing."

He stared for an instant at the people in the street. "Nothing" was a word his thought tripped on. He was used to mumbling it to himself as he walked alone in streets. And at his desk it often came to him and repeated itself. Now his thought murmured, "Nothing, nothing," and a sadness drew itself into his heart. He laughed with a sense of treating himself to a theatricalism.

"We haven't talked about God," he announced.

"God is one of my beliefs."

She was an idiot for frowning.

"I dislike to think of man as the product of evolution. It throws an onus on the whole of nature. Whereas with a God to blame the thing is simple."

She nodded, which was doubly idiotic, inasmuch as there was nothing to nod to. He went on:

"Life is too short for brevities—for details. I save time by thinking, if you can call it thinking, *en masse*—in generalities. For instance, I think of people frequently but always as a species. I wonder about them. My wonder is concerned chiefly with the manner in which they adjust themselves to the vision of their futility. Do they shriek aloud with horror in lonely bedrooms? There's a question there. How do people who are important to themselves reconcile themselves to their unimportance to others? And how are they able to forget their imbecility?"

They were walking idly as if dreamily intent upon the spectacle of the avenue. The nervous unrest that came to Dorn in streets and fermented words in his thought seemed to have deserted him. Assured of the admiration of his companion, he felt a quiet as if his energies had been turned off and he were coasting. He recognized several faces and saluted them as if overcome with a desire to relate a jest.

"Notice the men and women together," he resumed easily, almost unconscious of talking. "Observing married couples is a post-graduate course in pessimism. There's a pair arm in arm. Corpses grown together. There's no intimacy like that of cadavers. Yet at this and all other moments they're unaware of death. They move by us without thought, emotion, or words in them."

"They look very proud," she interrupted.

"It's the set expression of vacuity. Just as skeletons always seem mysteriously elate. Their pride is an absence of everything else—a sort of rigid finery they put on in lieu of a shroud. Never mind staring after them, please. They are Mr. and Mrs. Jalonick who live across the street from my home. I dislike staring even after truths. Listen, I have something more to say about them if you'll not look so serious. Your emotions are obviously infantile. I can give you a picture of marriage: two little husks bowing metronomically in a vacuum and anointing each other with pompous adjectives. Draw them a little flattened in the rear from sitting down too much and you'll have a masterpiece. It's amusing to remember that Mr. and Mrs. Jalonick were once in love with each other!" Dorn laughed good-naturedly. "Fancy them on a June night ten years ago before their eyes had become cotton, holding hands and trying to give a meaning to the moon. Are you tired?"

"No, please. Let's walk, if you haven't anything else to do."

"Nothing." It was the seventh anniversary of his marriage. An annoying thought. "You're an antidote for inertia. I marvel, as always, at my garrulity. Women usually inspire me with a desire to talk. I suppose it's a defensive instinct. Talk confuses women and renders them helpless. But that isn't it. I talk to women because they make the best sounding-boards. Do you object to being reduced to an acoustic? Yes, sex is a sort of irritant to the vocabulary. It's amusing to converse profoundly with a pretty woman whose sole contributions to any dialogue are a bit of silk hose and an oscillation of the breasts."

"You make me forget I'm a woman and agree with you."

"Because you're another kind of woman. The reflector. Or acoustic. I prefer them. I sometimes feel that I live only in mirrors and that my thoughts exist only as they enter the heads of others. As now, I speak out of a most complete emptiness of emotion or idea; and my words seem to take body in your silence—and actually give me a character."

"I always think of you as someone hiding from himself," she answered. Dorn smiled. They were old friends—a union between them.

"There's no place of concealment in me," he said after a pause. He had been thinking of something else. "But perhaps I hide in others. After talking like this I come away with a sort of echo of what I've said. As if someone had told me things that almost impressed me. I talk so damned much I'm unaware of ever having heard anybody else but myself express an opinion. And I swear I've never had an opinion in my life." He became silent and resumed, in a lighter voice, "Look at that man with whiskers. He's a notorious Don Juan. Whiskers undoubtedly lend mystery to a man. It's a marvel women haven't cultivated them—instead of corsets. But tell me why you've disdained art as an ideal. You're curious. It's a confessional I should think would appeal to you. I'm almost interested in you, you see. Another hour with you and you would flatter me into a state of silence."

Dorn paused, somewhat startled. Her dark lips parted, her eyes glowing toward the end of the street, the girl was walking in a radiant abstraction. She appeared to be listening to him without hearing what he said. Dorn contemplated her confusedly. He frowned at the thought of having bored her, and an impulse to step abruptly from her side and leave became a part of his anger. He hesitated in his walking and her fingers, timorous and unconscious of themselves, reached for his arm. He wondered with a deeper confusion what she was dreaming about. Her hand as it lay on his forearm gave him a sense of companionship which his words sought clumsily to understand.

"I was saying something about art when you fell asleep," he smiled.

Rachel threw back her head as if she were shaking a dream out of her eyes.

"I wasn't asleep," she denied. They moved on in the increasing crowd.

"Men and women," Dorn muttered. "The street's full of men and women going somewhere."

"Except us," the girl cried. Her eyes, alight, were thrusting against the cold, amused smile of his face. He would be late. Anna would be waiting. An anniversary. Anniversaries were somehow important. They revived interest in events which had died. But it was nice to drift in a crowd beside a girl who admired him. What did he think of her? Nothing . . . nothing. She seemed to warm him into a deeper sleep. It was a relief to be admired for one's silence. Admired, not loved. Love was a bore. Anna loved him, bored him. Her love was an applause that did not wait for him to perform—an unreasonable ovation.

He looked at the girl again. She was walking beside him, vivid eyes, dark lips—almost unaware of him, as if he had become a part of the dream that lived within her.

Chapter Five

WHEN she was a child she used to see a face in the dark as she was falling asleep. It was crude and misshapen, and leered at her, filling her heart with fear. Later, people had become like that to her.

When she was eighteen Rachel came to Chicago and studied art at an art school. She learned nothing and forgot nothing. She read books in English and in Russian—James, Conrad, Brusov, Tolstoi. Her reading failed to remove her repugnance to the touch of life. Instead, it lured her further from realities. She did not like to meet people or to hear them talk. At twenty she was able to earn her living by drawing posters for a commercial art firm and making occasional illustrations for magazines designed for female consumption.

As she matured, the repugnance to life that lay like a disease in her nerves, developed dangerously. She would sit in her room in the evening staring out of the window at the darkened city and thinking of people. There was an endless swathing of people, buildings, faces, words, that wound itself tightly about her. She would cover her face suddenly and whisper, "Oh, I must go away. I must."

She hurried through dragging days as if she were running away. But there were things she could not escape. Men smiled at her and established themselves as friends. Women were easy to get rid of. One had only to be frank and women vanished. But this same frankness, she found, had an opposite effect upon men. Insults likewise served only to interest men. They would become gradually more and more acquainted with her until it became impossible to talk to them. Then she would have to ignore them, turning quickly away when they addressed her and saying, "Goodbye, I must go."

At times she grew ashamed of her sensitiveness. She would sit alone in her room surrounded by a whimpering little silence. A melancholy would darken her heart. It wasn't because she was afraid of people. It was something else. She would try to think of it and would find herself whispering suddenly, "Oh, I must go away. I must."

To men, Rachel's beauty seemed always a doubtful quality. Her appeal itself was doubtful. The Indian symmetry of her face lay as behind a luminous shadow—an ill-mannered, nervous face that was likely to lure strangers and irritate familiars. In the streets and restaurants people looked at her with interest. But people who spoke to her often lost their interest. There was a silence about her like a night mist. She seemed in this silence preoccupied with something that did not concern them. Men found the recollection of her more pleasing than her presence. Something they remembered of her seemed always to be missing when they encountered her again. Lonely evening fields and weary peasants moving toward the distant lights of their homes spoke from her eyes. An exotic memory of simple things—of earth, sky, and sea—lay in her sudden gestures. A sense of these things men carried away with them. But when they came to talk to her they grew conscious only of the fact that she irritated them. These who persisted in their friendship grew to regard her solicitously and misunderstand their emotions toward her.

It was evening when Rachel came to her room after her walk with Erik Dorn. The long stroll had given her an aversion toward work. She glanced at several unfinished posters and moved to a chair near a window.

A glow of excitement brightened the dusk of her face. Her eyes, usually asleep in distances, had become alive. They gave themselves to the night.

Beyond the scratch of houses and the slant of home lights she watched the darkness lift against the sky. The city had dwindled into a huddle of streets. Noise had become silence. The great crowds were packed away in little rooms. Sitting before the window, unconscious of herself, she laughed softly. Her black hair felt tight and heavy. She shook her head till its loose coils dropped across her cheeks. She had felt confused when she entered the room, as if she had grown strange to herself.

"Who am I?" she whispered suddenly. She raised her hand and stared at it. Something intimate had left her. She remembered herself as in a dream. There had been another Rachel who used to sit in this chair looking out of the window. A memory came of people and days. But it was not her memory, because her mind felt free of the nausea it used to bring.

She stood up quickly and turned on a light. Her dexterous hands twisted her hair back into loose coils on her head. Strange, she did not know herself. That was because things seemed different. Here was her room, littered with books and canvasses and clothes, and the bed in which she slept, half hidden by the alcove curtains. But they were different. She began to hum a song. A tune had come back to her that men sang in Little Russia trudging home from the wheat fields. That was long ago when the world was a bad dream that frightened her at night. Now there was no world outside, but a darkness without faces or streets—a darkness with a deep meaning. It was something to be breathed in and felt.

She opened the window and stood wondering. She was lonely. Loneliness caressed her heart and drew dim fingers across her thought. She could never remember having been lonely before. But now there was a difference. She smiled.

Of course, it was Erik Dorn. He had pleased her. The things he had said returned to her mind. They seemed very important, as if she had said them herself. She would go out and walk again—fast. It was pleasant to be lonely. Her throat shivered as she breathed. Bewildered in the lighted room she laughed and her lips said aloud, "I don't know. I don't know!"

Among the men who had established themselves as friends of Rachel was a young attorney named George Hazlitt. He had gone to school with her in a small Wisconsin town. A year ago he had discovered her again in Chicago. The discovery had excited him. He was a young man with proprietory instincts. He had at once devoted them to Rachel. After several months he had begun to dream about her. They were correct and estimable dreams reflecting credit upon the correct and estimable stock from which he came.

He fell to courting Rachel tenaciously, torn between a certainty that she was insane and a conviction that a home, a husband's love, and the paraphernalia of what he termed clean, healthy living would restore her to sanity. Their meetings had been affairs of violence. In her presence he always felt a rage against what he called her neurasthenia—a word he frequently used in drawing up bills for divorce. He regarded neurasthenia not as a disease to be condoned like the mumps, but as a deliberate failing—particularly in Rachel.

The neurasthenia of the defendants he pursued in courts annoyed him only slightly. In Rachel it outraged him. It was his habit to inform her that her sufferings were nothing more than affectations and that her moods were shams and that the whole was a part and parcel of neurasthenia.

This unhappy desire of his to browbeat her into a state which he defined as normal, Rachel had accepted in numb helplessness. She had given up commanding him to leave her alone. His presence frequently became a nausea. Her enfevered senses had come to perceive in the conventionally clothed and spoken figure of the young attorney, a concentration of the repugnant things before which she cowered. During his courtship he had grown familiar to her as a penalty and his visits had become climaxes of loathsomeness.

But a stability of purpose peculiar to unsensitive and egoistic young men kept Hazlitt to his quest. His steady rise in his profession, the growing respect of his fellows for his name, fired him with a sense of success. Rachel had become the victim of this sense. Of all the men she knew Hazlitt grew to be the most unnecessary. But his persistence seemed to increase with her aversion for him. In a sort of mental self-defense against the nervous disgust he brought her, she forced herself to think of him and even to argue with him. By thinking of him she was able to keep the memory of him an impersonal one, and to convert him from an emotionally unbearable influence into an intellectually insufferable type. A conversion by which Hazlitt profited, for she tolerated him more easily as a result of her ruse. She thought of him. His youth was fast entrenching itself in platitudes and acquiring the vigor and directness that come as a reward of conformity. Life was nothing to wonder at or feel. Life shaped itself into definite images and inelastic values before him. To these images and values he conformed, not submissively, but with a militant enthusiasm. On summer mornings he saw himself as a knight of virtue advancing clear-eyed upon a bedeviled world. When he was among his own kind he summed up the bedevilments in the word "bunk." The politer word, to be used chivalrously, was "neurasthenia." The victims of these dedevilments were "nuts." A dreadful species like herself, given to wrong hair cuts, insanities, outrages upon decency and above all, common sense.

Hazlitt's attraction to Rachel in the face of her neurasthenia did not confuse him. Confusion was a quality foreign to Hazlitt. He courted her as a lover and proselyter. His proselyting consisted of vigorous denunciations of the things which contributed to the neurasthenia of his beloved. He declaimed his notions in round, rosy-cheeked sentences. There was about Hazlitt's wooing of Rachel the pathos which might distinguish the love affair of a Baptist angel and the hamadryad daughter of a Babayaga.

Yet, though in her presence he denounced her art, taste, sufferings, books, friends, affectations, away from her she came to him—beautiful eyed and fragile—bringing a fear and a longing into his heart. Dreaming of her over a pipe in his home at night, he saw her as something bewilderingly clean, different—vividly different from other women, with a difference that choked and saddened him. There was a virginity about her that extended beyond her body. This and her fragility haunted him. His youth had caught the vision of the night mist of her, the lonely fields of her eyes, the shadow dreams toward whose solitudes she seemed to be flying. Beside Rachel all other women were to him somehow coarse and ungainly fibered, and somehow unvirginal.

Out of his dream of her arose his desire to have her as his own, to come home and find her waiting, to have her known as Mrs. George Hazlitt. The thought of the Rachel he knew—mysterious, fugitive, neurasthenic—established normally across a breakfast table, smiling a normal goodbye at him with her arms normally about his neck, was a contrast that sharpened his desire. It offered a transformation that would be a victory not only for his love but for the shining, militant platitudes behind which Rachel had correctly pointed out to herself, he lived.

Bewildered in the lighted room, Rachel turned suddenly to the door. Someone was knocking—

loud. She hurried eagerly forward, wondering at an unfinished thought . . . "perhaps it is. . . ." Hazlitt, smiling with steady, solicitous eyes confronted her.

"I've been knocking for five minutes," he announced. "I heard you or I'd have gone away."

Rachel nodded. Of course, it would be Hazlitt. He was always appearing when least expected. But it would be nice to talk to someone. She smiled. This was surprising and she shook her head as if she were carrying on a conversation with herself. George Hazlitt was always unbearable. But that was a memory. It no longer applied.

"I'm glad you came," she greeted him. "I was lonely."

Hazlitt looked at her in surprise. Visiting Rachel was a matter that required an extreme of determination. He had come prepared as usual for the sullen, uncomfortable hour she offered.

"I was going out," she continued, "but I won't now. If you'll sit down I'll do some work. You won't mind."

She looked at him eagerly as if to tell him he must forget she had always hated him and that she was different now. At least for the moment. He understood nothing and remained staring at her. His manner proclaimed frankly that he was bewildered.

"Yes, certainly," he answered at length, and sat down. She hurried about, securing her paints and setting up one of the unfinished posters. Drawing a deep breath Hazlitt lighted a pipe and watched her. She was beautiful. He admitted it with less belligerency than usual. He sat thinking, "what the deuce has happened to her. She said she was glad to see me." He was afraid to start an inquiry. She had never before smiled at him, let alone voiced pleasure over his presence. It was a mistake of some sort but he would enjoy it for awhile. But perhaps it was the beginning of something.

Hazlitt sighed. He smoked, waited, and struggled to avoid the thoughts that crowded upon him.

"That's rather nice," he said. He would follow her mood, whatever it was. Rachel's eyes laughed toward him.

"I hope it doesn't bore you. If you hadn't come I would never have thought of working."

The thing was unbelievable. Yet he contemplated it serenely. He would talk to her soon and find out what was the matter. There was undoubtedly something the matter. His eyes stared at her furtively as she returned to her work. "There's something the matter," his thought cautioned him. Rachel resumed her talking. A naiveté and freshness were in her voice. She was letting her tongue speak for her and laughing at the sound of the curious remarks it made.

"Do you think that women are becoming barbarians? The way they mess up their hair and go in for savage colors! Sometimes I get to feeling that they will end up as—as psychopathic barbarians. With astrologer hats."

She regarded Hazlitt carelessly. Hazlitt, with fidgets in his thought, smiled. His eyes lost their solicitous air. They began to search shrewdly for some reason. The spectacle of a coquettish Rachel was beyond him, even as the sound of her laugh was an amazing music to his senses. But his shrewdness evaporated. It occurred to him that women were peculiar. Particularly Rachel. A direct and vigorous Hazlitt concluded that Rachel had succumbed to his superior guidance. There was nothing else to explain her tolerance. He called it tolerance, for he was still wary and her eyes shining eagerly, hungrily at him might be no more than a new kind of neurasthenia. He let her talk on without interruption. She would like to paint streets, houses, lights in the dark, city things. Blowing puffs of smoke carelessly toward the ceiling he answered finally, "If you didn't have to support youself, perhaps you could." A fear whirled in his heart with the sentence. He had never asked her outright to marry him. The thought that he had almost asked her, now made him feel dizzy.

"There! I guess that can rest now."

Rachel put aside her painting. She sat down near him. Her eyes narrowed and she listened with a sleepy smile as he began carefully to recite to her incidents that had happened during his day. But he became silent. She didn't mind that. She desired to sit as she was, her emotion a dream that escaped her thought. Hazlitt fumbled with his pipe. It was out. He dropped it into a pocket. His shrewdness and his weariness had left him. He felt almost that he was alone.

"You're wonderful," he whispered; and he grew frightened of his voice. Rachel saw his face light with an unusual expression. He would be kind now and let her smile.

"I'm glad you came," she sighed. "I don't know why. I feel different to-night."

She had a habit of short, begrudging sentences delivered in a quick monotone—a habit of speech against which Hazlitt had often raged. But now her words—flurried, breathless, begrudging as always—stirred him. They could be believed. She was a child that way. She spoke quickly thoughts that were uppermost in her mind.

"I never thought I could be glad to see you. But I am."

Hazlitt felt suddenly weak. Her face before him was something in a dream. It was turned away and he could watch her breathing. Bewilderedly he remembered a thousand Rachels, different from this one, who was glad he had come. But the beauty of her burned away uncomfortable memories. She was the Rachel of his loneliness. Out of George Hazlitt vanished the vigor and directness of a young man who knows his own soul. There came a vision—a thing uncertain and awesome, and he sat humbled before it.

He reached her hand and closed his fingers over it. An awe squeezed at his throat. Her hand lay without protest within his. He had never touched her before. She had been a symbol and a dream. Now he felt the marvel of the fact that she was a woman. Her hand, warm and alive, astonished him with the news.

Rachel, during his speechlessness, looked at him unbelievingly. The grip of his fingers was bringing an ache into her heart. It was sad. The night and the room were sad. She could feel sadness opening little wounds in her breasts. And before she had been happy. She heard him whispering, "I can't talk to you. I can't. Oh, you are beautiful!"

His eyes made her think he was suffering. Then he was sad, too. She stood up because his hand drew her. Why did he want her to stand up? His body touched her and she heard him gasp. Her heart seemed adrift. She was unreal. There was another Rachel somewhere else. He was saying, but he was not talking to her, "Oh, Rachel, I love you. I love you, Rachel!"

Still she waited unbelievingly, the ache in her dragging at her senses. She had fallen asleep and was dreaming something that was sad. But his face was suddenly too close. His eyes were too near and bright. They awakened her.

"Let me go, quick."

His hands clung. For an instant she failed to understand his resistance. He was saying jerkily, "No . . . no!"

She twisted out of his arms and stood breathless, as if she were choking. Hazlitt looked at her, a bit pensively. His heart lost in a dream and a rapture could only grimace a child's protest out of his stare. He hadn't kissed her. But that would come soon. Not everything at once. He must not be a brute. He smiled. His good-natured face glowed as if in a light. Then he heard her talking,

"Go away. At once. I never want to see you again. I'll die if I see you again."

Her hands were in her hair.

"Go away. Please. . . . Oh, God, I can't stand you. You—horrify me!"

The panic in Rachel's voice seemed to dull his ears to her words. He saw her for a vivid moment against the opened window and then he found himself alone, looking into a night that was haunted with an image of her. He remembered her going, but it seemed to him he still saw her against the window, his eyes bringing to him a vision of her face as she had looked.

He had grown white. In the memory of her face, as in an impossible mirror, he saw a loathsome image of himself. Her eyes had blazed with it. He sickened and his thought grew faint. Then the night came before him and the echo of the words Rachel had spoken beat in his head. He walked with his hat politely in his hand out of the door.

On the stairs his eyes grew weak and warm.

Erik Dorn

Tears rushed from them. He stumbled and clutched at the banister. She had led him on. She had looked at him with love. Love . . . but he had dreamed that. What was it, then? Her eyes burning toward him had told him he was loathsome. There was something wrong with him. He wept. He put his hat on mechanically. He dried his eyes. There was something wrong.

On her bed Rachel lay mumbling to herself, mumbling as if the words were a pain to her ears. "Erik Dorn . . . Erik Dorn."

Chapter Six

THE world in which Erik Dorn lived was compounded of many surfaces. Of them Anna, his wife, was the most familiar. It was a familiarity of absorption. Weeks of intimacy passed between them, of lover-like attentiveness during which Dorn remained unconscious of her existence. Her unending talk of her love for him—words and murmurs that seemed an inexhaustible overflow of her heart—passed through his mind as a part of his own thought. Hers was a more definite contribution to the emptiness of the life through which he moved.

Yet in his unconsciousness of her there lived a shadowy affection. On occasions in which they had been separated there had always awakened in him an uneasiness. In his nights alone he lay sleepless, oppressed, a nostalgia for her presence growing in him. With his eyes opened at the darkness of a strange room he experienced then an incompleteness as if he himself were not enough. The emptiness in which he was living became suddenly real. He would feel a despair. Words unlike the sophisticated patter of his usual thought would come to him. . . . "What is there . . . I would like something . . . what? . . ." A sense of life as an unpeopled vastness would frighten him vaguely. Night sounds . . . strange, shadow-hidden walls. They made him uneasy. Memories then; puzzling, mixed-up pictures that had lost their outlines. Things that had left no impression on his thought—sterile little incidents through which he had moved with automatic gestures—returned like sad little outcasts pleading with him. Faces he could not remember and that were yet familiar peered at him in his sleeplessness with poignant eyes that frightened.

There would come to him the memory of the time he had been a boy and had lain like this in his mother's home, startled with fears that sat like insanities in his throat. The memory of his being a boy seemed to restore him to the fears long forgotten. Words would come . . . "I was a boy . . ." and he would lie thinking of how people grew old; of how he had grown old without seeming to change, and yet changing—as if he had been gently vanishing from himself and even now was moving slowly away. He was like a house from which issued a dim procession of guests never pausing for farewells. He had been a boy, a youth, a man . . . each containing days and thoughts. And they moved slowly away from him—completed figures fully dressed. Slowly, without farewells, with faces intensely familiar yet no longer known. Thus he would continue to vanish from himself, remaining unchanged but diminishing, until there were no more guests to forsake and he stood alone waiting a last farewell —a curious, unimaginable good-bye to himself. Nothing . . . nothing. A long wait for a good-bye. And then nothing again. Already he was half shadow—half a procession of Erik Dorns walking away from him and growing dimmer.

In the dark of the strange room, his eyes staring and fearful, he would reach suddenly for Anna, embracing her almost as if she were beside him. Her smile that forever shone upon him like the light of lilies and candles from a sad, quiet altar; her words that forever flowed like a dream from her heart, the warmth of her body that she offered him as if it no longer existed for herself— to these his loneliness sought vainly to carry him. And he would find himself tormented by a desire for her, lying with her name on his lips and her image alone alive in the empty dread of his thought.

United again in their home, he lapsed into the unconsciousness of her, sometimes vaguely startled by the tears he felt on her cheeks as they lay together at night. Out of this unconsciousness he made continual love to her, giving her back her endearments and caresses. Of this he never tired. His kisses unaware of her, his tendernesses without meaning to him, he yet felt in her presence the shadow of a desire. The love that filled his wife seemed to animate his phrases with an amorous diction that echoed her own. He would hold her in his arms, bestowing kisses upon her, and watch as in wonder of some mysterious make-believe, the radiance that his meaningless gestures brought to her.

There were times, however, when Dorn became aware of his wife, when she thrust herself before him as a far-away-eyed and beautiful-faced stranger. He had frequently followed her in the street, watching her body sway as she walked, observing with quickening surprise her trim, lyre-like shoes, her silken ankles, the agile sensualism of her litheness under a stranger's dress. He had noticed that she had coils of red hair with bronze and gold lights slipping over it, that her face tilted itself with a hint of determination and her eyes walked proudly over the heads of the crowd. He watched other men glimpse her and turn for an instant to follow with their stares the promise of her body and lighted face. Dorn, walking out of her sight, got a confused sense of her as if she were speaking to the street, "I am a beautiful woman. In my head are thoughts. I am a stranger to you. You do not know what my body looks like or what dreams live in me. I have destinations and emotions that are mysterious to you. I am somebody different from yourselves."

On top of this sense of her had come each time a sudden vivid picture—Anna in their bedroom attaching her garters to the tops of her stockings; Anna tautening her body as she slipped out of her nightgown . . . or a picture of her pressing his head against her breasts and whispering passionately, "Erik, I adore you." The strangeness then would leave her and again she was something he had absorbed. When he looked for her she had vanished in the scribble of the crowd and he walked with the same curious unconsciousness of her existence as of his own.

There were times too in their home when Anna became a reality before his eyes—an external that startled him. This was such a time now. Rachel had come to visit them. She sat silent, fugitive-bodied amid overfed, perspiring-eyed guests. And he stood looking at Anna and listening to her.

He wondered why he looked at Anna and not at Rachel. But his wife in black velvet and silken pumps, like a well-limned character out of some work of stately fiction, held his attention. He desired to talk to her as if she were a stranger. She sat without surprise at his unusual verbal animation in her behalf, listening to his banter with an intent, almost preoccupied smile in her eyes. While he talked, asking her questions and pressing for answers, he thought. "She's not paying any attention to my words, but to me. Her love is like a robe about her, covering her completely." Yet she seemed strange. Behind this love lived a person capable of thinking and reasoning. Dorn, as sometimes happened, grew curious about her thoughts. He increased his efforts to rivet her attention, as if he were trying to coax a secret out of her. The easiest way to arouse her was to say things that frightened her, to make remarks that might give her the feeling he had some underlying idea in his head hostile to their happiness.

The company of faces in the room emitted laughter, uttered words of shocked contradiction, pressed themselves eagerly forward upon his phrases. A red-faced man whose vacuity startled from behind a pair of owlish glasses exclaimed, "That's all wrong, Dorn. Women don't want war. Your wife would rather cut off her arm than see you go to war. And mine, too."

The wife of the red-faced man giggled. A younger, unmarried woman posed carelessly on the black piano bench in an effort to exaggerate the charms of her body, spoke with a deliberate sigh.

"No, I don't agree with you, Mr. Harlan. Women are capable of sacrifice."

She thrust forward a lavender-stockinged leg and contemplated it with a far-away sacrificial light in her eyes. The red-faced one observed her with sudden owlish seriousness. His argument seemed routed.

"Of course that's true," he agreed. Mr. Harlan came of a race whose revolutionary notions expired apologetically before the first platitude to cross their path. "We must always bear in mind that women are capable of sacrifice; that women . . ." The lavender stocking was withdrawing itself and Mr. Harlan stammered like an orator witnessing a sudden exodus of his audience, "that women are really capable of remarkable things," he concluded.

Dorn was an uncommonly clever fellow, but a bit radical. He'd like to think of something to say to him just to show him there was another side to it. Not that he gave a damn. Some other time would do. The red face turned with a great attentiveness toward the hoarsely oracular Mr. Warren, his eyes dropping a furtive curtsy in the direction of the vanished stocking.

"I never agree with Dorn," Warren was remarking, "for fear of displeasing him."

He gazed belligerently at Anna whose eyes were attracting attention. She was watching her husband in a manner unbecoming a hostess. A middle-aged youth toying politely with the blue sash of a girl in a white dress—he had recently concluded a tense examination of the two antique rings on her fingers—saw an occasion for laughter and embraced it. The girl glanced somewhat timidly toward Anna and addressed her softly, as if desiring to engage in some conversation beyond the superficial excitement of the moment.

"I'm just mad about blue sashes," she whispered. "I think the sash is coming back, don't you?"

Anna nodded her head. Erik had resumed his talk, his eyes still on her.

"Women are two things—theory and fact," he was saying. "The theory of them demands war.

If we get into this squabble you'll find them cheering the loudest and waving the most flags. War is something that kills men; therefore, it is piquantly desirable to their subconscious hate of our sex." He smiled openly at Anna. "It's also something that plays up the valor and superiority of man and therefore offers a vindication for her submission to him."

"Oh," the lavender stocking was indignantly in evidence, "how awful!"

Dorn waited until the young woman had shifted her hips into a more protesting outline.

"I agree," the red face chimed in. "It's nonsense. Dorn's full of clever nonsense. I quite agree with you, Miss Dillingham." Miss Dillingham was the lavender stocking. The wife of the red face fidgeted, politely ominous. She announced pertly:

"I agree with what Mr. Dorn says." Which announcement her husband properly translated into a warning and a threat of future conversation on the theme, "You never pay any attention to me when there's anybody else around."

Dorn continued, "And it gives them a sense of generalities. Women live crowded between the narrow horizons of sex. They don't share in life. It's very sad, isn't it, Miss Williams?" Miss Williams removed her sash gently from the hands of the elderly youth and pouted. She was always indignant when men addressed her seriously. It gave her an uncomfortable feeling that they were making fun of her.

"Oh, I don't know," she answered. The elderly youth nodded his head enthusiastically and whispered close to her ear, "Exactly."

"The things that are an entirety to women," pursued Dorn, "milk bottles, butcher bills, babies, cleaning days, hello and good-bye kisses, are merely gestures to their husbands. So in a war they find themselves able to share what is known as the larger horizon of the male. One way is through sacrifice. They sacrifice their sons, lovers, husbands, uncles, and fathers with a high, firm spirit, announcing to the press that they are only sorry their supply of relatives is limited. The sacrificing brings them in contact with the world in which their males live. That's the theory of it."

Anna's smile continued to deny itself to his words. It said to him, "What does it matter what you say? I love you." And yet there was a thought behind it holding itself aloof.

"But the fact of woman is always denying her theory," he added. "That's what makes her confusing. The fact of her weeps at departures, shell shocks, amputations; grows timid and organizes pacifist societies. It's a case of sex instinct versus the personal complex."

The elderly young man straightened in his chair, removing his eyes from Miss Williams with the air of one returning to masculine worldliness.

"I don't know about that," he said. "It's all

very well to talk about such things flippantly. But when the time comes, we must admit . . ."

"That talk is foolish," interrupted Warren. He looked at Rachel and laughed. "As a matter of fact, if anybody else but Dorn said it, I'd believe it. But I never believe Dorn. Do you, Miss Laskin?"

Rachel answered, "Yes."

Dorn, piqued by the continual silence of his wife, felt a sudden discomfiture at the sound of Rachel's voice. Was Anna aware he was talking to her so as to avoid talking to Rachel? Perhaps. But Rachel's presence was diluted by the company. He caught a glimpse of her dark eyes opened towards him, and for a moment felt his words disintegrate. He continued hurriedly:

"War, in a way, is a noble business, in that it reduces us to a biological sanity—much the same as does Miss Dillingham's lavender stocking!"

The company swallowed this with an abrupt stiffening of necks. Isaac Dorn, who had been airing himself on the veranda, relieved a tension by appearing in the doorway and moving quietly toward an unoccupied chair. Anna reached her hand to the old man's and held it kindly. Miss Dillingham, surveying the stretch of hose which had been honored in her host's conversation, raised her eyes and replied quietly:

"Mr. Dorn is too clever to be really insulting."

The red-faced one clung to a sense of outrage. His cheeks had grown slightly distended, and with the grimace of indignant virtue bristling on his face, he turned the expression toward his wife for approval. She nodded her head and tightened the thin line of her lips.

"I only meant," laughed Dorn, "that it reduces us to the sort of sanity that wipes out the absurd, artificial notions of morality that keep cluttering up the thought of the race. War reminds us that civilization and murder are compatible. Lavender stockings, speaking in generalities, are reminders that good and evil walk on equally comely legs."

Mr. Harlan, having registered indignation, now struggled vainly against the preenings of his wit, and finally succumbed.

"In these days you can't tell Judy O'Grady and the Colonel's lady apart by their stockings, eh?" He hammered his point home with a laugh. Warren winked at Rachel as if to inform her of the mixed company they were in, and Mrs. Harlan endeavored to put an end to the isolated merriment of her husband with a "John, you're impossible!" The elderly youth, conscious of himself as the escort of a young virgin, lowered his eyes modestly to her ankles. Dorn, watching his wife's smile deepen, nodded his head at her. He knew her momentary thought. She labored under the pleasing conviction that his risqué remarks were invariably inspired by memories of her.

"Barring, of course, the unembattled stay-at-homes," he continued. "The sanity of battle-fields is in direct ratio to the insanity of the non-combatants. You can see it already in the press. We who stay at home endeavor to excuse the crime of war by attaching ludicrous ideals and purposes to its result. Thus every war is to its non-combatants a holy war. And we get a swivel-chair collection of nincompoops raving weirdly, as the casualty lists pour in, of humanity and democracy. It hasn't come yet, but it will."

"Then you don't believe in war?" said the red face, emerging triumphantly upon respectable ground.

"As a phenomenon inspired by ideals or resulting in anything more satisfactory than a wholesale loss of life, war is always a joke," Dorn answered. He wondered whether Rachel was considering him a pompous ass. "I have a whole-hearted respect for it, however, as a biological excitement."

The blue sash winced primly at the word biological, and appealed to her escort to protect her somehow from the indecencies of life. The elderly youth answered her appeal with a tightening of his features.

"War isn't biological," he retorted in her behalf.

Dorn, wearying of his talk, waited for some one of the company to relieve him of the burden. But the elderly youth had subsided, and fulfilling his functions as host—a business of diverting visitors from the fact that there was no reason for their presence in his home—Dorn was forced to continue:

"I can conceive of no better or saner way to die

than crawling around in the mud, shrieking like a savage, and assisting blindly in the depopulation of an enemy. But unless a man is forced to fight, I can conceive of nothing more horrible than war. Don't you think that, Anna?"

"You know what I think, Erik," she answered. "I hate it."

He was startled by a sudden similarity between Rachel and Anna. She too was looking at him with the indignant aloofness of his wife—with a rapt attention seemingly beyond the sound of his words. He caught the two women turn and smile to each other with an understanding that left him a stranger to both. He thought quickly, "Anna is the only one in the room intelligent enough for Rachel to understand." He felt a momentary pride in his wife, and wondered.

As the conversation, playing with the theme of war, spread itself in spasmodic blurs about the room, bursting in little crescendoes of conviction, pronouncements, suddenly serious and inviolable truths, Dorn found himself listening excitedly. An unusual energy pumped notions into his thought. But it was impossible to give vent to ideas before this collection of comedians. He desired to look at Rachel, but kept his eyes away. If they were alone, he could talk. He permitted himself the luxury of an explosive silence.

He sat for a time thinking. "Curious! She knows I have things to say to her. They are unimportant but I can say them to no one else.

She knows I avoid looking at her. There must be something—an attraction. She's a fool. I don't know. I should have put an end to our walks long ago."

His vocabulary, marshaling itself under a surprising force, charged with a rush through his thought. Sentences unrelated, bizarre combinations of words—a kaleidoscopic procession of astounding ideas—art, life, war, streets, people—he knew what they were all about. An illumination like a verbal ecstacy spread itself through him. Under it he continued to think as if with a separate set of words, "I don't know. She isn't beautiful. A stupid, nervous little girl. But it hasn't anything to do with her. It's something in me."

He stood up, his eyes unsmiling, and surveyed the animated faces as from a distance. Paper faces and paper eyes—fluttering masks suspended politely above fabrics that lounged in chairs. They were unreal—too unreal even to talk to. Beyond these figures in the room and the noises they made, lay something that was not unreal. It pulled at the sleep in him. He stood as if arrested by his own silence. The night outside the window came into his eyes, covering the words in his brain and leaving him alone.

He heard Anna speaking.

"What are you thinking about, Erik?"

Her eyes seemed to him laden with forebodings. Yet she was smiling. There was something that made her afraid. He turned toward Rachel and found her standing as if in imitation of himself, her face lifted toward the window, the taut line of her neck an attitude that brought him the image of a white bird's wing soaring. He felt himself unable to speak, as if a hand had been laid threateningly on his throat. Rachel was indiscreet to stand that way, to look that way. There was no mistaking. His thought, shaking itself free of words . . . "In love with me. In love with me!" He paused. A bewildering sense of infidelity. But he had done nothing—only walk with her a few afternoons. And talk. "A stupid, nervous little girl." It was some sort of game, not serious necessarily. He stepped abstractedly toward his wife, aware that the conversation had flattened.

"I wasn't thinking," he answered, searching guiltily for an epigram. "Won't you play?"

Anna stood up and brought her eyes to a level with his own. Again the light of foreboding, of unrevealed shadows flashed at him out of her smile. She understood something not clear in his own head; nor in hers. He grasped her hand as she passed and with a dolorous grimace of his heart felt it unresponsive in his fingers.

Anna was playing from a piano score of *Parsifal*. The music dropped a curtain. Dorn became conscious of himself in an overheated room surrounded by a group of awed and saccharine faces. Rachel was smiling at him with a meaning that he seemed to have forgotten. He stared back, pleasantly aware that a familiar sneer had returned to his eyes. In a corner his father sat watching Anna and he noticed that the old man's watery eyes turned in, as if gazing at images in his own thought. His father's smile, as always, touched Dorn with an irritation, and he hurried from it.

The others were more amusing. The spectacle of the faces wilting into maudlin abstractions under the caress of the music brought a grin to him. The sounds had drugged the polite little masks and left them poised morosely in a sleepy dream. The lavender stocking crept tenderly into evidence. The owlish glasses focused with noncommittal stoicism in its direction. The blue sash looked worried and the raised eyebrows of the elderly youth asked unhappy questions. Music made people sad and caused sighs to trickle from their ludicrously inanimate features. Melting hearts under lacquered skins, dissolving little whimpers under perfunctory attitudes.

He remembered his own mood of a few moments ago, and explained to himself. Something had given him a dream. The night shining through the window, the curve of Rachel's neck. Rachel . . . Rachel . . . He grew suddenly sick with the refrain of her name. It said itself longingly in his thought as if there was a meaning beyond it.

The playing had stopped. The listeners appeared to be lingering dejectedly among its echoes. Rachel slipped quickly to her feet, her arms thrust back as if she were poised for running. She passed abruptly across the room. Her behavior startled him. The faces looked at her curiously. She was running away.

Anna followed her quietly into the vestibule and the company burst into an incongruous babble. Dorn listened to their voices, again firm and self-sufficient, chattering formalities. He watched Rachel adjusting her hat with over-eager gestures. Her eyes were avoiding him. She seemed breathless, her head squirming under the necessity of having to remain for another moment before the eyes of the people in the room.

"I must go," she said suddenly. Her hand extended itself to Anna. A frightened smile widened her mouth. Dorn felt her eyes center excitedly on him. A confused desire to speak kept him silent. He stood up and entered the hall to play his little part as host. But Rachel was gone. The door had closed behind her and he stared at the panels, feeling that the house had emptied itself. Things were normal again. Anna was speaking to her guests, smoothly garrulous. They were putting on hats and saying good-bye. They would have to hurry to escape the rain. He assisted with wraps, his eyes furtively watching the door as if he expected to see it open again, with Rachel returning.

"I've really had a wonderful time," the lavender stocking was shrilling. He became solicitous and followed her to the door, walking with her down the housesteps. A moist summer night, promising rain.

But the street was empty of Rachel, and he returned.

Chapter Seven

THEY were in their bedroom undressing. Outside, the night rustled with an approaching storm. On the closed windows the rain began a rattle of water. A wind filled the darkness.

"What makes you act so strangely to-night, Erik?"

She looked at him as she stood uncovering herself. She desired to speak with a disarming casualness. Instead, her words came with a sound of tears in them. He was always strange—always going away from her until she had to close her eyes and love in the dark without trying to see him. Now he might go to war and be killed. Something would happen. "Something . . . something . . ." kept murmuring itself in her thought.

"I love to hear you play to a crowd," he answered good-humoredly.

"Why?" She could not get the languor out of her voice.

"When people listen to music it always reminds me we are descended from fish. God, what dolts! Minds like soft-bodied sea growths. I can actually see them sometimes."

"You always dislike my friends."

She would argue with him, and in his anger his strangeness would go away.

"Your friends?" He seemed pleased at the chance of growing angry. "Allow me to point out to you that the assemblage to-night had the distinction of being my friends. I discovered the collection. I brought them to the house first."

"They think you're wonderful." She would get him angry that way.

"A virtue, I admit. But it doesn't excuse their other stupidities."

They seemed to have nothing to argue about. Anna loosened her hair. The sight of it rolling in glistening bronzes and reds from her head invariably gave her a desire to cover Erik's face in it. With his face buried in the disordered masses of her hair she would feel an exquisite fullness of love.

"You don't think Rachel stupid, do you?"

Dorn felt a relief at the sound of her name. His thought was full of her, but he had been afraid to talk.

"Miss Laskin," he replied, concealing his eagerness for the topic with a drawl, "is partially insane."

"Yes, you like insane people, though. I can always tell when you like people. You never pay any attention to them then, but sort of come hanging around me—as if you were apologizing to yourself for liking them, and doing penance. Or you call them names."

"Miss Laskin," Dorn answered, delighted to

protract the conversation, "is a vivid sort of imbecile suffering from vacuous complexities. An hour alone in a room with her would drive even a philosopher to madness. She's one of the kind of people given to inappropriate silences. She reminds me of an emotion undergoing a major operation. Good Lord, Anna, don't tell me you're jealous of her?'

It was immaterial whether he denounced or upheld Rachel. To talk of her even with indignation was a delight.

Thunder rolled, and he became silent. Anna turned her nakedness to him. Her eyes, grown dark, beheld a yearning and a sorrow.

"Don't talk about people," she whispered. "I'm glad you hate them—all of them."

Her nudity always surprised Dorn. Her body seemed always to have grown more beautiful and impersonal. A shout of rain sounded in the night and a chill wind burst with a clatter in the darkness. He thought of Rachel as he darkened the room. There came to him a picture of her walking in the rain with her head raised and laughing.

Anna lay for a moment, awed by the suddenness of the storm. She turned quickly, her arms reaching hungrily about her husband.

"I love you," she whispered. "Oh, I love you so much. My own, my dearest!"

She felt his lips touch hers, and closed her eyes. "Tell me . . ."

Dorn murmured back to her, "I adore you."

A little laugh came, and tears reached her cheeks.

"You're so wonderful," she whispered. "Think of it! It's been the same since the first night. You love me—just as you did."

She paused questioningly—an old question to which he gave an old answer.

"I love you more."

"I know it. I can feel it. You won't ever get tired of loving me?"

"Never—never as long as I live."

"Oh, you make me so happy!"

A sigh almost like a moan came from her heart.

"Oh, I'm a fool. I get frightened sometimes—when I hear you talk. Something takes you away. You mustn't ever go away. Promise me. Listen, Erik." She dropped into a panic. "Promise me you won't go to war."

He laughed.

"That was only talk," he whispered. "You should know my talk by this time."

"I'll never know you."

"Please, Anna, don't. You hurt me when you say that."

"And when you were silent," she went on softly, "I felt—I felt something had happened. Erik, darling Erik. Oh, you're my whole life!"

"I adore you, sweetest," he murmured.

"I don't live except in you, Erik. And, oh, I'm a fool. Such a fool!"

"You're wonderful," he interrupted. He was making responses in an old ritual.

"No, I'm not. I'll make you tired of me. Tell me, please. Tell me you love me. I feel you've never told me it."

"I love you more than everything else in life. More than everything."

"Oh, do you, Erik?"

She pressed herself closer to him, and he felt her body like the heat of a flame avidly caress him.

"I don't want you any different, though," she whispered. "When I see other men I get horrified to think that you might become like them—if you didn't love me. Dead, creepy things. Oh, men are horrible. Talk to me, Erik."

"I can't. I love you. What else is there to say?" His voice trembled and her mouth pressed upon his.

"I don't deserve such happiness," she said. Tears from her eyes fell like warm wax on his shoulder. Her hands were fumbling distractedly over him.

"Erik," she gasped, "my Erik! I worship you."

The storm pounded through the night, leaping and bellowing in a halloo of sounds. Dorn tightened his arms mechanically about her warm flesh. His lips were murmuring tensely, dramatically, "I love you. I love you." And a sadness made a little warmth in his heart. He was alone in the night. His arms and words were engaged in an old make-believe. But this time he felt himself further away. There was no meaning. . . .

He tried vainly to think of Anna, but an emptiness crowded even her name out of his mind. His hands were returning her caresses, mimicking the eager distraction of her own. His mind, removed as if belonging elsewhere, was thinking aimless little words.

There was a storm outside. Lightning. . . . The war was taking up too much space in the paper. Crowding out important local news. The Germans would probably get to Paris soon and put an end to it. . . . Why did Rachel run away? Should he ask her? Sometime. When he saw her. Ask her. Ask her. . . . His thought drifted into a blank. Then it said . . . "The thing is meaningless. Meaningless. Houses, faces, streets. Nothing, nothing. There's nothing. . . ."

His wife lay silent, quivering with an ecstasy. Her arms were hungrily choking him. Dorn closed his eyes as if to hide himself. His lips still murmured in a monotone, vague as the voice of a stranger in his ears—responses in an old ritual—"I love you, I love you! Oh, I love you so much! . . ."

PART TWO

DREAM

Chapter One

IN the evening when women stand washing dishes in the kitchens of the city, men light their tobacco and open newspapers. Later, the women gather up the crumpled sheets and read.

The streets of the city spell easy words—poor, rich—neither.

Here in one part live the grimy-faced workers, their sagging, shapeless women and their litters of children. Their windows open upon broken little streets and bubbling alleys. Idiot-faced wooden houses sprawl over one another with their rumps in the mud. The years hammer away—digesting the paint from houses. The years grind away, yet life persists. Beneath the grinding of the years, life gropes, shrieks, sweats. And in the evening men light their tobacco and open newspapers.

Around a corner the boxes commence. One, two, three, four, and on into thousands stand houses made of stone, and their regimental masonry is like the ticking of a clock. Unvarying windows, doors identical—a stereotype of roofs and chimneys—these hold the homes of the crowds. Here the vague faces of the streets, the hurrying, enigmatic figures pumping in and out of offices and stores gather to sleep and breed.

In the evening the crowds drift into boxes. The multiple destinations dwindle suddenly into a monotone. The confusions of the city's traffic; the winding and unwinding herds that made a picture for the eyes of Erik Dorn, individualize into little human solitudes. The stone houses stand ticking away the years, and within them men and women tick. Doors open and shut, lights go on and off, day and night drop a ticktock across miles of roofs. And in the hour of the washing of dishes men kindle their tobacco and read the newspapers.

Slowly, timidly, the city moves away from the little stone boxes. Automobiles and trees appear. Here begin the ornaments. Marble, bronze, carved and painted brick—a filigree and a scrollwork—put forth claims. The lords of the city stand girthed in ornaments. Knight and satrap have changed somewhat. Moat and battlement grimace but faintly from behind their ornaments. The tick-tock sounds through the carouse. Sleek, suave men and languorous, desirable women sit amid elaborations, sleep and breed in ornamental beds. Power wears new masks. Leadership has improved its table manners, its plumbing, and its God.

Beautiful clocks, massive with griffiens and gargoyles, nymphs and scrollwork—they shelter heroes. But heroes have changed. Destiny no longer passes in the night—a masked horseman riding a lonely road. Instead, an old watchmaker winds up clocks, sleek men and desirable women. In the inner offices of the city the new heroes sit through the day, watchmakers themselves, winding and unwinding the immemorial crowds with new devices. But in the evening they too return to their ornamental boxes, and under Pompeian lamps, amid Renaissance tapestries, open newspapers.

Alley box and manor, the tick-tock of the city has them all. Paved streets and window-pitted walls beat out a monotone. Lust and dream turn sterile eyes to the night. The great multiple tick-tock of the city waits another hour to pass.

Wait, it reads a newspaper. On the west side of the city a man named Joseph Pryzalski has murdered a woman he loved, beating her head in with an ax, and subsequently cut his own throat with a razor. At the inquest there will be exhibited a note scribbled on a piece of wrapping-paper still redolent with herring . . . "God in heaven, forgive me! She is dead. It is better. Oh, God, now my turn!" Deplorable incident.

In the next column the exploits of three young men armed with guns. Entering a bank, the three young men shot and killed Henry J. Sloane, cashier; held half a dozen other names at bay, loaded their pockets with money, and escaped in a black automobile. The police are, fortunately, combing the city for the three young men and the black automobile. Thank God for the police moving cautiously through the streets with a large, a magnificent comb that will soon pick the three young men, their three guns, and their symbolical black automobile out of the city.

Next, the daily report of excitements in Europe. The Austrian army has been annihilated. A part of the German army, seemingly the most important part, has also been annihilated. Day by day the armies of the Allies continue to devour, obliterate, grind into dust the armies of the Kaiser. Bulletin—black type demanding quick eye—twenty thousand unsuspecting Prussians walking across a bridge on the Meuse were blown up and completely annihilated. This occurred on a Monday. In the teeth of these persistent and vigorous annihilations, the Huns still continue their atrocities. Shame! In Liége, on a Tuesday, the blood-dripping Huns added another horror to their list of revolting crimes. Three citizens of Liége were executed. They died like heroes. There are other items on this general subject, including a message from the Pope.

Alongside the war, as if in a next room, a woman has shot her lover on learning he was a married man. "Beauty Slays Soul-Mate; Shoots Self." . . . Annihilation on a smaller but more interesting scale, this.

A street-car has crashed into a brewery wagon and at the bottom of the column a taxi has run over a golden-haired little girl at play.

But why has Raymond S. Cotton, wealthy clubman and financier and prominent in northshore society circles, disappeared? Society circles are agog. Sometimes society circles are merely disturbed. But they are always active. Society circles are always running around waving lorgnettes and exclaiming, "Dear me, and what do you think of this? I am all agog." The police are combing the city for a woman in black last seen with the prominent Mr. Cotton in a notorious café. But a man is to be hanged in the County Jail. "The doomed man ate a hearty breakfast of ham and eggs and seemed in good spirits." Fancy that!

"Flames Destroy Warehouse, Two Firemen Hurt." This, in small apologetic type like a footnote on a timetable. Inconsiderate firemen who take up important space on a crowded day!

Apology ceases. Here is something that requires no apology. It is extremely important. Wilbur Jennings, prominent architect, has defied the world and departed for a Love Bungalow in Minnesota with another man's wife. A picture of Wilbur in flowing bow tie and set jaws defying the world. Also of his inamorata in a ball gown, eyes lowered to a rose drooping from her hand. Various wives and chubby-faced children, and the inamorata's Siberian hound, "Jasper." What he said. What she said. What they said. Opinions of three ministers, roused on the telephone by inquiring reporters. The three divines are unanimous. But Wilbur's tie remains defiant.

Arm in arm with Wilbur, his tie and his troubles, his epigrams and his Love Bungalow, sits an epidemic of clairvoyants. There is an epidemic of clairvoyants in the city. Five widows have been swindled. The police are combing the city for . . . a prominent professor of sociology on the faculty of the local university interrupts. The prominent professor has been captured in a leading Loop hotel whither he had gone to divert himself with a suitcase, a handbook on sex hygiene, and an admiring co-ed.

This, waiting for an hour to pass, the city reads. Crimes, scandals, horrors, holocausts, burglaries, arsons, murders, deceptions. The city reads with a vague, dull skepticism. Who are these people of the newspaper columns? Lusting scoundrels, bandits, heroes, wild lovers, madmen? Not in the streets or the houses that tick-tock through the night. . . . Somewhere else. A troupe of mummers wandering unseen behind the great clock face of the city—an always unknown troupe of rascally mummers for whom the police are continually combing and setting large dragnets.

In the evening men light their tobacco and read the little wooden phrases of the press that squeal and mumble the sagas of the lawbreakers. Women come from the washing of dishes and eating of food and pick up the crumpled pages. . . . A scavenger digging for the disgusts and abnormalities of life, is the press. A yellow journal of lies, idiocies, filth. Ignoring the wholesome, splendid things of life—the fine, edifying beat of the ticktock. Yet they read, glancing dully at headlines, devouring monotonously the luridness beneath headlines. They read with an irritation and a vague wonder. Tick, say the streets, and tock, say the houses; and within them men and women tick. To work and home again. Home again and to work. New shoes grow old. New seasons vanish. Years grind. Life sinks slowly away with a tick-tock on its lips.

Yet each evening comes the ragged twopenny minstrel—a blear-eyed, croaking minstrel, and the good folk give him ear. No pretty words in rhythms from his tongue. No mystic cadences quaver in his voice. Yet he comes squealing out his song of an endless "Extra! All about the mysteries and the torments of life. All about the raptures, lusts, and adventures that the day has spilled. Read 'em and weep! Read 'em and laugh! Here's the latest, hot off the presses, from dreamers and lawbreakers. Extra!"

Thus the city sits, baffled by itself, looking out upon a tick-tock of windows and reading with a wonder in its thought, "Who are these people? . . ."

Chapter Two

AT ten o'clock the courts of the city crowd up. The important gentlemen who devote themselves to sending people to jail and to preventing them from being sent to jail, appear with fat books under their arms and brief-cases in their hands. They have slept well and eaten well and have arrived at their tasks with clear heads containing arguments. These are arguments vastly more important than poems that writers make or histories that dreamers invent. For they are arrangements of words which function in the absence of God. God is not exactly absent, to be sure, since the memory of Him lingers in the hearts of men. But it is a vague memory and at times unreliable. It would appear that He was on earth only for a short interval and failed to make any decided impression.

Therefore, at ten o'clock, the courts crowd up and the important gentlemen bristling with substitute arrangements of words, address themselves to the daily business of demonstrating whether people have done right or wrong, and proving, or disproving also, how extensive are the sins which have been committed. Arrangements of words palaver with arrangements of words. There ensues a vast shuffling of words, a drone and a gurgle of syllables. The Case of the State of Illinois Versus Man. Order in the Court Room. "No talking, please . . ." "If it Please Your Honor, the Issue involved in this case is identical with the Issue as explicitly set forth in the Case of Matthews Versus Matthews, Illinois Sixth, Chapter Eight, Page ninety two, in which in the Third Paragraph the Supreme Court decided." The Court Instructs the Jury, "You are to be Guided by the Law as given You in these instructions and by the Facts as admitted in Evidence of the Case; the court Instructs the jury they are the judges of the law as well as of the fact but the Court further instructs the Jury before You decide for Yourselves that the Law is Otherwise than as given you by the Court, you are to exercise great Care and Caution in arriving at your decision. . . ." "Gentlemen, have you arrived at your verdict?" "We have." "Let the clerk be handed the verdict." "We the Jury find the Defendant . . ."

Thus the tick-tock of the great city grown stern and audible, grown verbose and insistent, speaks aloud in the courts. And here huddled on benches are the little troupes of mummers who have committed crimes. The mysterious sprinkling of marionettes not wound up by the watchmaker. Names that solidify for a moment into the ink headlines. Lusts, dreams, greeds, and manias sitting sad-faced and dolorous-eyed listening to a drone and a gurgle of words. Alas! The evil-doers and the doers of good bear a fatuous resemblance to each other. God Himself might well be confused by this curious fact. But fortunately there are arrangements of words capable of adjusting themselves to confusion, capable of tick-tocking in the midst of disorder. Tick, say the words and tock say the juries. Tick-tock, the cell door and the scaffold drop. Streets and windows, paintings of the Virgin Mary, beds of the fifty-cent prostitutes, cannon at Verdun and police whistles on crossings; the Pope in Rome, the President in Washington, the man hunting the alleys for a handout, the languorous women breeding in ornamental beds—all say a tick-tock. Behind the arrangements of words, confusion strikes a posture of guilt, strikes a posture of innocence. God Himself were a dolt to interfere. For if the song of the angels is somehow other than the tick-tock of men, the song of the angels is a music for heaven and the tick-tock of men is a restful drone in which the city hides the mysteries non-essential to the progress and pattern of its streets.

Chapter Three

IN and out of the crowded courtrooms of the city George Hazlitt pursued his career. Buried in the babble of words, his voice sounded from day to day with a firm, self-conscious vigor. To the thousand and one droners about him, the law was a remunerative game in which one matched platitude with bromide, legal precedent of the State of Illinois with legal precedent of the State of Indiana; in which right and wrong were a shuffle of words and the wages of sin dependent upon the depth of a counselor's wits.

There was in Hazlitt, however, a puritanical fervor which withstood the lure of expediency. He entered the courts not to juggle with words, fence for loopholes out of which to drag dubious acquittals for his clients. His profession was a part of his nature. He saw it as a battle ground on which, under the babbling and droning, good and evil stood at unending grips. Good always triumphing. Evil always going to jail despite habeas corpuses, writs, and duces tecums.

To question the nobility of the Hazlitt soul would be a sidestepping. There were among his friends, men of dubious integrity with elastic scruples and pliable consciences. But skepticism thrust in vain at the Hazlitt armor. In him had been authentically born the mania for conformity. He was a prosecutor by birth. Against that which did not conform, against all that squirmed for some expression beyond the tick-tock of life, he was a force—an apostle with a sword. Men pretending virtues as relentless as his own were often inclined to eye him askance. Virtue breeds skepticism among the virtuous. But there was a difference about Hazlitt.

The basis of his philosophy was twofold. It embraced a rage against dreamers and a rage against lawbreakers. Lawbreakers were men and women who sacrificed the welfare and safety of the many for the sating of their individual greeds and lusts. He viewed the activities of lawbreakers with a sense of personal outrage. He, Hazlitt, was a part of society—a conscious unit of a state of mind, which state of mind was carefully written out in text-book editorials, and on tablets handed down by God from a mountaintop. Men who robbed, cheated, beat their wives, deserted their families, seduced women, shirked responsibilities, were enemies on his own threshold. They must be punished, mentally, by him; physically by the society to which he belonged.

The punishing of evil-doers did more than eliminate them from his threshold. It vindicated his own virtue. Virtue increases in direct proportion with its ability to distinguish evil. The denunciation of evil-doers was the boasting of George

Hazlitt, "I am not one of them." The more vigorous the denunciation, the more vigorous the boast. The hanging of a man for the crime of murder was a reward paid to George Hazlitt for his abstinence from bloodshed. The jailing of a seducer offered a tangible recompense for the self-denial which he, as a non-seducer, practiced.

Apart from the satisfactions his virtue derived in establishing its superiority by assisting spiritually in the punishment of the unvirtuous, his rage against lawbreakers found itself equally on his devotion to law. He perceived in the orderly streets, in the miles of houses, in the smoothly functioning commerce and government of his day, a triumph of man over his baser selves. The baser selves of man were instincts that yearned for disorder. Of this triumph Hazlitt felt himself a part.

Disorder he thought not only illegal, but debasing. The same virtue which prevented him from promenading in his pajamas in the boulevard stirred with a feeling of outrage against the confusion attending a street-car strike. His intelligence, clinging like some militant parasite to the stability of life, resented all agitations, material or spiritual, all violators who violated the equilibrium to which he was fastened.

Against dreamers his rage was even deeper and more a part of his fiber. In the tick-tock of life Hazlitt saw a perfection—an evolution out of centuries of mania and disorder. The tick-tock was a perfection whose basic principle was a respect for others. This respect evolved out of man's fear of man and insuring a mutual protection against his predatory habits, was to Hazlitt a religion. He denied himself pleasures and convenient expressions for his impulses in order to spare others displeasure and inconvenience. And his nature demanded a similar sacrifice of his fellows —as a reward and a symbol of his own correctness. Such explanation of his conduct as, it is easier to follow the desires of others than to give expression to the desires of one's self, would have been, to Hazlitt, spiritual and legal sacrilege.

In dreamers, the rising young attorney sensed a poorly concealed effort to evade this primal responsibility toward him and the society of which he was an inseparable part. Men who walked with their heads in the clouds were certain to step on one's feet. Dreamers were scoundrels or lunatics who sought to justify their unfitness for society by ridiculing it as unworthy and by phantasizing over new values and standards which would be more amiable to their weaknesses. There were political dreamers and dreamers in morals and art. Hazlitt bunched them together, branded them with an identical rage, and spat them out in one word, "nuts."

Dreamers challenged his sense of superiority by hinting at soul states and social states superior to those he already occupied. Dreamers disturbed him. For this he perhaps hated them most. Their phantasies sometimes lifted him into moments of disorder, moments of doubt as revolting to his spirit as were sores revolting to his skin. Then also, dreamers had their champions—men and women who applauded their lunatic writings and cheered their lunatic theories.

The punishment of lawbreakers vindicated his own virtue. But his rage against dreamers was such that their punishing offered him no sense of satisfactory vindication. His railing and ridicule against creatures who yearned, grimaced—neurasthenics, in short— left him with no fine feeling of the victorious sufficiency of himself. Thus to conceal himself from doubts always threatening an appearance, it was necessary for him to assume a viciousness of attitude not entirely sincere. So he read with unction political speeches and art reviews denouncing the phantasts of his day, and from them he borrowed elaborate invective. Yet his invective seemed like a vague defense of himself who should need no defense and thus again doubt raised a dim triumph in his heart.

"Yes, I'm a reactionary," he would say. "I'm for the good old things of life. Things that mean something." And even this definition of faith would leave him unsatisfied.

The paradox of George Hazlitt lay in the fact that he was himself a dreamer. Champions of order and champions of disorder share somewhat in a similarity of imaginative impulses.

Six months had passed since Hazlitt had wept on the stairs as he left Rachel's room. Dry-eyed now and clear-headed, he sat one winter afternoon against his chosen background—the swarm and clutter of a law court. His brief-cases were packed. His law books had been bundled back to his office.

He was waiting beside a vivid-faced young woman who sat twisting a tear-damp handkerchief in her hands. The jury that had listened for three weeks to the tale of the young woman's murder of a hospital interne who had seduced and subsequently refused to marry her, had sauntered out of the jury-box to determine now whether the young woman should be hanged, imprisoned, or liberated. The excitements attending the trial had brought a reaction to Hazlitt. He seemed suddenly to have lost interest in the business of his defense of the wronged young woman. This despite that he had for three weeks maintained a high pitch of rage against the scoundrel who had violated his client and subsequently driven her insane by even more abominable cruelties.

Hazlitt's concluding remarks to the jury on the subject of dishonored womanhood and the merciless bestiality of certain male types had been more than a legal oration. He had expressed himself in it and had spent two full days lost in admiration of the echoes of his bombast. . . . "Men who follow the vile dictates of their lower natures, who sow the whirlwind and expect to reap the roses thereby; cynical, soulless men who take a woman as one takes a glove, to wear, admire, and discard;

depraved men who prowl like demons at the heels of virtue, fawning their ways into the pure heart of innocence and glutting their beastly hungers upon the finest fruits of life—the beauty and sacrifice of a maiden's first love—are such creatures men or fiends, gentlemen of the jury?" And then . . . "spurned, taunted by the sneers of one of these vipers, her pleadings answered with laughter and blows of a fist, the soul of Pauline Pollard grew suddenly dark. Where had been sanity, innocence, and love, now came insanity. Her girl's mind—like sweet bells jangled out of tune—brought no longer the high message of reason into her heart. We sitting here in this sunny courtroom, gentlemen, can think and reason. But Pauline Pollard, struggling in the embrace of a leering savage, listening to his fiendish mockeries of her virtue—the virtue he had stolen from her—ah! the soul and brain of Pauline Pollard vanished in a darkness. The law is the law, gentlemen. There is no one respects it more than I. If this girl killed a man coldly and with reason functioning in her mind, she is guilty. Hang her, gentlemen of the jury! But, gentlemen, the law under which we live, you and I and all of us, also says, and says wisely, that a mind not responsible for its acts, a soul whose balance has been destroyed by the shrieking voices of mania, shall not be held guilty. . . ."

The jury that had listened with ill-concealed envy to the recital of the amorous interne's promiscuous exploits, listened to Hazlitt and experienced suddenly a fine rage against the deceased. Out of the young attorney's florid utterings a question fired itself into the minds of the jurors. The deceased had done what they all desired to do, but dared not. This grinning, unscrupulous fiend of a hospital interne had blithely taken what he desired and blithely discarded what he did not desire. The twelve good men and true bethought them of their wives whom they did not desire and yet kept. And of the young women and the things of flesh and spirit they desired with every life-beat in them and yet did not take. Was this terrible denial which, for reasons beyond their incomplete brains, they imposed upon themselves, a meaningless, profitless business? The bland interne was dead and unfortunately beyond their punishment. Yet the fact that he had lived at all called for a protest—some definitely framed expression which would throw a halo about their own submission to women they did not desire, and their own denial to women they did desire. The law, whose arrangements of words are omniscient, provided such a halo.

Dr. Hamel, the interne under discussion, was dead and buried, and therefore, properly speaking, not on trial. Nor yet was Pauline Pollard on trial. The persons on trial were twelve good men and true who were being called upon to decide, somewhat dramatically, whether they were right in living in a manner persistently repugnant to them; whether somebody else could get away with something which they themselves, not daring to attempt, bitterly identified as sin.

In thirty minutes the still outraged jury was to file in and utter its dignified protest. Pauline Pollard would again be free. And twelve men would return to their homes with a high sense of having meted out justice, not to Pauline or her amorous interne, but to themselves.

Enticing speculation, the yes or no of these twelve men, three days ago. But now Hazlitt sat with an odd indifference in his thought. The crowd waiting avidly for the dramatic moment of the verdict; living vicariously the suspense of the defendant—depressed him. The newspaper reporters buzzing around, forming themselves into relays between the press table and the door, further depressed him. He felt himself somewhere else, and the scene was a reality which intruded.

There was a dream in Hazlitt which sometimes turned itself on like a light and revealed the emptiness of life without Rachel, the emptiness of courtrooms, verdicts, crowds. Yes, even the emptiness of the struggle between good and evil. He sat thinking of her now, contrasting the virginal figure of her with the coarseness of the thing in which he had been engaged. There was something about her . . . something . . . something. And the old refrain of his dream like a haunting popular ballad, started again here in the crowded courtroom.

He remembered the eyes of Rachel, the quick

gestures of her full-grown hands that moved always as in sudden afterthoughts. Virginal was the word that came most often to his thought. Not the virginity that spells a piquant preface to sensualism. She would always be virginal, even after they were married. In his arms she would remain virginal, because there was something in her, something beyond flesh. His heart choked at the memory of it, and his face saddened. Something he could not see or place in a circle of words, that did not exist for his eyes or his thought, and yet that he must follow. Even after he had won her there would be this thing he could not see; that trailed a dream song in his heart and kept him groping toward the far lips of the singer. Yes, they would marry. She had refused to see him twice since the night he had wept on the stair, leaving her. But the memories of that night had adjusted themselves. He had seen love in the eyes of Rachel as he held her hand. She had laughed love to him, given him for an instant the vision of beauty-lighted places waiting for him. The rest had been . . . neurasthenia. Thus he had forgotten her words and his tears and the vivid moment when he had seen himself reflected in her eyes as a horror. He had tried twice to see her. He would continue trying, and some day she would again open the door to him, laughing, whispering . . . "I'm so lonely. I'm glad you've come." In the meantime he would continue sending her letters. Once each week he had been writing her, saying he loved her. No answers had come. But this, curiously, did not anger him. He wrote not so much to Rachel as to a dream of her. She remained intact in her silence . . . as he knew her . . . an aloof, virginal being whose presence in the world was its own song.

There was a commotion. Hazlitt looked about him and saw strange faces light up, strange eyes gleam out of the electric-glowing dusk. Snow was falling outside. Pauline's hand gripped his forearm. Her fingers burned. Raps of a gavel for silence. The judge spoke. A sad-faced man, with a heavy mustache combating his words, stood up in the jury-box and spoke. In a vast silence a clerk beside the judge's bench cleared his voice. moistened his lips, and spoke.

So he had won another case. Pauline was free. Snow outside and rows of lighted windows. She was overwrought. Let her weep for a spell. Snow outside. Three weeks and one day. Everybody seemed happy with the verdict. People were good at heart. A triumph for decency cheered them. People were not revengeful at heart, only decent. Congratulations . . . "Thank you, thank you! No, Miss Pollard has nothing to say now. She is too overcome. Tomorrow . . ." The persistent press! What did they expect her to say? Absurd the way they kept interviewing her. The snow would probably tie up traffic. Eat down-town . . .

"If you're ready, Miss Pollard."

"Oh, I must thank the jurors."

Handshakes. Twelve good men with relaxed faces. "There, there, little woman. Start over. We only did our duty and what was right by you."

Everybody stretched his legs. Mrs. Hamel was sobbing. Well, she was his mother. It would only have satisfied her lower instincts of vengeance to have jailed Pauline.

"All right, Miss Pollard." He took her arm. Curious, what a difference the verdict had made in her. She was a woman like any other woman now. . . . His overcoat might do for another season. . . . Pretty girl. Hard to get used to the idea she wasn't a defendant.

"This way, Miss Pollard." . . Take her to a cab and send her home. If she'd ever get started. What satisfaction did women find in kissing and hugging each other? "Thank God, Pauline. Oh, I'm so glad." . . . Girl friends. Well, she'd be back among them in a few days, and in a month or so the thing would be over.

At last! Hazlitt blinked. The whirl of snow and crowds emptying out of buildings gave him a sense for an instant of having stepped into a strange world. The sharp cold restored his wandering energies and a realization of his victory in the court-room brought him a belated glow. He was young, on an upgrade, able to command success.

Hazlitt felt a sudden lusty kinship toward the

swarm of bodies unwinding itself through the snowfall. A contact with other . . . a pleasant, comforting contact. What more was life, anyway? A warmth in the heart that came from the knowledge of work well and honestly done. Look the world squarely in the eyes and say, "You have no secrets and I have no secrets. We're friends."

"Shall we go to your office, Mr. Hazlitt?"

Why there? Hazlitt smiled at the young woman. She was free. He patted the gloved hand on his arm and was surprised to see her eyes grow alive with tears.

"I would like to talk to you—now that it's over. I feel lost. Really." She returned his smile as one determined to be brave, though lost.

The snow hid the buildings and left their window lights drifting. Faces passing smiled as if saying, "Hello, we're all together in the same snow with no secrets from each other. . . . All friends." . . . Hazlitt walked with the girl through the streets. The traffic and the crowds were intimate friends and he spoke to them by patting Pauline's hand. An all's-well-with-the-world pat.

"Eighth floor, please. . . ."

The elevator jiggled to a stop and they stepped into the corridor. Scrawny-faced women were crawling patiently down the floor. They slopped wet brushes before them, wrung mops out over pails, and crawled an inch farther down the floor. Hazlitt smiled. This, too, was a part of life—

keeping the floors of the building scrubbed. He won law cases. Old women scrubbed floors. It fitted into an orderly pattern with a great meaning to its order. He paused for a moment to admire the cleanliness of the washed surface. Homage to the work of others—of old women on their knees scrubbing floors.

"Well, it's all over, Miss Pollard."

She was sitting beside the desk where she had sat the first time they had discussed her defense. Hazlitt, unloading his brief-case, looked at her. Uncommonly pretty. Trusting eyes. What a rotten fellow, the interne!

"I don't know why I wanted to come here." Pauline's eyes stared sadly about the room. "I'm free, but . . ." She covered her face and wept.

"Now, now, Miss Pollard!"

"Oh, it's still awful."

"You'll forget soon."

"I'll go away. Somewhere. Alone." A louder sob.

"Please don't cry."

Hazlitt watched her tenderly. The weeping increased. A lonesomeness and a vagueness were in the girl's heart. The tick-tock of the city had a foreign sound. She was a stranger in its streets. There had been something else, and now it was gone. A wilderness, a tension, the familiar face of Frankie Hamel telling her to go to hell one night and stop bothering him with her damned wailing . . . and Frankie dying at her feet whispering,

"What the devil, Pauline?" Then the trial. Hot and cold hours. A roomful of silent, open-mouthed faces listening to her weep, watching her squirm with proper shame and anguish as she told her story to the jurors . . . the details of the abortion. "And then I couldn't stand it. I don't remember what happened. Oh, I loved him! I don't remember. He cursed me. He called me a . . . Oh, God, names. Awful names! I told him I was going to kill myself. I couldn't live, disgraced . . . without his love. I'd bought a gun to kill myself. And he laughed. I don't remember after that; except that somehow he was . . . he was dead. And I wasn't . . ."

These things were gone. The trial was over and done. Now there was nothing left but the city with its street-cars and offices.

"Oh, everything's so changed," she murmured. Hazlitt stood behind her chair, hand on her shoulder. Poor child! The law could not free her from the remorse for her crime and mistake. Lawlessness carried its own punishment. Virtue its own rewards, sin its own torments.

"You'll forget," he answered softly. The law sometimes punished. But after all this was the real punishment . . . beyond the power of the law to mete out. Punishment of sin. Conscience. Poor child! Inexorable fruit of evil. Despair, remorse. . . .

"You must forget. You're young. You can begin over. Please don't cry."

Erik Dorn

Thus Hazlitt comforted her who was weeping not with remorse for what had been, but that it had gone. No word consciousness stirred her grief. An unintelligible sorrow, it swelled in her heart and filled her with helplessness. Life had gone from her. She was mourning for it. Mourning for a murderess and a sinner who had gone, abandoned her and left her a naked, uninteresting Pauline Pollard again—a nobody surrounded by nobodies. And once it had been different. Lighted faces listening to her in a room. Frankie whispering, "What the devil, Pauline?"

A fresh burst of tears brought Hazlitt in front of her. Gently he moved her hands from her face.

"You mustn't," he began over again.

"Oh, I won't ever be able to . . ."

"Yes you will, little girl."

"No, no!"

She was standing. Snow outside. Rows of lighted windows drifting. Thoughts slipped out of his head. Traffic probably tied up.

"Please don't cry."

She dropped her head against his shoulder and wept anew. It was nice to have somebody asking her not to cry. It made it easier and more purposeful to weep.

Hazlitt sighed. Tears . . . tears . . . the live odor of hair. Arms that felt soft. She was mumbling close to him, "I can't help it. Please forgive me."

"Yes, yes! There, there!" Of course he would

forgive her. Forgiveness made him glow. But as he spoke his voice depressed him. What should he do? Could he help her? What was life, anyway? Snow outside and rows of lighted windows drifting. Her body close, warm, and saddening. The firmness of his nerves dissolved. He had his sorrow too . . . Rachel. Far away. Drifting like the snow outside. Rachel . . . the odor of hair brought her back. Should he cry? Her knees had touched him once like this. She had held her arm about his shoulder once, like this. But, oh, so different! . . . The girl seemed to come closer to him.

He had been holding a stranger politely. Now the stranger relaxed. Soft, warm, familiar body. He grew frightened. Somehow the clinging of the girl's body, the murmur of her tears, brought a sorrow into his heart. I am not Rachel, but I am like her. . . . What made him think that? Yes, she was like her, warm, soft, and woman. Like her—like her. Why had they kissed? And her hands clasping nervously at his shoulders? She was not in love? Not Rachel. But she wanted something. And he too. Something that was a dream song. Here were the lips of the singer, eager, reaching to his own. Pressing, asking more. How had this happened? Should he speak? But what? Nothing to say. Had he forgotten Rachel? Remembering Rachel? Who was this? The questions blurred. Rachel, sang his heart. For a moment he embraced the warm shadow of a dream. And then a woman was offering herself to him. No dream now. Her thighs riveted themselves against him. Under her clothes her body seemed to be moving, coming to him.

Hazlitt grew dizzy. He had been consoling her. No more. Now what? He threw his strength into his embrace. Their bodies moved together.

"Oh . . ." A moan as if she were still weeping. Her lips parted in desperate surrender. Her kiss took the breath out of him.

"Dearest!" His voice carried him out of her arms. He knew suddenly that but for the word and the familiar sound of his voice he would have possessed her. But the word rang an alarm in his ears. Fright, nausea, relaxed muscles. A wiliness in his thought. . . . "Do you feel better now?"

She failed to hear. Her fingers still clutched.

"There . . . there, don't cry!" He felt cold. His hands on her arms pressed them gently away, his fingers patting them with a fatherly diapason. George Hazlitt, attorney-at-law.

"Better now, Pauline?" An error to have called her Pauline. Look bad in the record. Committed him to "Pauline."

"Oh, George!"

The thought of Rachel listened in amazement . . . George . . . Pauline. Dearest! He must be careful. She had grown numb against him. A numb woman sewed to his lapels. He lowered her as if she were lifeless and he fearful of disturbing her. She looked harmless in a chair. Was it possible to talk now? Not yet. Take her hand; careful not to squeeze it. Pat it as he'd done in the street. An all's-well-with-the-world pat.

Somebody rattled the doorknob. Hazlitt started eagerly. Relief. But, good God, no lights in the office. The cleaners would come in and think things. Her hair in disorder and her face smeared with weeping would make them think things. An oath disentangled itself from his confusion. The door opened. Two scrawny-faced women with mops and brooms. . . .

"It's all right. Go ahead. We're just leaving. Are you ready, Miss Pollard?"

The Miss Pollard was a masterpiece. But did it deceive the mops and brooms? Damn them! They walked arm in arm down the corridor.

"I think the elevators have stopped. Wouldn't it be a joke if we had to walk down?"

She refused to answer. Witness remains silent. Why couldn't she be interested in jokes? . . . the woman of it. Nothing had happened. She had nothing to think about. Why not jokes? He frowned at the grilling of the elevator door. An elevator bobbed up.

In the street, "I'll get a cab, Miss Pollard." Take a firm stand and not call her Pauline again. But she was silent. Nothing had happened. He grew frightened. She was trying to bulldoze him by pretending. Bundle her into a cab and get rid of her.

Suddenly, as if he'd been thinking it out when he hadn't, "You must forgive me for—that. I didn't mean to, please."

Anything rather than her silence. Even an apology. Nothing had happened, but he would apologize anyway to be on the safe side. She looked at him and said, "Oh!"

"Please, Miss Pollard, you make me feel like a cur."

A chauffeur leaned forward from his seat and thrust open the cab door. Pauline entered without hesitation. She might have the decency to hesitate when he was apologizing for nothing. Hazlitt stuck his head in after her. The thing was ludicrously unfinished and he was making an ass of himself. She should have hesitated.

"Tell your mother I hope she'll be better soon."

"Where to, mister?"

He gave an address and added, "Just a minute, please."

Hazlitt reëntered the cab with his head. The thing was still unfinished. Wishing good health to her mother made it worse—as if he were trying to cover up something. He must be frank. Drag everything into the open and show he wasn't afraid. But she was weeping again. He paused in consternation. Her hand reached toward him. A voice, vibrant and soft with tears, whispered in the gloom of the cab. A love voice. "Goodby, George!"

He watched the tail light dart through the traffic and then began his defense. Gentleman of the jury . . . jury . . . he had done nothing. It was she who had suggested the office. A low, vulgar ruse to trap him. The evidence was plain on that point. Overruled. But he had attempted only to console her. Irrelevant and immaterial to the facts at issue in the case. But she had flung her arms around him. Not he! Never he! The woman was mad. Yes, a mad woman. Dangerous. She had done the same to the interne. Overruled. Overruled. What? Frank Hamel, gentleman of the jury, glutting his beastly hungers on the finest fruit of life—the innocence and sacrifice of a maiden's first love. No, not Hamel. Hazlitt. Are such creatures men or fiends? What was he thinking about Oh, yes, the interne. Dead, buried . . . we, the jury, find the defendant not guilty. . . . But the dead interne was saying something.

For moments George Hazlitt looked out upon a new world—a miserable world—vast, blurred, upside down. People were moving in it. Dead internes. They passed with faces intent upon their own solitudes. Buildings were in it. They burst a skyrocket of windows into the night. There was snow. It fell twisting itself out of the darkness. Familiar faces, buildings, snow. Theater façades making a jangle of light through the storm.

Entrances, exits, cars clanging, figures hurrying, signs sputtering confusion in the snow. All familiar, all a part of the great tick-tock of the city.

Hazlitt stopped and stared at the familiar night of the streets. A gleam and a flurry were sweeping his eyes. Snow. But faces and buildings and lights were a part of it. They swarmed and danced about him, sending a shout to his heart. "We're upside down . . . we're upside down . . . heels in air. . . . She made love to the interne as she did to you . . . and the fiend is dead. Lies . . . lies . . . but who gives a damn?"

The horn of a motor screeched. A woman and a man pattered by on a run, leaving a trail of laughter. From afar came the sound of voices—of street evangels singing hymns on a corner. The soul of George Hazlitt grew sick. Night hands fastened themselves about his throat. Upside down . . . heels in air. The things he had said to the jury were lies. Lies and disorder. Right and wrong. God in heaven, what were they, if not right and wrong?

The thing came to Hazlitt without words, with a gleam and a flurry as of snow. He stood blind —a little snow-covered figure shivering and lost in a lighted, crowded street. All because a woman, warm and clinging, had kissed him on the mouth and moved her body. But once she had kissed another man thus—on the mouth, with her body moving, and therein lay a new world—a world of flying-haired Mænads and growling satyrs that lived behind the tick-tock of windows. Standing in the snowstorm an insane notion took possession of Hazlitt. It had to do with Evil. Order was an accident. Men and women were evil. The tick-tock was a pretense.

The notion passed. Doubt needs thought to feed upon, and Hazlitt gave it none. Or he would have ended as Hazlitt and become someone else. He walked again with a silence in his head. Another block, and life had again focused itself into tableaux. The moment of doubt had shaken him as if rough hands had reached from an alley and clutched wildly at his throat. But it had gone, and the memory of it too was gone. Hands that had nobody behind them; emotion that came without the stabilizing outline of words. So the world stood again on its feet. Tick-tock, said the world to George Hazlitt; and his brain gave an answer, "Tick-tock!"

For the paradox of Hazlitt was not that he was a thinker, but a dreamer. His puritanism had put an end to his brain. Like his fellows for whose respect and admiration he worked, he had bartered his intelligence for a thing he proudly called Americanism, and thought for him had become a placid agitation of platitudes. But he could still dream. His emotions avenged his stupidity. Walking in the street—he felt a desire to walk—he shut himself in. It seemed to him now that his love had become a part of the snow and the far-away dark of the sky. Rachel . . . Rachel, his thought called as if summoning something back.

It came to him slowly—the image of the virginal one—doubly sweet and beautiful now that he was unclean. How had it happened? She had been weeping; he comforting her. Two strangers, they had sat in his office. One a murderess weeping for her sins; the other a kindly hearted, clean-minded attorney consoling her, pointing to her the way of hope. And then like two animals they had stood sucking at each other's breath. God, what could he do? Nothing. He was unclean. He recalled with a dread the thought that had come to him in the embrace . . . was she Rachel? Yes, she had been Rachel and he had lowered his dream to her lips, as if in the lust of a strange woman's kiss there lay the image of Rachel, the virginal mystery of Rachel. If he had been man enough not to drag the memory of Rachel into it, it would be easy now. But he would look squarely at the facts, anyway. That must be his punishment and his penance. Yes, say it . . . it was with his love for Rachel he had embraced and almost possessed the body of a stranger.

Hazlitt quickened his walking. He was confronted with the intricate business of forgiving himself. He felt shame, but shame was something that could be walked off. Faster . . . with an amorous mumble soothing him and the hurt. After all, was it so important? Yes . . . no. Forgive himself, but not too quickly. He walked. . . . Words made circles in his head —abject and sorrowful circles about the dream of the virginal one.

A man with a curious smile stopped in front of him to light a pipe. Hazlitt paused and looked at the street. He would take a car. His legs were tired. The wind and snow put out the match of the man who was lighting a pipe. Hazlitt looked at him. What was he smiling about? We're all in the snow . . . all without secrets in the snow. Hail fellows of the street . . . Curious, he should feel sad for a man who was smiling on a street corner. Tiredness. The man was cursing the snow good-humoredly. Suddenly the pipe was lighted and the man seemed to have forgotten it. His eyes gleamed for an instant across Hazlitt's face, and with an abrupt nod of recognition the man passed on. Walking swiftly, bent forward, vanishing behind a flurry of snow.

Hazlitt peered down the track for his car. He wondered how the man knew him. It pleased his vanity to be recognized by people he couldn't place. It showed he was somebody. Yes, George Hazlitt, attorney-at-law. He recalled . . . they had met once in an office. A newspaperman— editor or something. Probably looking for news. Hazlitt was glad he had been recognized. The man would think of him as he walked on in the snow—of his victory in the court-room and his future. That was part of life, to be thought of and envied by others.

Beside him a newsboy raised a shout . . . "Extra! Pauline Pollard acquitted! . . ." People would read about it in their homes. His name. Wonder who he was. A voice across the street answered, "Extra! Germans bombard Paris! . . ." The damned Huns! Why didn't America put an end to their dirty business by rushing in?

He stepped into the warm street-car and sat staring moodily out of the window. He was a part of life, but there was something beyond—a —mystery. "Extra! . . ." He should have bought a paper. There was the newspaper fellow again, still walking swiftly, bent forward, staring into the snow. . . . Oh, yes, Erik Dorn. He had met him once. . . . The car passed on.

Chapter Four

ERIK DORN laughed as he walked swiftly through the snow in the street. It seemed to him he had been laughing incessantly for a week, and that he would continue to laugh forever. His thought played delightedly with his emotions . . . a precocious child with new fantastic toys. He was in love. A laughable business!

Five months of uncertainty had preceded the laugh. An irritated, inexplicable moodiness as if the shadow of a disease had come into his blood. On top of this moodiness a violence of temper, a stewing, cursing, fuming about. A five months' quarrel with his wife. . . .

His love-making had been somewhat curious. Walks with Rachel—a whirligig of streets, faces, words. A dance and a flash of words, as if he were exploding into phrases. As if his vocabulary desired to empty itself before Rachel. His garrulity amazed him. Everything had to be talked about. There was a desperate need for talk. And when there was nothing to talk about for the moment, his words abhorring idleness, fell to inventing emotions—a complete set of emotions for himself and for Rachel. These were discussed, explained, and forgotten.

Finally the strange talk that had ended a week ago—a last desperate concealment of emotion and desire in a burst of glittering phrases. Phrases that whirled like the exotic decorations about the wild body of a dancer, becoming a dance in themselves, deriving a movement and a meaning beyond themselves. Then the end of concealment. An exhausted vocabulary sighed, collapsed. A frantic discarding of ornaments and the nude body of the dancer stood posturing naïvely, timidly. Therewith an end to mystery. The thing was known.

It had happened during one of their walks. Leaden clouds over day-dark pavements. Warehouses, railroad tracks, factories—a street toiling through a dismantled world. Their hands together, they paused and remained staring as if at a third person. He had reached out rather impersonally and taken her hand. The contact had shocked him into silence. It was difficult to breathe.

"Rachel, do you love me?"

She nodded her head and pressed his hand against her cheek. They walked on in silence. This brought an end to talk. Talk concealed. There was nothing more to conceal. His vocabulary sighed as if admitting defeat and uselessness. At a corner grown noisy with wagons and trucks Rachel stopped. Her eyes opened to him. He looked at her and said, as if he had fallen asleep "I too am in love." He laughed dreamily. "Yes, I've been since the beginning. Curious!"

She might laugh at him. It was evident he had avoided making love to her during the five months in fear of that. The only reason he hadn't embraced, kissed, and protested affection five months ago was the possibility that she would laugh—and perhaps go away.

Even now, despite the absence of laughter, a part of the fear he had still lingered. He was no longer Erik Dorn, man of words and mirror of nothings. He had said he loved her. Avoiding, of course, the direct remark. But he had indicated it rather definitely. It would undoubtedly lessen him to her, make him human. She had admired him because he was different. Now he was like everybody else saying an "I love you" to a woman. Perhaps he should unsay it. Again, a dreamy laugh. But it made him happy. A drifting, childish happiness. He looked at her. Her eyes struck him as marvelously large and bright. Yet in a curious way he seemed unaware of her. No excitement came to him. Decidedly there was something unsensual about his love— if it was love. It might be something else. It is difficult for an extremely married man to distinguish offhand. He desired nothing more than to stand still and close his eyes and permit himself to shine. Vague words traced his emotions. A fullness. A completion. An end of nothing. Thrills in his fingers. Remarkable disturbance of the diaphragm. To be likened to the languorous effects of some almost stimulating drug.

In a great calm he slowly forgot himself, his words, and Rachel. Standing thus he heard her murmur something and felt his hand once more against her cheek. A pretty gesture. Then she was walking down the dark street, running from him. She had said good-bye. He awoke and cursed. A bewildering sensation of being still at her side as if he had gone out of himself and were following her. He remained thus watching the figure of Rachel until it disappeared and the street grew suddenly cold and empty. A strange scene mocked him. Strange smoke, strange warehouses, strange railroad tracks. Cupid awaking in a cinder patch.

He walked on, still bewildered. Nothing had happened to him. Instead, something had happened to the streets. The city had suffered an amputation. There was something incomplete about its streets and crowds. His eye felt annoyed by it. He was not thinking of Rachel. He felt as if she had suddenly ceased to exist and left behind her an unexistence. It was this emptiness outside that for the moment annoyed and then frightened him. An emptiness that had something to give him now. His senses reached eagerly toward the figures of people and buildings and received nothing. What did he want of them? They were a pattern, intricate and precise, with nothing to give. Yet he wanted. Good God, he wanted something out of the streets of the city. Then he remembered, as if recalling some algebraic formula, "I'm in love." His laughter had started at that moment.

At home it continued in him. Anna had gone to visit relatives in Wisconsin. He spent an hour writing her a long amorous letter. He was in love with Rachel, but a new notion had planted itself in him. Whatever happened, Anna must not be made unhappy. Love was not a reality. Anna and her happiness were the realities that must be carefully considered. This thing that had popped into life in the cinder patch was a mood—comparable to the mood of a thirsty man taking his first sip of water.

" . . . the memory of you comes before me," he scribbled to his wife, "and I feel sad. I am incomplete without you. Dear one, I love you. The streets seem empty and the hours drag. . . ."

In writing to his wife he seemed to recover a sense of virtue. He smiled as he sealed the envelope. "It must be an old instinct," he thought. "People are kindest to those they deceive. Thus good and evil balance."

His father, sitting before a grate fire, desired to talk. He would talk to him in circles that would irritate the old man and make his eyes water more.

"People don't live," he began. "To live is to have a dream behind the hours. To have the world offering something."

"Yes, my son. Something . . ."

"Then the people outside one take on meaningful outlines. There comes a contact. One is a part of something—of a force that moves the stars, eh?"

The old man nodded, and mumbled in his beard. Dorn felt a warmth toward his father. His stupidity delighted him. He would be able henceforth to talk to the old man and say, "I love Rachel," and the old man would think he was coining phrases for a profitless amusement. It would be the same with Anna. He would be able to make love to Anna differently hereafter. A rather cynical idea. He laughed and beamed at Isaac Dorn. Did it matter much whom one kissed as long as one had a desire for kissing? In fact, his desire for Rachel seemed at an end, now that he had mentioned it to her. A handclasp, a silence trembling with emotion, a sudden light in the heart—properly speaking, this was all there was to love. The rest was undoubtedly a make-believe. As he walked out to post the letter he tried to recall the emotions or ideas that had inspired him to marry Anna. There had undoubtedly been something of the sort then. But it had left no memory. Their honeymoon, of which she was always speaking, even after seven years, with a mist in her eyes—good Lord, had there been a honeymoon?

He spent the next afternoon with Rachel. A silence of familiarity had fallen upon them. There was a totality in silence. Walking through the streets beside her, Dorn mused, "Undoubtedly the thing is over. It begins even to bore a bit."

He noted curiously that he was unconscious of the streets. No tracing their pictures with phrases. They were streets, and that was an end of it. They belonged where they were.

His eyes dropped to his companion. A face with moonlight grown upon it. Beautiful, yes. Sometime he would tell her. Pour it out in words. There was a paradox about the situation. He was obviously somewhat bored. Yet to leave her, to put an end to their strolling through the strange moments, would hurt. Had he ever lived before? Banal question. "No, I've never lived before. Living is somewhat of a bore, a beautiful bore."

When they parted she stood looking at him as one transfixed.

"Erik!"

She made his name mean something—a world, a heaven. For an instant his laughter ended and a sadness engulfed him. Then once more he was alone and laughing. Rachel was walking away, something rather ridiculously normal about her step. Yes, he would laugh forever. Lord, what a jest! Like water coming out of a stone. Laugh at the crowds and buildings that desired to annoy him by sweeping toward him the memory of Rachel saying "Erik!" He diverted himself, as he hurried to his home, by staring into people's eyes and saying, "This one has a dream. That one hasn't. This one loves. The streets hurt him. That one is dead. The streets bury him."

On the third day the bombardment of Paris interfered with his plans. He remained too late in the office to walk with Rachel. As he sauntered about the shop, assisting and directing at the extras and replates, he vaguely forgot her. Word had come from the chief to hold the paper open until nine o'clock. If Paris failed to fall by nine everybody could go home and spend the rest of the night wrangling with his wife or looking at a movie. If it fell by nine there would be a final extra.

"I hope the damned town falls five minutes after nine," growled Warren, "if it's got to fall. Let it fall for the morning papers. What the hell are they for, anyway? I've got a rotten headache."

Dorn told him to run along. "I'll handle the copy, if there is any. A history of Paris out of the almanac will answer the purpose, I guess."

Warren folded his newspapers and left. Dorn sat scribbling possible headlines for the next replate: "Germans Bombard Paris . . ." and then a bank in smaller type: "French Capital Silent. Communication Cut Off." He paused and added with a sudden elation, "Civilization on Its Knees."

The hum and suspense of the night-watch pleased him. He liked the idea of sitting in a noisy place waiting to flash the news of the fall of Paris to the city. And the next day the four afternoon papers would carry a small box on the front page announcing to the public that, as usual, each of them had been first on the street with the important announcement. The fall of Paris! His thought mused. Babylon Falls. . . . Civilization on Its Knees. The City Wall of Jericho Collapses. Carthage Reduced to Ashes. Rome Sacked by Huns. Yes, there had been magnificent headlines in the past. Now a new headline—Paris. There would be a sudden flurry; boys running between desks; Crowley trying to shout and achieving a frightful whisper; a smeared printer announcing some ghastly mistake in the composing room; and Paris would be down—fallen. Nothing left to do except grin at the idea of the morning papers cursing their luck. He sat, vaguely hoping there might be tidal waves, earthquakes, cataclysms. On this night his energies seemed to demand more work than the mere fall of Paris would occasion. "Might as well do the thing up brown and put an end to the world—all in one extra," he smiled.

A messenger boy brought a telegram. He opened it and read,

"I am going away. RACHEL."

All a part of the night's work. Killing off Paris. Answering telegrams to vanishing sweethearts. He stuffed the message into his pocket. On second thought he tore it up. Anna was coming home the next day. "Wife Finds Tell-tale Telegram. . . ." Another headline.

"Wait a minute, boy."

Erik Dorn 121

The messenger lounged into an editor's chair. Dorn scribbled on a telegraph blank:

"Wait till Friday. I must see you once more. I will call for you at seven o'clock Thursday. We have never been together in the night. ERIK."

The messenger boy and the telegram disappeared. Still the laughter persisted. There was a jest in the world. Paris seemed a part of it. Everything belonged to it.

"I wonder what the writers of Paris are saying," Crowley inquired.

"Enjoying themselves, as usual," Dorn answered. "I'll tell you a secret. We live in a mad and inspiring world."

There was no final headline that night. Wednesday brought problems of conduct. It was obvious that Rachel was going away because of Anna. Her departure was a fact which presented itself with no finality. It resembled an insincere thought of suicide. Rachel, having gone, would still remain. The emotional prospects of the farewell closed his thought to the future. He spent Wednesday waiting for a seven o'clock on Thursday. An hour had detached itself from hours that went before and that followed. At home in the evening he endeavored to avoid his wife. His letters to her during her visit in Wisconsin had brought her back violently joyous. She desired love-making. He listened to her pour out ardent phrases and wondered why he felt no sense of betrayal toward her. "Conscience," he thought, "seems to be a vastly over-advertised commodity." He sat beside Anna, caressing her hand, smiling back into her passion-filled eyes, and gently checking an impulse in him to confide to her that he was in love with Rachel. It would be pleasant to tell her that, provided she would nod her head understandingly, smile, and stroke his hair; and answer something like, "You mean Rachel is in love with you. Well, I can't blame her. I'm horribly jealous, but it doesn't matter." An incongruous sanity warned him to avoid confessions, so he contented himself by rolling the situation over on his tongue, tasting the jealousy of his wife, the drama of the dénouement, and remaining peacefully smiling in his leather chair.

Thursday arrived. The afternoon dragged. He sat at his desk wondering whether he was sorrowful or not. The thought of meeting Rachel elated him. The thought that she was leaving and that he would not see her again seemed a vague thing. He put it out of his mind with ease and devoted himself to dreaming what he would say, the manner in which he would bid farewell.

Walking now swiftly in the street toward Rachel's home his thought still played with his emotions. It was this that partially caused his laughter. Also, now that he was going to see her, there was again the sense of fullness. An unthinking calm, complete and vibrant, wrapped him in an embrace. The fullness and the calm brought laughter. His thought amused him with the words, "There's a flaming absurdity about everything."

He delighted in dressing his emotions in absurd phrases, in words that grimaced behind the rouge of tawdry ballads. Thinking of Rachel and feeling the sudden lift of sadness and bewilderment in his blood, he murmured aloud: "You never know you have a heart till it begins to break." The words amused him. There were other song titles that seemed to fit. He tried them all. "I don't know why I love you, but I do-o-o." Delightful diversion—airing the mystic desires of his soul in the tattered words of the cabaret yodelers. "Just a smile, a sigh, a kiss. . . ." A sort of revenge, as if his vocabulary with its intricate verbal sophistications were avenging itself upon interloping emotions. And, too, because of a vague shame which inspired him to taunt his surrender; to combat it with an irony such as lay in the ridiculous phrases. This irony gave him a sense of being still outside his emotions and not a submissive part of them. "I am still Erik Dorn, master of my fate and captain of my soul," he smiled. But perhaps it was most of all the reaction of a verbal vanity. His love was not yet pumping rhapsodies into his thought. Instead, the words that came seemed to him somehow banal and commonplace. "I love you. I want to be with you all the time. When we are together things grow strange and desirable." Amorous mediocrities! So he edited them into a further banality and thus concealed his inability to give lofty utterance to his emotions by amusing himself with deliberately cheapened insincerities. "Saving my linguistic face," he thought suddenly, and laughed again.

Rachel was sad. They left her home in silence.

"We'll go toward the park," he announced. It irritated him to utter matter-of-fact directions. Why when he had had nothing to talk about had he been able to talk? And now when there was something, there seemed little to say? Words were obviously the delicate fruit of insincerity. Silence, the dark flower of emotion.

"I must go away." Rachel slipped her arm into his. He stared at her. She seemed more sorrowful than tears. This annoyed. It was ungrateful for her to look like weeping. But she was going from him. He tried to think of her and himself after they had parted, and succeeded only in remembering she was at his side. So he laughed quietly.

"Yes, to-morrow the guillotine falls," he answered. "To-night we dance in each other's arms. Immemorial tableau. Laughter, love, and song against the perfect background—death. Let's not cheat ourselves by being sad. To-morrow will be time enough."

He realized he was collapsing into a pluck-ye-the-roses-while-ye-may strain, and stopped irritated. There was something he should talk to her about—the causes of her departure. Plans. Their future. Was there a future? Undoubtedly some-

Erik Dorn   125

thing would have to be arranged. But his mind eluded responsibilities.

"I'm happy," he whispered. "I talk like a fool because I feel like one. Heedless. Irresponsible. You've given me something and I can only look at it almost without thought."

"It seems so strange that you should love me," she answered. "Because I've loved you always and never dreamed of you loving." She had become melting, as if her sadness were dissolving into caresses. "Let's just walk and I'll remember we're together and be happy, too."

Thoughts vanished from him. He released her hand and they walked in silence with their arms together. A sleep descended. Their faces, tranquil and lighted by the snow, offered solitudes to each other.

It was now snowing heavily. A thick white lattice raised itself from the streets against the darkness. The little black hectagonals of night danced between its spaces. Long white curtains painted themselves on the shadows of the city. The lovers walked unaware of the street. The snow crowded gently about them, moving patiently like a white and silent dream over their heads. Phantom houses stared after them. Slanting rooftops spread wings of silver in the night and drifted toward the moon. The half-closed leaden eyes of windows watched from another world.

The snow grew heavier, winding itself about the yellow lights of street lamps and crawling with sudden life through the blur of window rays. Beneath, the pavements opened like white and narrow fans in a far-away hand. Black figures leaning forward emerged for an instant from behind the falling snow and disappeared again.

Still the lovers moved without words—two black figures themselves, arms together, leaning forward, staring with burning hearts and tranquil faces out of a dream, as if they did not exist, had never existed; as if in the snow and night they had become an unreality, walking deeper into mists— yet never quite vanishing but growing only more unreal. Snow and two lovers walking together with the world like a dream over their heads, with life lingering in their eyes like a delicately absent- minded guest—the thought drifted like a memory through their hearts.

Then slowly consciousness of themselves returned, bringing with it no relief of words. Their hearts seemed to have grown weak with tears, and in their minds existed nothing but the dark vagueness of despair—the despair of things that die with their eyes open and questing. Faces drifting like circles of light in the storm. At the end of the street a park. Here they would vanish from each other. The snow would continue falling gently, patiently, upon an empty world.

The cold of Rachel's fingers pressed upon his hand. Her face turned itself to him. A moment of happiness halted them both as if they had been embraced. A wonder—the why and where of her leaving. But an indifference deprived him of words.

"This is all of life," he muttered. Rachel staring at him nodded her head in echo. They were standing motionless as if they had forgotten how to live. Beyond this there were no gestures to make, nowhere to go. They had come to a horizon—an end. Here was ecstasy. What else? Nothing. Everything, here. Sky and night and snow had fallen about their heads in an ending. They stood as if clinging to themselves. Dorn heard a soft laugh from her.

"I thought I had died," Rachel was murmuring. He nodded his head in echo.

A lighted window lost in the snow drew their eyes. People sat in a room—warm, stiff figures. The lovers stood smiling toward it. Words, soft and mocking, formed themselves in Dorn. A pain was pulling his heart away. The ecstasy that had raised him beyond his emotions seemed suddenly to have cast him into the fury of them. He would say mocking things—absurd phrases to which he might cling. Or else he must weep because of the pain in him. "Two waifs adrift in a storm, peering into a bakery window at the cookies." That was the key. A laugh at the dolorous asininity of life. "Face to face with the Roman Pop U Lace. We who are about to die salute you." Laugh, a phrase of laughter or he would stand blubbering like an imbecile.

He struggled for the theatric gesture and found

himself shivering at Rachel's side, his arm clinging about her shoulders. Lord, what a jest! After the moment they had lived through, to stand round-eyed and blubbering before the gingerbread vision of joys behind a lighted window. The whine of a barrel-organ. The sentimental whimpering of a street-corner *Miserere*. And he must weep because of it—he who had stood with his head thrust through the sky. His thought, like an indignant monitor, collapsed with scoldings. Let it come, then! With a sigh he gave himself to tears, and they stood together weeping.

The little lighted room seemed an enchantment floating in the scurry of the storm. It reached with warm fingers into their hearts, whispering a broken barrel-organ lullaby to them. Life shone upon them out of the lighted window and behind it the world of rocking-chairs and fireplaces, wall pictures and table lamps, lay like a haven smiling a good-by to them. Their hearts become tombs, closed slowly and forever upon a vision.

"The world will be a black sky and the memory of you like a shining star that I watch endlessly." He listened to his words. They brought a dim gladness. His phrases had finally capitulated to his love. He could talk now without the artifice of banality to hide behind. Talk, say the unsayable, bring his love in misty word lines before his eyes; look and forget a moment.

Rachel's voice at his side said, "I love you so. Oh, I love you so!"

Yes, he could talk now. His heart wagged a tongue. The pain in him had found words. The mystic desires and torments—words, words.

"We'll remember, years later, and be grateful we didn't bury our love behind lighted windows, but left it to wander forever and remain forever alive. Rachel, my dear one."

"I love you so!" she wept.

More words . . . "it would have been always the same. We've lived one moment and in all of life there's nothing more than what we've had. Lovers who grow old together live only in their yesterdays. And their yesterdays are only a moment—till the time comes when their yesterdays die. Then they become little, half-dead people, who wait in lighted rooms, empty handed, fumbling greedily with trifles. . . ."

"I love you!" She made a refrain for him. "I don't know the things you do. I only love you."

"Rachel . . ." He had no belief in what he was saying. The things he knew? What? Nothing but pain and torment. Yet his heart went on wagging out words: "All life is a parting—a continual and monotonous parting. And most hideous of all, a parting with dead things. A saying good-by to things that no longer exist. We part with living things, and so keep them, somehow. Your face makes life for the moment familiar. Visions bloom like sad flowers in my heart. Your body against mine brings a torment even into my words. Oh, your weeping's the sound of my own heart dying. Rachel, you are more wonderful than life. I love you! I feel as if I must die when you go away. Crowds, streets, buildings—all empty outlines. Empty before you came, emptier when you have gone."

He paused. His thought whispered: "I'll remember things I say. I mustn't say too much. I'm sad. Oh, God, what a mess!"

They walked into the park. A sudden matter-of-factness came into Dorn's mind. He had sung something from his heart. Yet he remembered with astonishment it had been a wary song. He had not asked her to stay. Had he asked her she would have remained. Curious, how he acquiesced in her going. A sense of drama seemed to demand it. When he had received her message the night in the office he had agreed at once. Why? Because he was not in love? This too, a make-believe, more colored, more persuasive than the others? Wrong. Something else. Anna. Anna was sending her away. The figure of Anna loomed behind their ecstasies. It stood nodding its head sorrowfully at a good-by in the snow.

They were deep in the park. Trees made still gestures about them. The ivory silhouettes of trees haunted the distance. A spectral summer painted itself upon the barren lilac bushes. Beneath, the lawn slopes raised moon faces to the night. Deep in the storm the ghost of a bronze fountain emerged and remained staring at the scene.

It was cold. The wind had died and the snow hung without motion, like a cloud of ribbons in the air. The white park gleamed as if under the swinging light of blue and silver lanterns. The night, lost in a dream wandered away among strange sculptures. In the distance a curtain of porphyry and bisque drew its shadow across the moon.

Rachel pointed suddenly with her finger.

"Look!" she whispered. She remained as if in terror, pointing.

Three figures were converging toward them— black figures out of the distant snow. Figures of men, without faces, like three bundles of clothes, they came toiling across the unbroken white of the park, an air of intense destinations about them. Above the desolate field of white the three figures seemed suddenly to loom into heroic sizes. They reared to a height and zigzagged across a nowhere.

"See, see!" Rachel cried. She was still pointing. Her voice rang brokenly. "They're coming for me, Erik. Erik, don't you see? People wandering toward me. Horrible strangers. Oh, I know, I know!" She laughed. "My grandmother was a gypsy and she's telling my fortune in the snow. Things that will jump out of space and come at me, after you're gone."

The three men, puffing with exertion, converged upon the walk and passed on with a morose stare at the lovers. Dorn sighed, relieved. He had caught a strange foreboding sense out of the tableau of the white field and the three converging black figures. . . . If he loved her why was he letting her go? If he loved her. . . .

He walked on suddenly wearied, saddened, uncertain. It was no more than a dream that had touched his senses, a breath of a dream that lingered for a moment upon his mirror. It would pass, as all things pass. And he would fall back into the pattern of streets and faces, watching as before the emptiness of life make geometrical figures of itself. Yes, it was better to have her go —simpler. Perhaps a desire would remain, a breath, a moonlit memory of her loveliness to mumble over now and then, like a line of poetry always unwritten. Let her go. Beautiful . . . wonderful. . . . These were words. Was he even sad? She was—what? Another woman.

In the shadow of a snow-covered wall he paused. The snow had ended.

"Come closer," he whispered. She remained silent as he removed her overcoat. He dropped it in the snow and threw his own beside it.

"We'll be warm for a minute against each other."

She was a flower in his arms. She seemed to vanish and become mist. Slowly he became aware of her touch, of her arms holding him and her lips. She was saying:

"I am yours—always—everywhere. I will be a shrine to you. And whenever you want me I will come crawling on my knees to you."

Dying, dying! She was dying. Another moment and the mist of her would be gone. Rachel. . . . Rachel. I love you. I send you away. Oh, God, why do I send you away?"

She was out of his arms. Undressed, naked, emptied, he stood unknown to himself. No words. Her kiss alone lived on his lips. She was looking at him with burning wild eyes. Expression seemed to have left her. There was something else in her face.

"I must look at you. To remember, to remember!" she gasped. "Oh, to remember you! I have never looked at you. I have never seen you. It's a dream. Who is Erik Dorn? Who am I? Oh, let me look at you. . . ."

The eyes of Rachel grew marvelously bright. Burned . . . burned.

Dorn stared into an empty park. Gone! Her coat still in the snow. His own beside it. He stood smiling, confused. His lips made an apology. He walked off. Oh, yes, their coats together in the snow. A symbol. He stumbled and a sudden terror engulfed him. "Her face," he mumbled, "like a mirror of stars." He felt himself sicken. What had her eyes said? Eyes that burned and devoured him and vanished. "Rachel," he wept, "forever!" He wondered why he spoke.

The park, white, gleaming, desolate, gave him back her face. Out of the empty night, her face. In the trees it drifted, haunting him. The print of a face was upon the world. He went stumbling toward it in the snow. He covered his eyes with his hands as he walked.

"Her face," he mumbled, "her face was beautiful. . . ."

Chapter Five

IN a dining-room of the city known as the Blue Inn, Anna Dorn sat waiting for her husband. Opposite her a laughing-eyed man was talking. She listened without intelligence. He was part of old memories—crowded rooms in which lights had been turned off. They had danced together in their youth. She had worn his fraternity pin and walked with him one night under a moon and kissed him, saying: "I will always love you. The other boys are different. You are so nice and kind, Eddie." And Eddie had gone away east to continue a complacent quest for erudition in a university. Almost forgotten days and places when there had been no Erik Dorn, and when one debated which pumps to wear to the dance. Erik had blotted them out. A whimsical, moody young Mr. Dorn, laughing and carousing about the city and singling her out one night at a party. . . . "We must get out of here or we'll choke to death. Come, we'll go down to the lake and laugh at the stars. They're the only laughable things in the world."

She looked sadly at the man whose kindly voice sought to rally her out of a gloom. Before the laughing stars there had been another day—other stars, another Anna. All part of another world. Eddie Meredith and another world sat dimly apparent across the white linen of the table. Anecdotes of old friends they had shared, forgotten names and incidents reached through the shadows of her thought and stirred an alien memory. He hadn't changed. Ten years—and he was still Eddie Meredith, with eyes that looked for simple pleasures and seemed to find them. He had always found something to laugh about. Not the way Erik laughed. Erik's laugh was something that had never ceased to hurt. Strange that Eddie's voice had never grown tired of laughing during the ten years.

The ache in her heart lightened and she listened with almost a smile—the ghost of another Anna smiling. It was the other Anna who had walked through youth with a joyous indifference to life, to everything but youth. Buried now deep under years, Eddie warmed it back. Eddie sat talking to the ghost that had been Anna Winthrop and that could not answer him.

He was a poor talker. She was too used to Erik. Simple, threadbare phrases, yet she had once thought him brilliant. Perhaps he was—a different kind of brilliance. She noted how his words seemed stimulated with an enthusiasm beyond their sense. Trifles assumed an importance. For moments she felt herself looking at the joyousness of an old friend and forgetting. Then as always through the day and night. . . . "Erik,

Erik," murmured itself in her mind . . . "he doesn't love me. Erik, dear Erik!" Over and over, weaving itself into all she said and saw. Sometimes it started a panic in her. She would feel herself grow dark, wild. Often it seemed to bring death. Things would become vague and she would move through the hours unaware of them.

The joyousness of Eddie drifted away. She remained smiling blankly at him. His words slipped past her ear. Inside, she was wandering—disheveled thoughts were wandering through a darkness. At night she lay beside him as he slept, with her eyes wide open and her lips praying, "Dear Jesus, sweet brother Jesus, give Erik back to me!" . . . Or she would crawl out of bed and walk into a deserted room to weep. Here she could mumble his name till the anguish of her tears choked her. As the cold streets grew gray she would hurry to bathe her face, even rouging her cheeks, and return to their bed to wait for Erik to awake, that she might caress him, warm something back in him with her kisses, and perhaps hear him whisper her name as he used to do. But he drew himself away, his eyes sometimes filling with tears. "It's nothing, Anna, nothing. Please don't ask. I don't know what it is. My head or something. I feel black inside. . . ." And he would hurry to work, not waiting for her to join him at breakfast.

Then there had been nights when he held her in his arms thinking she was asleep, and she felt his tears dropping over her face—tears of silence. She would lie trembling with a wild joy, yet not daring to open her eyes or speak, knowing he would move away. These moments, feigning sleep and listening to Erik weeping softly against her cheek, had been her only happiness in the four black months since the change had come to him. He still loved her. Yes. . . . Oh, God, it was something else. Perhaps madness. She would drift to sleep as his weeping ceased, long after it ceased, and half dreams would come to her of nursing him through terrible darknesses, of warming him with her life, of magically driving away the things that were tormenting him out of his mind— great black things. Through the day she hungered for his return from work, that she might look at him again, even though the sight of him, dark and aloof, tore at her heart till she grew faint.

She had never thought of questioning him calmly. There had been no suspicion of "someone else." That was a thing beyond even the wildest disorder of her imaginings. It was only that Erik was restless, perhaps tired of his home, of her too much loving and longing to go somewhere—away. Her awe of his brain, of his strange, always impenetrable character, adjusted itself to the change in him. There were mysterious things in Erik—things she couldn't hope to understand. Now these unknown things had grown too big in him. He was different from other men, not to be questioned as one might question other men. So she must wander about blindly, carefully, and drive things away.

She came out of her sorrow reveries and smiled. Eddie was still talking. The music of a violin, harp, and piano was playing with a rollicking wistfulness through the clatter and laughter of the café. Eddie was saying, "There, that's better. That makes you look like Anna. You were looking like somebody else."

His jolly eyes had a keenness. She must dissemble better. Erik would come in a moment and Eddie must never think. . . .

"I've heard about your husband, the lucky dog!" Eddie beamed at her impudently. "Think," he exploded, "of meeting you accidentally after ten years. Wow! Ten years! They say themselves quickly, don't they? By the way, there's a curious fellow coming to meet me here. I'll drag him in. If your Erik don't like it I'll sit on him till he does. His name's Tesla—Emil Tesla. Bomb-thrower or something. I don't know exactly. He's helped me with my collection. Oh, I forgot. You don't know about that. I keep thinking that you know me. You see nothing has changed in me. I'm still the same Eddie—richer, balder, foolisher, perhaps. It seems you ought to know all about the ten years without being told. But I'll tell you. I'm an art collector on the sly. Pictures—horrible things that don't look like anything. I don't know why I collect them, honestly. Pictures mean nothing to me. Never did. Particularly the kind I pick up. But it's a habit that keeps me cheerful. Better than collecting stamps. Cubist, futurist, expressionist. Ever see the damn things? I gobble them up. I guess because they're cheap. Here he is—the young fellow with the soft face."

Meredith rose and jubilantly waved a napkin. A stocky man in loose clothes nodded at him and approached.

"Not Mrs. Erik Dorn," he repeated. Anna nodded. The sound of her husband's name on others' lips always elated her, even now. She lost for a moment the aversion she felt at the touch of Tesla's hand. It seemed boneless. . . . They would all eat together. Anna was an old school friend. Years ago, ah! many years.

Tesla fastened a repugnantly appreciative eye upon her, as if he were becoming privy to an exclusive secret. She frowned inwardly. An ugly man with something bubbly about him.

"I was telling Mrs. Dorn you were a bomb-thrower or something," Meredith announced. His good spirits frisked about the table like a troupe of frolicsome puppies.

"Only an apprentice," Tesla's soft voice—a voice like his hands—answered. "But why talk of such things in the presence of a beautiful lady." He bowed his head at her. She thought, "An unbearable man, completely out of place. How in the world could Eddie. . . ."

The music had changed. Muted cornets,

banjos and saxophones were wailing out a tom-tom adagio. People were rising from tables and moving toward a dancing space. Eddie stood beside her bowing with elaborate stiffness.

"My next dance, Miss Winthrop."

Anna looked up blankly.

"Good Lord, have you forgotten your own name? Come on. You know Dorn, don't you, Emil? Well, throw a fork at him when he shows up. Come, we haven't danced together for ten years. The last time was. . . ."

"The last time was the senior prom," Anna interrupted quickly. "You see I haven't forgotten." She stood mechanically.

As they walked between tables and diners, he said, "I sure feel like a boy again seeing you."

"I'm afraid I've almost forgotten how to dance, Eddie. My husband doesn't dance much."

"Here we are! Like old days, eh? Remember Jimmie Goodland, my deadly rival for your hand?"

They were dancing.

"Well, he's married. Three kids."

"And how many children have you, Eddie?"

"Me?" He laughed. "Have I forgotten to tell you that? Well, I'm still at large, untrammeled, free. There've been women, but not *the* woman."

His voice put on a pleasing facetiousness.

"Mustn't mind an old friend getting sentimental. But after you they had to measure up to something—and didn't."

Since the night Erik had singled her out at the party no man had spoken to her that way. She listened slightly amazed. It confused her. His eyes, as they danced, were jolly and polite. But they watched her too keenly. Erik might misunderstand. Her love somehow resented being looked at and spoken to like that. She hurried back to their first topic.

"What became of Millie Pugh, Eddie?"

"Married. A Spaniard or something. Two kids and an automobile. Saw them in Brazil somewhere."

"And Arthur Stearns?"

"Fatter than an alderman. Runs a gas works or something in Detroit. Married. One kid."

Anna laughed. "You sound like an almanac of dooms."

"Well, all married but me—little Eddie, the boy bachelor, faithful unto death to the memories of his childhood. Do you remember the night we ran Mazurine's out of ice-cream?"

This was another world, another Anna. She closed her eyes dreamily to the movement of the dance and music—delicious drugs.

"Faster," she whispered.

They broke into quicker steps. "Erik. . . . Erik. . . . my own. Love me again. Come back to me. . . ." Still in her thought, but fainter, deeper down. Not words but a sigh that moved to the rhythm of the music.

"And how may children have you?"

She answered without emotion, as if she were talking with a distant part of herself. "There was a little boy. He died as a baby. We haven't any."

Deep, kindly eyes looking at her as they danced. "I'm so sorry, Anna."

She whispered again, "Faster!" A shadow over his face. She must be careful of his eyes—eyes that laughed, but keen, almost as keen as Erik's. "My Erik . . . my own. . . ." It was all a dream, a nightmare of her own inventing. Nothing had happened. Imaginings. Erik loved her. Why else should he weep and kiss her when he thought her asleep? He loved her, he loved her!

Her face grew bright. Faster. Always to dance and dream of Erik. She must tell Eddie. . . .

"Erik is wonderful. I'm dying to have you meet him. Oh, Eddie, he's wonderful!"

Now she could laugh and enjoy herself. Something had emptied out of her breasts—cold iron, warm lead. She was lighter, easy to bend and glide to the music. Everything was easy. Her face lighted by something deeper than a smile, she danced in silence. Eddie was far away—ten years away. His eyes that were smiling at her were no eyes at all. They were part of the music and movement that caressed her with the sweetness of life, of being loved by Erik. . . .

Tesla watched his friend lead the red-haired lady away to dance. For a while there lingered about him the air of unctious submission that had revolted Anna. Then it vanished. His face as he sat alone seemed to tighten. The flabbiness of his eyes became something else. Diners at other tables caught glimpses of him while they ate. A commanding figure, rugged, youthful-faced. Features that made definite lines, compelling lines, in the blur of other features. A man of certainties, yet with something weak about him. His eyes were like a child's. They did not quite belong in his face. There, eyes should have gleamed, stared with intensities. Instead, eyes purred—abstract, tender eyes; the kind that attracted women sometimes because they were almost like a women's eyes dreaming of lovers.

"Hello, Tesla!"

Again the fawning lights, smiles, bowings. This was Dorn—a Somebody. Somebodies always changed Tesla. There was a thing in him that smirked before Somebodies, as if he were a timorous puppy wagging its tail and leaping about on flabby legs.

"Mrs. Dorn is sitting here with a friend. They're dancing. We're all at this table, Mr. Dorn."

Dorn caught the eager innuendo of his voice. He knew Tesla vaguely as a radical, an author of pamphlets. Tesla continued to talk, a sycophantic purr in his words. . . . The war was financed by international bankers. Didn't he think so? America was being drawn in by Wall Street—to make the loans to the Allies stand up. But something was going to happen. The eyes of the workers were opening slowly all over the world. In Russia already a beginning of realities. Ah, think of the millions dying for nothing, advancing or improving nothing by their death. Soldiers, heroes, workingmen, all blind acrobats in another man's circus. But something was happening. Revolution. This grewsome horseplay in Europe's front yard would start it. And then —watch out!

The voice of Emil Tesla, eager, fawning, had yet another quality in it. It promised, as if it could not do justice to the things it was saying and must be careful, soft, polite. Dorn felt the man and his power. Not a puppy on flabby legs but a brute mastiff with a wild bay that must come out in little whines, because the music was playing, because he was talking to Somebody. A man physically beaten by life, his body scraping, bowing; his words mumbling confusedly in the presence of other words. Yet a powerful man with a tremendous urge that might some day hurl him against the stars. He had something. . . .

To Tesla's sentences Dorn dropped a yes or no. Tesla needed no replies. He purred on eagerly before his listener, seeming to whine for his appreciation and good will, yet unconscious of him. A waiter brought wine. Dorn stared at the topaz tint in his glass. His eyes had changed. They no longer smiled. A heaviness gleamed from them. The thing in his heart would not go. Heavy hands turning him over and over, as if life were tearing him, crowds and streets pulling at him. There had been no rest since Rachel had gone.

He sat almost oblivious of Tesla. In the back of his brain the city tumbled—an elephantine grimace, a wilderness of angles, a swarm of gestures that beat at his thought. But before his eyes there were no longer the precise patterns of another day. He was no longer outside. He had been sucked into something, the something that he had been used to refer to condescendingly as life. People sitting in a room like this had been furniture that amused him. Now they were alive, repulsive, with a meaning to them that sickened him. Streets had once been stone and gesture. Now they, too, were meanings that sickened. A sanity in which he alone was insane, surrounded him; a completion in which he alone seemed incomplete. Men and women together—tired faces, lighted faces—all with destinations that satisfied them. And he wandering, knocked from place to place by heavy hands, pushed through crowds, dropped into chairs. Time itself a torment into which he kept thrusting himself deeper.

The change in Erik Dorn had come to him with

a cynicism of its own. It laughed with its own laughter. A mind foreign to him spoke to him through the day. . . . "You would smile at life, Erik; well, here it is. Easy for a sleeper to smile. But smile now. Life is a surface, eh? shifting about into designs for the delectation of your eyes. Watch it shifting then. Darkness and emptiness in a can-can. Watch the tumbling streets that have no meanings. No meanings? Yet there's a torment in them that can hoist you up by your placid little heels and swing you round . . . round, and send you flying. A witch's flight with the scream of stars whistling through it. Flight that has no ending and no direction . . . no face of Rachel at its ending. Burning eyes, devouring eyes . . . face like a mirror of stars. There's a face in the world and you go after it, heels in air, tongue frozen, breathing always an emptiness that chokes. Easy for sleepers to dawdle with words and say carelessly life is this, life is that. What the hell's the difference what life is? It means nothing to me. People and their posturings mean nothing. But what about now? A contact, a tying up with posturings, and the streets and crowds tearing you into gestures not your own. . . ."

Aloud he would say, "My love for her has given me a soul and I've become a fool along with other fools."

He did not think of Rachel in words. There were moments of dream when he made plans—a fantastic amorous rigmarole of Rachel and himself walking together over the heads of the world; child dreams that substituted themselves for the realities he demanded. But these were infrequent. He was learning to avoid them as one avoids a drug that soothes and then doubles the hunger of the nerves.

As now in the café, listening to Tesla, watching with dark eyes the scene, there was a turning of heavy hands in him to which he must not give thought. Watch the café, listen to Tesla, talk, eat and spit out a disgust for the things of which he was a part—things from which he demanded Rachel and a surcease to the pain in him. And that only stifled with the emptiness of her.

Out of the wretchedness of garbled emotions that had become the whole of Erik Dorn, his vocabulary arose with a facile paint brush and painted upon his thought. His phrases wandered about looking for subjects as if he must taunt himself with details that forever brought him loathing.

Before he had seen pictures complete, rhythmic pictures of streets and crowds, pleasantly blurred and in motion. Now he saw them as if life was in a state of continual pause—an arrested cinematograph; grotesquely detailed and with the meaning of motion out of it. A picture waiting something to set it moving. This something he could not give it. Helplessly his words continued to trace themselves over the outlines of scenes about him, as if trying to stir them into a life.

This scene consciousness had become almost a mania in the four months. But in the mechanical, phraseological movement of his thought he was able to hide himself. Thus he listened to Tesla and looked at the café. The inn was filled with people—elaborately dresssed women and shiningly groomed men—grouped about white-linened, silver-laden tables; an ornamental grimacing little multitude come to the café as to some grave rite, moving to the tables with an unctious nonchalance. Women dressed in effulgent silks, their flesh gleaming among the spaces of exotic plumage, gleaming through the flares of luxurious satin distortions. A company that gestured, grimaced with the charm of lustful marionettes. Flesh reduced to secrecy. Lust, dream in hiding. From the secret world they inhabited, moist bodies beckoned with a luscious, perverse denial of artifice.

The picture of it shot into his eyes, arousing a hate in his thought. He heard Tesla . . . "life has changed with the industrialization of society. It is no longer a question of who shall run the court. The court is an atrophied institution, a circus surviving in the backyard of history. It's a question of who shall run the factory. Democracy is a thing that touches only politicians. The factory touches people. Democracy cleared the way but it's not a way in itself. It's still the court idea of government. Steam, gas, and electricity made the French revolution obsolete even before it was ended. This war . . . good God, Dorn, blood pouring over toys we've outgrown! . . ."

Still fawning voiced, but with a bay underneath. Dorn listened and remained elsewhere—among a turning of heavy hands. Yet he thought of Tesla, "He makes an impression on me. I'll remember his words. A man of power, rooted in visions." He replied suddenly, "I'm convinced the weak will rule some day, if that's what you're driving at. The race can survive only as long as its weakest survive. Christianity started it. Socialism will carry it a step further. The fight against the individual. What else is any institutionalism? A struggle to circumvent the biological destiny of man, which is the same as the biological destiny of fish—extinction. That's what we're primarily engaged in. The race must protect its weak, so it invents laws to curb the instincts and power of its strong. And we obey the laws—a matter of adjusting ourselves ludicrously to our weaknesses and endowing these adjustments with high names. Bolshevism will be the law of to-morrow and wear even a higher name than Christianity. Yesterday it was, 'only the poor shall inherit heaven, only crippled brains and weaker visions shall see God.' To-morrow the slogan will have been brought down to earth. Yes, they'll run the factories—your masses. There's the strength in them of logic—a logic opposed to evolution. They'll run the factories as they now run heaven —an Institution nicely accommodated to their fears and weaknesses."

Dorn paused. He was not thinking. People said things. An automatic box of phrases in him released answers. Tesla was replying, not so fawningly, the bay beneath his soft words mastering his sycophantic tones. Let him talk. He had something to talk about. He saw something. There was a new tableau in Tesla's brain. Let him keep murmuring things about it—suavely, unctuously letting off steam.

Like a man returning drearily to his game of solitaire, Dorn fastened his eyes again upon the scene. Looking at things would keep him from thinking. To think was to cry out. He had learned this. His eyes, dark and heavy, fastened themselves upon the walls of the inn lost in shadows, painted with nymphs and satyrs sprawling over tapestried landscapes. He devoured their details, his heart searching in them for the mystery of Rachel and finding only a deeper emptiness—insistently naked bodies of nymphs lying like newly bathed housemaids amid stiff park sceneries. Miracles of photographic lechery. Would people about him look like that naked? Thank God they were dressed! An ankle in silk was better than a thigh in sunlight. An old saw . . . beauty lay in the imagination. Women removed their beauty with their clothes.

The nymphs on the wall reminded one chiefly that they were careful to scrub their legs all the way up.

He sighed and watched the eyes of diners look at the walls. Her face—a mirror of stars. What else was there but her face? Other faces, of course. A revulsion of other strange faces. Men studying the naked figures on the walls with profound but aloof interest, eyeing the women near them shrewdly as they turned away. Women with serious, unconcentrated eyes upon the paintings, turning tenderly towards their escorts. He would die of looking at faces that were not hers. A love-sick schoolboy. God, what an ass! Tesla was becoming an insufferable bore. What in God's name did he have to do with masses raising their skinny arms from a smoking field and crying aloud, "Bread!" Tesla had a lot to do with it. The skinny arms, the smoking field, and the balloon with the word "bread" in it were Tesla's soul. But his soul was different—heavy hands turning.

Dorn drank wine from his glass. Anna, dancing with a plump, laughing stranger, flitted through the distance. A deeper turning over of iron in his heart at the glimpse of her. The scene no longer could divert him. The thought of Anna dropped like a curtain upon a picture. What could he do? What? At night he grew sick lying beside her. It wasn't conscience. There was nothing wrong about loving someone else. But there was an uncanniness about it. Lying beside a woman who didn't know what was in his mind. He would lie thinking, "Oh, Rachel, I love Rachel," repeating almost idiotic love words for Rachel in his mind. And Anna would smile patiently at him, unaware. That was the most intolerable thing. The fact she didn't know. And also the fact that he must remain inarticulate. He must sit with his heart choking him and his head in a blaze, and keep stuffing words back down his throat. Through the day he tormented himself with the thought, "I must tell her. I can't keep this thing up any longer." But when he saw her it was impossible to tell her. A single phrase would end it. He held the phrase on his lips—as if it were a knife balanced over Anna's heart. "I love Rachel." That would end it. But it was impossible. He couldn't say it. Why? He sat, trying to get a glimpse of her dancing again and tried to avoid answering himself. It was something he mustn't answer. He must get away from his damned thought. His eyes fastened themselves upon the fountain in the center of the room. It was Anna that tormented him, not Rachel. Anna . . . Anna. . . . The tension broke. He was looking at the fountain surmounted by a marble nude crouched in a posture of surprise; probably disturbed by her nudity. It was necessary for nudity to be disturbed by itself. Did virgins eyeing themselves in mirrors blush with shame? Unquestionably.

The nude peered into the water of a large tiled basin. A gush of water over her managed to veil her unsuccessfully in an endless spray. Water filled the air with an odorless spice.

". . . the first blow will come out of Russia, Dorn. The Russians have not been side-tracked into the phantasms of democracy. They still think straight. Civilization hasn't crippled them with phrases. They are still what you would call biological. And dreams live in them. Yes, I know what you'll say . . . heavy dreams. But here in America there are no dreams—yet. Nothing but paper. Paper thoughts. Paper morals. Everything paper. Russia will send out fire to burn up this paper. Destroy it. Leave nothing behind—not even ashes."

True enough. Why answer it? But what difference did it make if paper burned? Was man after all a creature consecrated to institutions, doomed to expend himself upon institutions? A hundred million nervous systems, each capable of ecstasies and torments, devoting themselves to the business of political brick-laying. Always yowling about new bricks. Politics—a deformity of the imagination; a game of tiddledy-winks played with guns and souls.

He breathed with relief. Abstractions were a drug. But his thinking ended. Blue electric lights cast an amorous glow—an artificial moonlight—upon tables surrounding the fountain. Beneath the cobalt water of the basin, colored fish gliding like a weaving procession of little fat Mandarins. The remainder of the room also blue from shaded lights. That was why they dubbed it the Blue Inn. Blue lights made the Blue Inn. The air was heavy with the uncoiling lavender tinsel of tobacco smoke. A luxurious suppression as about some priapic altar . . . artificial shadows, painted lights, forlorn fountain ripplings.

"Oh, Erik, I've been dancing. This is Mr. Meredith. I once told you about him. The music is simply wonderful here."

Tesla, flabby-eyed and almost maliciously polite, as if he would expose the innate absurdity of politeness, tipped over a water glass in his floppings. Anna, still alive with the joyousness that had come to her, seated herself beside her husband. Her hand rested eagerly on his arm. He must love her . . . must. Must. It had been only a nightmare she'd invented. Oh, God, did anything matter as long as they loved each other?

"Tired, dearest?"

He looked at her and tried to lighten his eyes.

"Yes, a little. The damned war."

"I'm so sorry."

She mustn't ask him to dance. He was tired. She would coddle him. He was only a baby— tired, sleepy, sad. She must ask no questions. Only love. Before her love the darkness of his face would clear away as before sunshine.

"I'm so happy, Erik darling!"

Her fingers quivered on his arm. He looked at

her and smiled out of misty eyes. Of all the unbearable things in an unbearable world her happiness was the most unbearable. She nodded, as if she understood. Her pretense of understanding was a ghastly business. But Anna smiled. Poor Erik, he was only a boy. If only they were alone! If Eddie and Tesla and the whole world would go away and leave her with him, to kiss his eyes and stroke his hair. Sleep, baby, sleep. . . . What a crazy, wild thing, thinking that Erik no longer loved her. No longer loved her! Dear God, she was only a part of him. He must love her. . . . Must!

The talk kept on—words bubbling from Tesla, Eddie frisking with laughter.

"You must dance with me, Erik. It's been so long since we danced." There—she shouldn't have asked. She didn't mean to. Her eyes apologized. When he answered, "No, I'm tired," there was wine from a glass that warmed the little coldness his words dropped into her.

Listening to her, answering with words he tried to soften and make alive, Dorn tried to occupy himself with the details of the scene again. Could he keep on living as two persons—one of them turning over and over in a fire that consumed him —and the other making phrases, gestures, as if there were no fire consuming him? If he kept his eyes working, perhaps. He hated Anna. But that was because he couldn't bear the thought of her suffering. He hated her because he must be kind to her.

Meredith was ordering the dinner. **Dorn stared** out over the room.

Anna was watching him with her senses. Why didn't he speak to her as Eddie did? Perhaps he was going mad. His eyes suffered. He looked at things and seemed to hurt himself with looking. She kept her voice vibrant with a hope of joyousness. "I mustn't give in to the nightmare. It's only imagining. . . ."

"Erik, dearest, do eat something. Let me order for you."

Talk, talk! Dorn listened. Anna was saying, "Eddie thinks as you do about the war, Erik. Isn't that odd?" Yes, that anybody should be able to think as he did. He was a God. A super-God. If only she hated him. A moment of hate in her eyes would be heaven.

"A plain case of accepting an evil and making the best of it," laughed Meredith. "If we go in all I ask is for God's sake let's keep our eyes open and not slobber around."

Soft remonstrances from Tesla with polite references to Wall Street. Food on platters. An air of slight excitement with Anna directing the talk and serving. What made her so vivacious? The sight of an old friend, Meredith? Meredith . . . oh, yes, school days, long ago. A wild hope unfolded itself in Dorn. He looked at the man anew. Fantastic notion. But throw them together, day and night. Cafés, dancing, music, propinquity. He was her type—kindly, unselfish, prosperously elate over life. He'd help her on with her wraps and be polite over doorways. Perhaps. He turned to his wife and laughed softly. A way out. Give her to the man. Give her away. End her love for him—her damned, torturing love that made him turn over inside and weep at night when she was asleep; that hounded him like an unclean memory. It was only her love that made him unclean. He looked at her with his eyes lighted.

"Dancing makes a difference, doesn't it, dear? I'd dance myself, only my legs are tired."

He smiled as he spoke with the unctuousness of a villain administering poison in a bouquet of roses. But a way to get rid of her love. He didn't mind her, but the thing in her. That was the whole of it. Why hide from it? God, if he could only kill it he'd be free. Otherwise he'd never be free. Even if he went away there'd be the thought of her love. . . . Anna's face bloomed with joy at his words.

"We'll come here another night when you're not tired, honey."

"Yes," he answered, "make a party of it. How about that, Mr. Meredith?"

"Surest thing."

They forgot Tesla.

"Oh, Erik!" She embraced his arm with both her hands. Under the table she pressed her thigh trembling against him.

The music from the platform had changed. Cornets, banjos, saxophones, again. The boom and jerk of voices arose as if in greeting. Foreheads of diners glistening with a fine sweat. Sweat on the backs of women's necks, on their chins, under their raised arms; gleaming on the cool intervals of breasts, white and bulbous breasts peeping out of a secret world.

"If I may, Anna . . ."

Eddie was taking her away. The plot was working. Dorn's heart warmed toward the man. A rescuer, a savior. He nodded his head at his wife. He must make it look as if he were sorry it wasn't he going to dance with her; smile with proper wistfulness; shake his head sadly.

Anna, suddenly beside herself, laughed, and, leaning over touched his hair quickly with her lips. Damned idiot, he'd overdone it! No. Perhaps she was guilty. Apologizing for impulses away from him toward Meredith? He sat hoping feverishly, caressing a diagnosis as if he could establish it by repeating it over and over.

Tesla again, this time on art. Art of the proletaire. Damn the proletaire and Tesla both! He had a plot working out. Would their hands touch, linger, sigh against each other? Of course. They were human—at least their hands were. And then, dances every night. What a miserable banal plot! Another day-dream. Forget. Beyond Tesla's soft voice . . . an opening and shutting of mouths swollen in delicious discomforts. Look at them. Identify mouths. Tell himself the angles they made. People . . .

people . . . a wriggling of bodies in a growing satiety of tepid lusts.

"True art, Dorn, is something beyond decoration. Dreams made real. But the right kind of dreams—things that touch people. The other art was for sick men. That is—men sickened of life. The new art will be for healthy men, men reaching out of everything about them. And we must give them bread, soup, and art."

Yes, that might as well be true as anything else. Anything was truth. Anything and everything. Here he was in a scene that had no relation to him. Yet he wasn't detached.

"Speaking of art, Dorn, we've found a new artist, a wonder. She's going to do some things for *The Cry*. I got her interested. I must tell Meredith about her. Maybe you know her— Rachel Laskin. One of her things is coming out in the next issue. I'll send you a copy."

Coolly, amazedly, Dorn thought, "What preposterous thing makes it possible for this man to talk of Rachel as if she were a reality . . . like the people in the café? To him she's like the people in the café. He knows her like the people in the café."

He answered carelessly, "Oh, yes; Miss Laskin. I remember her well. That reminds me: you don't happen to have her address? I've got some things she left at the office we can't use."

Tesla dug an address out of a soiled stack of papers. His pockets seemed alive with soiled papers. Rachel's address was a piece of soiled paper like any other piece of soiled paper. Mumbling silently, Dorn sighed. Just in time. Anna again, and Meredith. He looked at them, recalling his plot. Were they in love? Tesla—the blundering idiot—"I was telling Dorn of a new artist I've found, Eddie. Rachel Laskin, a sort of Blake and Beardsley and something else. Thin lines, screechy things. You'll like them."

"Oh, yes, I always like them," Meredith smiled.

And Anna, "Oh, I know Rachel Laskin well. We're old friends. She's a charming, wonderful girl. I liked her so much. Where is she?"

"In New York."

"I'll have to look at her work," Meredith added. "That's me. Always looking at other people's work and saying, fine, great, and never knowing a thing about it. Ye true art collector, eh, Emil?"

Anna went on, "Erik was amused with her. She is rather odd, you know, and sort of wearing on the nerves. But you can't help liking her."

An amazing description of a face of stars. Dorn smiled.

Tesla said, "I only saw her once. A nervous girl, and she seemed upset."

More from Anna: "I hope she'll come back to Chicago. She was such fun. I really miss her. . . ."

All mad. Babbling of Rachel. Dorn stared cautiously about him. The torment in him became a secret swollen beyond its proper dimensions. They would look at him now and understand that he was not Erik Dorn, but somebody else huddled up, burning and flopping around inside. Love was a virulent form of idiocy. It meant nothing to people outside. Everything inside. Anna talking about Rachel started a panic in him. She was playing with memories of Rachel. Do you remember this? and that? As if he, of course, had forgotten her. Yes, there was an "of course" about it. A gruesome "of course." Gruesome—an excellent word. It meant Anna petting and laughing over a knife that was to plunge itself into her heart. When? Soon . . . soon. He had an address copied from a soiled piece of paper.

They bundled out of the café. Waiters, wraps. Eddie helped with the wraps. Alien streets, dark waiting buildings, lights, and then good-nights. The moments whirled mysteriously away. What did the moments matter? He was going to Rachel. Ah! When had he decided that? He didn't remember reaching any decision in the matter.

They entered a cab alone. The cab rolled away over snow-packed streets. But he couldn't leave Anna. Yes he could. Why not? No. Impossible. A faint thought like a storm packed into a nutshell. . . . "I will."

"You were wonderful to-night, Erik. When I see you with other men I just thank God for you."

That was the intolerable thing—his wonderfulness, his damned wonderfulness. It existed in her. He couldn't leave it behind.

Her hand lay warm in his.

"Kiss me, dearest!"

He kissed her and laughed. He was happy, then? Oh, yes, he was going to Rachel. Simple. Four months of misery, making a weeping idiot out of himself. And now, a decision had been reached. His head on her shoulder, she wanted it so, she was whispering caresses to him. This was Anna. But it would soon be Rachel. What difference did such things make? One woman, another woman. . . .

"You're like Jimmie was."

Happy tears filled her eyes, to be noted and remembered now that he was going to Rachel. Jimmie was a baby who had died—his baby. Offspring was a more humorous word. To be noted and remembered. What a dream!

"I'm so happy, Erik. Everything seems wonderful again when you smile and laugh like this. Your cheeks make such a nice little curve and your head on my shoulder, where it belongs . . . for always and ever. . . ."

Let her sing. He could stand it. What did it matter? But would she die when he left. He would have to say something outright. God, what a thing to say outright. Kill not only her but the wonderful selves of him that lived in her. That didn't mean anything. Anyway, it was rather silly to waste time thinking. . . . To-night, after the ride . . . going to Rachel. He had her address. He would walk up, ring the bell. She would answer and her face would look in surprise at him.

"My Erik, my own sweet little one!"

Dreaming of Jimmie, of him and Jimmie together. . . . "I don't ever want to move. I want us to keep on riding like this forever and ever. . . ."

Quite exquisite tragedy. A bit crude. But reality was always rather crude. Crude or not, what was more exquisite than happiness laughing with an unseen knife moving toward its heart? At least he was an appreciative audience. With his head on her shoulder. Why not? Life demanded that one be an audience sometimes . . . sit back and listen to the fates whispering. What a ride! Dark waiting houses moving by. Seven years together, growing closer and more subtly together—yet not together at all. Anyway, he was sick of living that way. Even without Rachel . . . a mess. Night lies. Passion lies. A dirty business. No, not that. She was beautiful. Anna, not Rachel. He was the unclean one.

"Are you happy, beloved?"

"Yes."

Lord, what an answer to give her. A prayer! Insufferably exquisite gods of drama—she was praying. Tears rushing from her eyes.

"Sweet Jesus . . . sweet brother Jesus . . . thanks for everything. Oh, I've been so unfaithful. Not to believe. Thanks for my wonderful Erik."

He must kill her, swiftly, before she could know that prayers were vain. Easier to kill her body than to listen to this. How, though? With his hands about her throat. Murder was an old business. It would be mercy to her. But he was too much a coward. A cowardly audience listening to words . . . far away from him.

"Beloved . . . darling. Oh, it's so good to have you back again."

"Don't talk." He put his arm tightly around her, his fingers fumbling at her bare neck. But that was only a pretense, a bit of insipid melodrama —his fingers. He was an actor frightened by his part.

The taxi driver was demanding $4.50—an outrage.

"That's too much, Erik."

But he paid. Should he tell him to wait? He would need him in a few minutes. No, too cold-blooded to tell him to wait. And anyway, Anna was listening. He was still an audience. He would jump on the stage and begin acting later. Soon.

"Keep the change."

"Thanks, sir."

An insane world . . . a polite and jovial taxicab driver carrying lunatics about the streets.

"Oh, dear, look! Father's sitting up." She

was disappointed. "And I wanted to kiss and hug you before we went upstairs."

Dorn unlocked the door of his house. He still had a house and could unlock its door without its meaning anything. To-morrow he would have no house. That was the difference between to-day and to-morrow. The old man would be there. That would make it easier. He shivered. "I'm going to do something then". . . . This was alarming.

Anna's arms were around him before he could remove his coat. She clung, laughing, kissing. Let her. . . . "The doomed man ate a hearty breakfast of ham and eggs and seemed in good spirits." Reporters, with a sense of the dramatic, usually wrote it that way. Ham and eggs were a symbol. Should he mull around for extenuating epigrams—a fervid rigmarole on the mysteries and ethics of life? Or strike swift, short? . . . "Death was instantaneous. The drop fell at 10:08 A.M. sharp." Always sharp. Damn his reporters!

"Anna . . ."

She bloomed at the sound of her name.

"I want to talk, Anna."

"No, let's not talk. I'm so happy. . . . Aren't you up rather late, father?"

Thank God she was getting nervous. One can't kill a smile.

"Anna, come to me."

An old phrase of their love-making. He hadn't

meant to use it. But phrases that have been used for seven years get so they say themselves. She moved quickly toward him. His father—smiling beyond her shoulder. Now for the slaughter. . . .

"Do you love me enough to make me happy, Anna?"

"I would give my life for you."

He was deplorably calm—too calm. His eyes were looking at books on shelves, at chairs, at pictures on the walls, as if everything was of an identical importance.

"I know, but that isn't it."

"What then, Erik?"

He couldn't say it. Particularly with his father smiling—an irritating old man who would never die. Should he fall at her feet and whimper? He couldn't. Her face was his, her eyes his. It wasn't leaving Anna. Himself, though. Yes, he was confronting himself. Seven years of selves. All wonderful. Everything he had said and done for seven years lived in Anna. So he must kill seven years of himself with a phrase. No. Yet he was talking on. It soothed him, untightened the agony in him.

"Listen, Anna. I can't tell you, but I must. My words circle away from me. They run away from what I want to tell you. Anna . . . I must go away—leave you."

Tears in his eyes, over his face. His voice, warm, blurring with tears. He choked, paused.

"Erik. . . ."

A white sound. Something bursting.
"If I stay, I'll go mad."
"No . . . no . . . Erik . . ."
Still white sounds, only whiter. Blank sounds, caused by speechlessness. Sounds of speechlessness.

"I may come back, if you'll take me back sometime. . . ."

A man was always an imbecile. Imbecility is a trademark. But there were no sounds now. His eyes tried to turn away from her. A face had ceased to live and give forth sounds. He remained looking at it. A cold, emptied face, like a picture frame with a picture recently torn out of it.

"Anna, for God's sake, hate me. Hate me. Loathe me the rest of your life. I've lied and lied to you—nothing but lies. . . . No, that's not true. But now it is. Think of me as vile when I go away. . . . Otherwise . . ."

Tears blubbered out of him.

. . . "otherwise I'll die thinking of you. Don't look at me that way? Yell at me. . . . You've known it. I can't help it. . . . It's something. I can't help it."

Behind this voice he thought: "It's not me alone. Nights of love . . . kisses . . . Jimmie . . . seven years. . . . Little things. Oh, God, little things. We're all leaving her—pulling ourselves out of her."

"Where are you going, my son?"

Could he lie now? Yes, anything that made it easier.

"Nowhere. Anywhere. I must go. Otherwise I'll choke to death. Take care of her. There's money. All hers. I'll write later about it. Anna . . . don't please."

The thing was a botch. Wrong, all wrong. But that didn't matter. His coat and hat mattered more than phrases. Looking for a coat and hat when he should be winding up the scene properly. These were preposterous banalities that distinguished life, unedited, from melodrama. Where was his hat? His hat . . . hat . . . Life, Fate, Tragedy had mislaid his insufferable hat. Ah . . . on the floor.

She was standing staring at him. Would she die on her feet? Quick, before the shriek. It was coming . . . a madness that would frighten him forever if he heard it. What a scoundrel he was! Why deny it? But in a few years he would be dead and no longer a scoundrel, and all this so much forgotten dust.

"Write to us, my son. And come back soon."

He closed the door softly behind him and started to walk. But his legs ran. It had been easy . . . easy. He stumbled, sprawled upon the iced pavement, bruising his face. He picked himself up unaware that he had stopped running. Night, houses, streets, what matter? In a few years—dust. But he had left in time. That was the important thing. Another minute and he would have heard her. A terrible unheard sound. He had left it behind. He had left her unfinished. Why was he running? Oh, yes—Anna.

He paused and held his eyes from staring back at his house. His eyes would pull him back to the door. Little things—oh, the little things made hurts. He must turn a corner. Light does not travel around corners.

Gone. The house was gone with all its little things. One jerk and he had ripped away. . . .

He walked slowly. A coldness suddenly fell into him. Rachel. He had forgotten about Rachel. Never a thought for Rachel. Disloyal. Where was she—the mirror of stars? Nowhere. He didn't love her. Was he insane? He loved Anna, not Rachel. He must go back. The thing was lopsided—pretense. He'd been pretending he was in love with Rachel. Love . . . schoolboy business. Mirror of stars! Something scribbled on a valentine. That was love. Rachel. No. . . . There was another face. Cold, emptied—a circle of deaths. Anna's face. But he must remember Rachel because he was going to Rachel—remember something about her. Say her name over and over. But that wasn't Rachel. That was a word like . . . like pocketbook. Something about her. . . .

Ah! yes. Her coat lying in the snow. He sighed with a determined effort at sadness . . . **her little coat in the snow!**

PART THREE

WINGS

Chapter One

"BOOM, boom," said the city of New York, "we have gone to war!"

And all the other cities, big and little, said a boom-boom of their own. A mighty nation had gone to war.

A time of singing. Songs on the lips of crowds. Lights in their eyes. High-pitched, garbled words, brass bands, flags, speeches. . . . Mine eyes have seen the coming of the glory of the Lord but we don't want the Bacon, All we Want is a Piece of the Rhine(d). . . . A brass monkey playing "Nearer, My God, to Thee" on a red banjo. . . . *Allons, les enfants . . . le jour de gloire est arrivé!* You tell 'em, kid! Store fronts, cabarets, hotel lobbies, sign-boards, office buildings all become shining citadels of righteousness beleaguered by the powers of darkness. Newspaper headlines exploding like firecrackers on the corners. A bonfire of faces in the streets. A bonfire of flags above the streets.

Boom, boom! . . . societies for the relief of martyred Belgium. Societies for Rolling Cigarettes, Bandages, Exterminating Hun Spies, Exterminating Yellow Dogs and Slackers. . . . Wah, don't let anybody be a slacker! A slacker is a dirty dog who does what I wanna do but am afraid to do. Who lies down. Who won't stand up on his hind legs and cheer when he's supposed to. . . . Societies for Knitting Sweaters, Giving Bazaars, Spotting Hun Propaganda. A bonfire of committees, communes, Jabberwocks, clubs, Green Walruses, False Whiskers, Snickersnees, War Boards, and Eagles Shrieking from their Mountain Heights with an obligato by the Avon Comedy Four—I'm a Jazz Baby. . . .

A mighty nation had gone to war. Humpty Dumpty and the March Hare wheeled out the Home Guards. Said the Débutante to her Soldier Boy in the moonlight, "To Hell with the chaperone, War is War. . . ." Somebody lost Eighty Hundred Billion Dollars trying to build aeroplanes out of Flypaper and a new kind of Cement. And the Press, slapping Fright Wig No. 7 on its bald head, announced to the Four Winds, ". . . once more glory, common cause, sacrifice, welded peoples of America, invincible host, lay common blood, altar liberty, sacred principle, government of the people by the people for the people perish earth" . . . And the Pulpits obliged with an "O God who art in Heaven girthed in shining armor before Thee Thy cause Liberty Humanity Democracy Thy blessing inspire light of sacrifice brave women and hero men give us strength O Lord not falter see way of Righteousness stern hearts bear great burden Thou has given us carry on till powers of darkness routed   virtue again triumphant Thy will done on earth as it is in Heaven. . . ."

And the soldiers entraining for the cantonments —clerks and salesmen, rail-splitters and window-washers with the curve of youth on their faces— the soldiers said, "Whasamatter with Uncle Sam? Rah . . . Wow . . . Good-bye . . . We'll treat 'em rough . . . ashes to ashes and dust to dust if the Camels don't get you the Fatimas must. . . ." And in the cantonments the soldiers said, ". . . this lousy son of a badwoman of a shavetail can't put nothin' over on me . . . say . . . oh, I hate to get up in the morning, oh, how I long to remain in bed. . . ." And in France the soldiers sang ". . . there are smiles that make you happy there are smiles that make you sad. . . . The Knights of Columbus are all right but the Y. M. C. A. is a son of a badwoman of a grafting mess. . . ."

"Yanks Land in France . . . Yanks in Big Battle . . . Yanks Sink Submarines" . . . bang banged the headlines. Don't eat meat on Tuesdays and Thursdays. Help the Red Cross buy Doughnuts for the Salvation Army and keep an eye on Your Austrian Janitor. . . . Elephants, tom-cats, and chorus-girls; a hallelujah with a red putty nose, Seventy-six Thousand Press Agents Walking on their Hands, Jabberwocks, Horned Toads, and Prima Donnas

. . . here comes the Liberty Loan Drive . . .

A mighty nation had gone to war. Boom! Boom! And in a moon-lighted room overlooking a fanfare of roofs, Erik Dorn whispered one night to Rachel,

"You have given me wings!"

Chapter Two

TIME to get up. An oblong of sunlight squeezing through beneath the drawn blind and slapping itself boldly on the gloomy carpet . . . "shame on all sleepy heads. Here's another day. . . ."

Rachel smiled as she opened her eyes. She lay quietly, smiling. It was as it was yesterday—as the day before. One opened one's eyes and life came quickly back with a "Hello, here I am—where you left me." So one lay, fearful to move, like a cup of wine that is too full and mustn't be joggled with even a kick at the bed sheets.

One lay and smiled. Thoughts and stockings side by side somewhere on the floor. Put on stockings in a minute. Put on thoughts in a minute. Dress oneself up in phrases, hats, skyscrapers, and become somebody.

Rachel's eyes livened slowly. Pleasant to be nobody—a bodyless, meaningless smile awake in the morning. Opened eyes on a pillow. A deep, deep sigh on a pillow. An oblong of sunshine on the floor. A happy bed. A happy ceiling. A happy door. Nothing else. Nobody else.

But a hat, a blue straw hat with a jauntily curved brim, sat on a candlestick and winked. Which reminded one that one was alive. After all, one was somebody. Time to get up. All the king's horses and all the king's men demanded of one to arise and get dressed and go out and be somebody. Rachel kicked at the sheets. Protest against the Decrees of Destiny. ". . . those are my feet kicking. Hello, here I am."

There was a note on the pillow adjacent. It read: "At eight o'clock to-night I'll return. Please don't get run over in the streets. ERIK."

Well, why not kiss the note, embrace the pillow and sigh? Why try to be anything but an idiot? . . . "Yes, Mr. Erik Dorn, I will be very careful and not let myself get run over in the streets."

Rachel's head fell on the adjacent pillow and she lay whispering, "I love you," until the sound of her voice caused her to laugh. . . . Time to get up. Dear me! She closed her eyes and rolled herself out of bed. . . . "Ouch! . . ." She sat up on the floor, legs extended, and stared at a shoe. Alas! a shoe is a crestfallen memory. A crestfallen yesterday lurks in old shoes. Shoes are always crestfallen. Even the shoes of lovers waiting under the bed weep and snivel all night. But why sit naked on the floor, stark, idiotically naked on the floor with legs thrust out like a surprised illustration in *La Vie Parisienne* and toes curling philosophically toward a shoe? . . . "I'll do as I please. Very well."

Sanity demanded clothes. But a sudden memory started her to her feet. She stood up

lightly and hurried toward the large oval mirror.
. . . "Your breasts are white birds dreaming under the stars. Your body is like the Queens of China parading through the moon. . . ."

She looked at herself in the mirror. Yes. But why not the Emperors of Afghanistan Walking on Their Hands? Thus . . . "my Body is like the Presidents of the United States Riding Horseback. . . ."

She placed her hands on her slim hips and tautened her figure. When Erik was away all one could do was play with the things he had said. Was she as beautiful as he thought? A joyousness flowed through her. The mirror gave her back a memory of Erik. She was a memory of Erik.

When she looked at herself in the mirror she saw only something that lived in the admiring eyes of Erik. Beautiful legs, beautiful body and "eyes like the courts of Solomon at night, like circles of incense." . . . All were memories of Erik.

She whispered softly to the figure in the mirror, "Erik knows your eyes. They are the beckoning hands of dreams." Thus Erik spoke of them. "I mustn't laugh at myself. I am more beautiful than anything or anybody in the whole world. There is nobody as beautiful as the woman Erik Dorn loves."

If she were only in a forest now where she could run, jump in the air, scream at birds, and end by hurling herself into dim, cool water. Instead, an absurd business of fastening her silk slip.

She seated herself on the bed, her stockings hanging from her hand, and fell again to listening to Erik. His word made an endless echo in her head. . . ."Perrin's a droll species. A sort of indomitable ass. Refuses to succumb to his intelligence. If you think he's in love with your Mary you're a downright imbecile. The man adjusts his passions to his phrases as neatly as a pretty woman pulling on her stockings. . . ." She didn't like Erik to refer to pretty women pulling on their stockings. What an idiot! If Erik wanted to he could go out and help all the pretty women in New York pull on their stockings. As if that had anything to do with their love. Somebody else's stockings! A scornful exclamation point. Now her skirt, waist, shoes, and hat, and she was somebody.

Somebody walking out of a house, in a street, looking, smiling, swinging along. The beautiful one, the desired one out for a promenade, embarrassed somehow by the fact that she was alive, that people looked at her and street-cars made frowning overtures to her. This was not her world. Yet she must move around in it as if she were a fatuous part of its grimacings and artifices. Shop windows that snickered into her eyes . . . "shoes $8 to-day. Hats, $10.50. . . . Traveling-cases only $19. . . ." She must be polite and recognize its existence by composing her features, wearing a hat, saying "pardon me" when she trod on anyone's feet or bumped an elbow into a stomach. A stranger's world—gentlemen in straw hats; gentlemen in proud uniforms marching off to war; a fretwork of gentlemen, signs, windows, hats, and automobiles and a lot of other things, all continually tangling themselves up in front of her nose. A city pouring itself out of the morning sky and landing with a splash and a leap of windows around her feet. Thus the beautiful one, out for a promenade and moving excitedly through a superfluous world.

She plunged into a perilous traffic knot and emerged unscathed. But that was wasting time. Time—another superfluous element, a tick-tock for the little wingless ones to crawl by. Then she remembered—a moon-lighted room . . . "you have given me wings!" Her thought traced itself excitedly about the memory. This had happened. That had been said. Yesterday, to-day and to-morrow—all the same. Memories mixing with dreams. Wings! Yes, wings that beat, beat on the air and left one moving behind a blue dress, under a jaunty hat like all other jaunty hats. But something else moved elsewhere. There were two worlds for her. But not for Erik. One world for Erik. Where would his wings take him? Beyond life there was still life. A wall of life that never came to an end or a top. That was the one world for Erik. Hurl himself against it, higher, higher. Soar till the superfluous ones became little dots on a ribbon of streets.

Tears came into her eyes. The strange world drifted away—a flutter of faces. A silence seemed to descend upon the streets as if their roaring were not a noise but the opened mouth of a dumb man. Erik had come to her. Arm in arm, smiling tears at him she walked through the spinning crowd in a path hidden from all snickering windows and revolving faces. A dream walk. These were her wings.

Consciousness returned. She rubbed her eyes with the knuckles of her hands and laughed softly. She must not excite herself with hysterical worries. Wondering about Erik. There had been days when she had moved like a corpse through the streets, a corpse always finding new and further deaths. Death days with her heart tearing at empty hours, with time like a disease in her veins. Days before he had come. Now all life was in her. Why invent new causes of grief? She must talk sane words to herself. But the sane words bowed a polite adieu and putting on their hats walked away and sat down behind the snickering windows. . . . Other words arrived quickly, breathlessly. . . . There was something in his eyes that frightened, something that did not rest with her but seemed to reach on further. In the midst of their ecstasies his eyes, burning, unsatisfied, making her suddenly chill with fear, would whisper to her, "There is something more."

In each other's arms it was she who came to an ending, not he. His kisses, his "I love you," were the clawing of fingers high up on the wall. For her they were the obliteration, the ending beyond life.

The street unraveled itself about her with a bang of crowds and a whirl of flags, a zigzag of eyes like innumerable little tongues licking at the air. The tension of her thought relaxed. She remembered that when he walked in streets he was always making pictures. She thought of his words. . . . "It's a part of me that love hasn't changed, except to increase. A pestiferous sanity keeps demanding of me that I translate incoherent things into words. The city keeps handing itself to me like a blank piece of paper to write on. And I scribble away."

She would do as he did, scribble words over faces and buildings as she walked. The city was a . . . a swarm of humanity. Swarm of humanity. My God, had she lost the power of thought? Imagine telling Erik, "A crowd of people I saw to-day reminded me of a swarm of humanity." There was no sanity in her demanding words. Because there was no incoherence outside. Things weren't incoherent but nonexistent. The city was no mystery. There was nothing to translate. It was an alien, superfluous world. That was the difference between them. To Erik it was not alien or superfluous. Even in their ecstasies there was still a world for him, like some mocking rival laughing at him, saying, 'You can embrace Rachel. But what can you do to me? See if you can embrace me and swallow me with a kiss. . . ."

That's why he stayed away till eight o'clock, moving among men, writing, talking, doing work on the magazine. But there was nothing for her to do. She inhabited a world named Erik Dorn, a perfect world in which there was no room even for thought.

Erik had written her a note from the office once . . . "my heart is a dancing star above the graves of your absence. . . ." But that was almost a lie because it was true only for one moment. Things occupied him that could not occupy her.

Another block. Four more blocks. Noisy aliveness of streets that meant nothing. She thought, "People look at me and envy me because I'm in a hurry as if I had somewhere important to go. People envy everybody who is in a hurry to get somewhere. Because for them there are no destinations—only halting places for their drifting. Perhaps I should go home and paint something so as to have it to show him when he comes; or sit down somewhere and think up words to give him. I won't be able to talk to-night. I must just be . . . without thinking . . . of anything but him. Why doesn't he sometimes mention Anna? Is he afraid it might offend me to remind me of Anna? Would it? No. Many people live in the world. Another woman lived in Erik Dorn and he was unaware of her as the sky is unaware of me. And she died. But she isn't dead. Only her world died. Her sky fell down. . . ."

Tears came to Rachel's eyes. Her hands clenched. . . . "Anna, Anna, forgive me! I'm so happy. You must understand. . . ."

She felt a revulsion. She had thought something weak, silly. "Who is Anna that I must apologize to her? A woman. A woman Erik never loved. Do I ask apologies of her for having lived with him—kissed him?"

There was a luncheon appointment with Mary James. Mary would bring a man. Perrin, maybe. Mary always brought a man. Without a man, Mary was incomplete. With a man she was even more incomplete. Mary insisted on lunching. Rachel hurried toward the rendezvous. She thought, "People can make me do anything now. Mary or anybody else. I was able once to walk over them. Now they lead me around. Because nothing matters. And people don't sicken me with their faces and talk. They're like noises in another room that one hears, sometimes sees, but never listens to or looks at. They ask questions. And you sit in a secret world beyond them with your hat and dress, properly attentive."

Here was the hotel for the rendezvous. Mary out of breath,

"Rachel! Hello! Wait a minute. Whee! What do you think you're doing? Pulling off a track meet or something? Been tryin' to catch up to you for an hour."

Rachel looked at her. She was a golden-haired monkey full of words.

"Charlie's at the Red Cat." A man. "We're going to lunch there. What in God's name's the matter with you?" A pause in the thick of the crowd. "Heavens, Rachel, are you well? I mean. . . ."

Rachel laughed. If you laughed people thought you were making answers.

They arrived at the Red Cat. Small red circular tables. Black walls. A painstaking non-conformity about the decoration. A sprinkling of diners saying, "We eat, but not amid normal surroundings. We are emancipated from normal surroundings. It is extremely important that we eat off little red circular tables instead of big brown square tables in order to conform with our mission, which is that of non-conformity."

Mary led the way to a table occupied by a tall, broad-shouldered youth with a crooked nose and humorously indignant eyes. He resembled a football player who has gone into the advertising business and remained a football player. Mary referred to him with a possessive "Charlie."

Charlie said, "Why do you always pick out these joints to eat in, Mary? Been sittin' here for ten minutes scared to death one of these females would begin crawlin' around on the walls. There's a waiter here with long hair and two teeth missin' that I'm goin' to bust in the nose if he doesn't stop."

"Stop what, Charlie?"

"Oh, lookin' at me. . . ."

The luncheon progressed. Olives, watery soup, delicate sandwiches. . . .

An air of breathlessness about Rachel seemed to discommode her friends. Charlie, piqued at her inattentiveness, essayed a volubility foreign to his words. He was not so "nice a young man" as Hazlitt. But he boasted among friends that girls had had a chance with him. They could stay decent if they insisted but he let them understand it wouldn't do them any good so far as marrying them was concerned because he wasn't out for matrimony. There was too much to see.

Mary interspersed her eating with quotations from advanced literature, omitting the quotation marks. A slim, shining-haired girl—men adored her hair—pretty-faced, silken-ankled, Mary had a mission in life. It was the utilizing of vivacious arguments on art, God, morals, economics, as exciting preliminaries for hand-holding and kissing with eyes closed, lips murmuring, "Ah, what is life?" Technically a virgin, but devoted exclusively to the satisfying of her sex—a satisfying that did not demand the completion of intercourse but the stimulus of its suggestion, Mary utilized the arts among which she dabbled as a bed for artificial immoralities. In this bed she had managed for several years to remain an adroitly chaste courtesan. Her pride was almost concentrated in her chastity. She guarded it with a precocious skill, parading it through conversation, hinting slyly of it when its existence seemed for the moment to have become unimportant. Her chastity, in fact, had become under skillful management the most immoral thing about her. She had learned the trick of exciting men with her virginity.

The thing had become for her an unconscious business. After several years of it she evolved into a flushed, nervous victim of her own technique. She managed, however, to preserve her self-esteem by looking upon the perversion of her normal sexual instincts into a species of verbal nymphomania as an indication of a superior soul state. Radical books excited her mind as ordinarily her body might have been excited by radical caresses. Amateur theatricals, publicity work for charitable organizations, an allowance from her home in Des Moines, provided her with a practical background.

Charlie was her latest catch. Later he would hold her hand, slip an arm around her, press her breasts gently and with a proper unconsciousness of what he was doing, and she would let him kiss her . . . while music played somewhere . . . preferably on a pier. Then she would murmur as he paused, out of breath, "Ah, what is life, Charlie?" And if instead of playing the game decently Charlie abandoned pretense and made an adventurous sortie, there would ensue the usual dénouement . . . "Charlie . . . Oh, how could you? I'm . . . I'm so disappointed. I thought you were different and that love to you meant something deeper and finer than—just that." And she would stand before him, her body alive with a sexual ardor that seemed to find its satisfaction in the discomfiture of the man, in his apologetic stammers, in her own virtuous words; and reach its climax in the contrite embrace which usually followed and the words, "Forgive me, dearest. I didn't mean. . . . Oh, will you marry me?"

These were things in store for Charlie. But he must listen first. There were essential preliminaries)—a routine of the chase. Her trimly shod foot crawled carefully against his ankle. There were really two types of men. Men who blushed when you touched their ankle under the table, and men who pretended not to blush. Charlie blushed with a soup-spoon at his lips. He glanced nervously at Rachel but she seemed breathlessly asleep with her eyes open—a paradoxical condition which baffled Charlie and caused him to withdraw disdainfully from further consideration of her.

Rachel, eating without hunger, was remembering an actress in vaudeville making a preliminary curtain announcement to her "Moments from Great Plays" . . . "Lady Godiva accordingly rode na-aked through the streets of Coventry, but, howevah, retained her vuhtue. . . ."

"Oh, but Charlie, you're not listening," explained Mary. "I was saying that chastity in woman is something man has insisted upon in order to show his capacity for waste. He likes the world to know that all his possessions are new and that he can command the purchase of new things because it shows his capacity for waste by which his standard of respectability is gauged in the eyes of his fellows. . . ."

Charlie lent an ear to the garbled veblenisms and gave it up. The mutterings and verbal excitements of women in general were mysteries beyond Charlie's desire to comprehend. They had, for Charlie, nothing to do with the case. It was pleasing, though, to have her talk of chastity. Chastity had a connection with the case. It was closely related to unchastity. He nodded his head vaguely and focused his attention on questing for the foot under the table that had withdrawn itself. The long-haired waiter with the missing teeth was an annoyance. He turned and glowered at him.

"Don't you think so, Rachel?" Mary pursued.

A monkey chattering. Another monkey kicking at her toes under the table. A room full of monkeys and all the monkeys looking at her, talk- to her, kicking her foot, inspired by the curious hallucination that she was a part of their monkey world. Rachel laughed and eyes turned to her. People were always startled by laughter that sounded so sudden. There must be preliminaries to laughter so as to get the atmosphere prepared for it.

"Rachel, I'm talking to you, if you please."

Mary, puckering her forehead very importantly, was informing her that Mary existed and was demanding proof of the fact. That was the secret of people. They didn't really exist to themselves until somebody recognized them and proved they were alive—by answering their questions. People lived only when somebody talked to them—anybody. The rest of the time they went along with nothing inside them except stomachs that grew hungry.

She answered Mary, "Oh, there are lots of things you don't know." And laughed, this time careful of not sounding too sudden. She meant there was something that lived behind hours, there was a dream world in which the words and faces of people were ridiculously non-existent. But Mary was a literal-minded monkey and thought she was referring to quotations from books superior to the ones she used.

"Oh, is that so?" said Mary.

Charlie, also literal-minded and still after the foot, echoed Rachel, "You bet your life it is."

"And I suppose you know all about them, Miss Laskin." Very sarcastic. An inflection that had made her a conversational terror in the Des Moines High School.

Mary was always conscious of not having read enough and of therefore being secretly inferior to more omnivorous readers. She did not think Rachel read much, but Rachel was different.

Rachel was an artist and had ideas. Mary respected artists and was always sarcastic toward them. It usually made them talk a lot—particularly male artists—and thus enabled her to find out what their ideas were and use them as her own. Nevertheless, despite her most careful parrotings the artists always managed to have other ideas always different from the ones she stole from them. Fearing some devastating rejoinder from Rachel—Rachel was the kind of person who could blurt out things that landed on you like a ton of bricks—she sought to fortify Charlie's opinion of her by replacing her foot against his ankle.

"Well, what are they, Rachel?"

What were the things Mary knew nothing about? A large order. Rachel's tongue began to wag in her mind. Stand up and make a speech. Fling her arms about. High-sailing words. Absurd! A laugh would answer. Laughs always answered. Rachel laughed. She would suffocate among such people, exasperating strangers with inquisitive faces and nervous feet.

At the conclusion of the luncheon Charlie had reached a new stage in his amorous maneuverings. He had paid no further attention to Rachel, although vividly conscious of her. But Mary offered definite horizons. A bird in the hand. There was something exciting about Mary not to be encountered in the Junos and Aphrodites of his cabaret quests. Mary appeared virtuous—and yet promised otherwise. She used frank words—

lust, chastity, virginity, sexuality. Charlie quivered. The words sticking out of long, twisted sentences, detached themselves and came to him like furtively indecent caresses. Mary promised. So he agreed to go with her to the Players' Studio where she was rehearsing in some kind of nut show.

"You must come too, Rachel. Frank Brander has done some gorgeous settings for the next bill."

Long hours before eight o'clock.

"I've got some important things on at the office," Charlie hesitated.

"Yes, I'll go," Rachel answered. This, mysteriously, seemed to decide Charlie. He would go too.

In the buzzing little auditorium of the Players' Studio, Charlie endeavored to further his quest. But the atmosphere seemed, paradoxically enough, a handicap. A free-and-easy atmosphere with men and women in odd-looking rigs sauntering about. The place was as immoral as a honky-tonk. Charlie stared at the young women in smocks and bobbed hair, smoking cigarettes, sitting with their legs showing. They should have been prostitutes but they weren't. Or maybe they were, only he wasn't used to that kind. Too damn gabby. Mary had jumped up on the small stage and was talking with a group of young men and women. He moved to follow, but hesitated. He didn't have the hang of this kind of thing. The sick-looking youths loitering around, casually embracing the gals and rubbing their arms, seemed to know the lingo. Charlie sat down in disgust and yielded himself to a feeling of stiffly superior virtue.

In a corner Rachel listened to Frank Brander.

"We've got quite a promising outfit here, Miss Laskin. Why don't you come around and help with the drops or something? The more the merrier. We're putting on a thing by Chekov next week and a strong thing by Elvenah Jack. Lives down the street. Know her? Oh, it isn't much." He smiled good-naturedly at the miniature theater. "But it's fun. I'll show you around."

Rachel submitted. Brander was a friend of Emil Tesla. He drew things for *The Cry*. He had a wide mouth and ugly eyes that took things for granted—that took her for granted. She was a woman and therefore interested in talking to a man. He held her arm too much and kept saying in her thought, "We've got to pretend we're decent, but we're not. We're a man and woman." But what did that matter? Long hours before eight o'clock.

On the stage Brander became a personality. A group of nondescript faces deferred to him. A woman with stringy hair and an elocutionist's mouth, grew dramatic as he passed. They paused before Mary. Brander had stopped abruptly in his talk. He turned toward Mary and stared at her until she began to grow pink. Rachel wondered. Mary wanted to run away, but couldn't. Brander finally said shortly, "Hello, you!" His eyes blazed for an instant and then grew angry.

"Come on, Miss Laskin." He jerked her and she followed. In the wings half hidden from the group that crowded the tiny stage Brander said, "Do you know that girl?"

Rachel nodded.

"She's no good," he grinned. "I like women one thing or the other. She's both. And no good. I got her number."

Rachel noticed that he had moved his hand up on her arm and was gently pressing the flesh under her shoulder. He kept saying to her now in her thought, "I've got a man's body and you've got a woman's body. There's that difference between us. Why hide it?" His voice became soft and he said aloud, "Don't you like men to be one kind or the other? And not both?"

Rachel looked at him blankly. She must pretend she didn't know what he was talking about. Otherwise she would begin to talk. He was a man to whom one talked because he demanded it. His face, ugly and boyish, seemed to have rid itself of many expressions and retained a certainty. The certainty said, "I'm a man looking for women."

Brander laughed.

"Oh, you're one of the other kind," he said. "Beg pardon. No harm done. Let's go out front."

Out front in the half-lighted auditorium Brander suddenly left her. She saw him a few minutes later standing close to a nervous-voiced woman who was saying, "Oh, dear! Dear me! I'll never get this part. I won't! I just know it!"

Brander was toying idly with a chain that hung about the woman's neck. He was looking at her intently. Mary approached, bearing Charlie along. She began whispering to Rachel, "That man's a beast. I hate him. He thinks he's an artist, but he's a beast. You'll find out if you're not careful."

Rachel asked, "Who?"

"Brander," Mary answered.

Charlie interrupted, indignation rumbling in his voice,

"A bunch of freaks, all of them. I don't see why a decent girl wants to hang around in a dump like this."

He was more grieved than indignant. A woman with dark hair and long gypsy earrings had suddenly laughed at him when he sat down beside her. Mary patted his arm.

"I know, Charlie. But you don't understand. My turn in a few minutes, Rachel. We'll wait here till the Chekov thing comes on. Do you know Felixson? He's got a wonderful thing for the bill after this. A religious play. Awfully strong. That's him with the bushy hair. You must know him."

Charlie grunted.

"You don't mean you act in this damn joint?"

"Oh, I'm just helping out for next week. It's lots of fun, Charlie."

Rachel stood up suddenly from the uncomfortable bench seat.

"I must go," she murmured. "I'm sorry."

Turning quickly she walked out of the place. Behind her Charlie laughed. "A wild little thing."

Mary with her body pressed closely against him combated an influence that seemed at work upon Charlie.

"She's changed a great deal, poor girl," said Mary.

"What is she?"

"An artist. She says wonderful things sometimes. Awfully strong things and just hates people."

"A nut," agreed Charlie.

"Oh, she's sort of strange. Puts on a lot, of course." Mary felt uncomfortable. Rachel had managed to leave behind a feeling of the unimportance of everybody but Rachel. She was leaning against Charlie for vindication. His body, trembling at the contact, provided it; but his words annoyed her.

"Well, she's different from the gang in here— I'll say that for her."

"Oh, let's forget her," Mary whispered. "I don't like this place. Really, I . . ." She hesitated and thought, "Rachel thinks she's mysterious and enigmatic and everything, but she's an awful fool. She can't put it over on me." Yet she sat, despite the vindication of Charlie's amorous embarrassment, and wondered, parrot fashion, "Ah, what is life?"

Outside Rachel was walking again. The memory of her meeting with Mary, of Brander's ugly appealing face that whispered frankly of his sex, was dead in her. Little toy people playing at games. Erik hated them. Erik said . . . well, it was something too indecent to repeat. She couldn't get used to Erik's indecent comparisons. But they were like that—the toy people in the little toy village. She didn't hate them the way Erik did. Some of them were just playing. But there were others. Why think of them? Walk, walk. Just be. A perfect circle. . . . "There's nothing to do. I don't want anything. To-night he'll talk to me. And I'll make real answers." Why did she want to be kissed? Kisses were for people like Mary. "Oh, he'll kiss me and I'll become alive."

It was late afternoon. Still, long hours before eight o'clock. It pleased Erik when she told him how empty the day had been. But she mustn't harp too much on that. It would sound as if she were making demands on him. No demands. He was free. They weren't married. A crowd was solidifying in 10th Street. She walked slowly, watching the people gathering at the corner. The office of *The Cry* was there. She remembered this and hurried forward.

Something was happening. An excitement was jerking people out of their silences. Blank, silent faces around her suddenly opened and dropped masks. Bodies drifting carelessly up and down the street broke into runnings.

Around the corner people were shouting, pressed into a ball of wild faces and waving arms. It was in front of the office of *The Cry* that something was happening.

"Kill the dirty rascal! Make the son-of-a —— kiss the flag!"

Words screeched out of a bay of sound.

"Kill him! Kill the son-of-a —— String him up!"

On the edge of the ball that was growing larger and seeming about to burst into some wild activity, Rachel stood tip-toed. She could see two burly-looking men dragging a bloody figure out of a doorway. Blood dropped from him, leaving stains on the top step. The two men were twisting his wrists as if they wanted them to come off. Yet they didn't act as if they were twisting anybody's wrists off. They seemed to be just waiting.

It was Tesla between them. His face was cut. One of his arms hung limp. Blood began to spurt from his wrists and drop from his fingers as if he were writing something on the top step in a foolish way. At the sight of him the noises increased. The ball of faces grew angrier. Policemen swung sticks. They yelled, "Back, there! Everybody back!" Runners were coming from all directions as if the city had suddenly found a place to go and was pouring itself into 10th Street.

"Hey . . . hey . . . they've got him!"

Nobody asked who, but came running with a shout.

The street broke over Rachel. Tesla vanished. Roaring in her ears, faces tumbling, lifting in a wildness about her. A make-believe of horror. Her thought gasped, "Where am I? What is this?" Her feet were carrying her into the boiling center of a vat of bodies. Then she saw Tesla again, standing above them. A blood-smeared man with a broken arm, his head raised. But he was somebody else.

Caught in the pack she became far away, seeing things move as with an almost lifeless deliberateness. Tesla's face was the center. His swollen eyes were trying to open. His paralyzed mouth was trying to form itself back into a mouth. A mist covered him as if the raging street and the many voices focused into a film and hid him. Behind this film he was doing something slowly. Then he became vivid. He was shouting,

"Comrades . . . workers . . ."

A roar from the street concealed him and his voice. But the vividness of him lingered and emerged again.

"Comrades!"

A fist struck against his mouth. His head wabbled. Another fist struck against his eye.

The two men holding his wrists were striking into his uncovered face with their fists. A gleeful, joyous sound went up. Rachel stared at the wabbling head of Tesla. The street laughed. Fists hammered at an uncovered face. People were coming on a run to see. A bell clanged. Beside her a man shrieked, "Make him kiss the flag, the dirty anarchist!"

Things slowed again. A film was over the scene. Tesla was being dragged down the steps. His head kept falling back as if he wanted to go to sleep. Then something happened. A laugh, high like a scream, lit the air. It made her cold. The men dragging Tesla down the steps paused, and their fists moving with a leisureliness struck into his face, making no sound and not doing anything. It was Tesla who had laughed. The fists kept moving through a film. But he laughed again—a high laugh like a scream that lit the air with mystery.

When the pack began to sift and sweep her into strange directions she felt that Tesla was still laughing, though she could no longer hear him. The street became shapeless. Something had ended. A bell clanged away. People were again walking. They had dull faces and were quiet. She caught a glimpse of the step on which Tesla had stood behind a mist and cried, "Comrades!" She remembered often having stood on the step herself in coming to the office of *The Cry*. This made her sicken. It was her wrists that had been twisted, her uncovered face that had been struck by fists.

The emotion left her as a hand tugged eagerly at her arm. It pulled her up on the crowded curbing.

"Good God, Rachel, what are you doing here?"

She looked up and saw Hazlitt in uniform. He kept pulling her. Why should Hazlitt be pulling her out of a crowd in 10th Street? She tried to jerk away. She must run from Hazlitt before he began talking. He would make her scream.

Turning to him with a quiet in her voice she said carefully:

"Please let me go. You hurt my arm."

But his hand remained. His eyes, shining and indignant, prodded at her. . . . The street was quiet. Nothing had happened. Unconscious buildings, unconscious traffic, faces wrapped in solitudes—these were in the streets again. She turned and looked with amazement at her companion. People do not fall out of the sky and seize you by the arm. There was something stark about Hazlitt pulling her out of the street mob and holding her arm. He was an amputation. You pulled yourself out of a filth of faces and sprawled suddenly into a quiet, cheerful street holding an arm in your hand, as if it had come loose from the pack. It seemed part of some arrangement—Tesla, the pack, Hazlitt's **arm.** Her amazement died. Hazlitt was saying:

"I knew you'd be in that mob. I thought when I saw them haul that dirty beggar out . . ."

He halted, pained by a memory. Rachel nodded. The curious sense of having been Tesla came again to her. He had laughed in a way that reminded her of herself. She would laugh like that if they struck at her face. Her eyes turned frightenedly toward Hazlitt. What was he going to do? Arrest her? He was in uniform. But why should he arrest her? His eyes had the fixed light of somebody performing a duty. He was arresting her, and Erik would come home and not find her. Her lithe body became possessed of an astounding strength. With a vicious grimace she tore herself from his grip and confronted him, her eyes on fire.

"Please, Rachel. Come with me till I can talk. You must . . ."

A white-faced Hazlitt, with suffering eyes. Then he was not arresting her. The street bobbed along indifferently.

"I'm going away in an hour. You'll maybe never see me again. But I can't go away till I've talked to you. Please."

It didn't matter then. She would be home in time. And it was easier to obey the desperate whine of his voice then run into the crowd. He would chase after her, whining louder and louder. They entered a hotel lobby. Hazlitt picked out a secluded corner as if arranging for some rite.

Erik Dorn 205

He was going to do something. Rachel walked after him, annoyed, indifferent. What did it matter? This was George Hazlitt—a name that meant nothing and yet could talk to her.

Sitting opposite her the name began, "Now you must promise me you won't get up and run away till I'm through—no matter what I say."

She promised with a nod. She must be polite. Being polite was part of the idiotic penalties attached to adventuring outside her real world, in unreal superfluous streets. What had made Tesla laugh? His laugh had not been unreal. Almost as if it were a part of her. Blood dropping from his fingers. A bleeding man.

"I'm leaving for France, Rachel. I couldn't go away without seeing you. I've spent a week trying to find you and this morning they told me to inquire at *The Cry*."

Was he apologizing for Tesla? She remembered the faces that had swept by in 10th Street. His had been one of them. Hazlitt had twisted Tesla's wrists and struck into his uncovered face.

Rachel slipped to her feet and stared about her. A hand caught at her arm and pulled her into the chair.

"You promised. You can't leave till you hear me."

She sank back.

"Give me five minutes. I'm unworthy of them. But I've found you and must talk now. I can't go across without telling you."

She looked up. Tears almost in his eyes. His voice grown low. He seemed to be whispering something that didn't belong to the sanity of the hotel lobby and the two large potted palms in the corner.

"I'm unclean. I've been looking for you to ask you to forgive me."

Hazlitt's hands crept over his knees.

"Oh, God, you must listen and forgive me."

This was a mad monkey uttering noises too unintelligible for even an attentive hat, dress, and pair of shoes to make anything of.

"Rachel, I love you. I don't know how to say it. There's something I've got to say. Because . . . otherwise I can't love you. I can't love you with the thing unsaid."

He looked bewilderedly about him and gulped, his face red, his eyes tortured.

"It's about a woman."

"Perhaps," she thought, "he's going to boast. No, he's going to cry. What does he want?"

The sound of his voice made her ill. If he were going to make love why didn't he start instead of gulping and covering his face and choking with tears in a hotel lobby as if he were an actor?

"I was drawn into it. I couldn't help it. One afternoon in my office after the trial. Then she kept after me. The thought of you has been like knives in me. I've loved you all through it and hated myself for thinking of you, dragging you into it. I dragged the thought of you down with

Erik Dorn

me. But she wouldn't let me go. God, I could kill her now. I broke away after weeks. She got somebody else. I've been living in hell ever since—on account of you. I'm unclean and can't love you any more. If it hadn't been for my going across I'd not have come to you. But the war's given me my chance. I can't explain it. I went in to—to wipe it out. But I had to find you and tell you. I didn't want to think of dying and having insulted you and not . . ."

He stopped, overcome. Rachel was nodding her head. She must make an answer to this. It was a riddle asking an answer.

"For God's sake, Rachel, don't look like that. Oh, you're so clean and pure. I can't tell you. You're like a star shining and me in the mud. You've always hated me. But it's different now. I'm going to France to die. I don't want to live. If you forgive me it'll be easier. That's why I had to talk, Rachel, forgive me. And then it won't matter what happens."

She let him take her hand. It was an easy way to make an answer. A desire to giggle had to be overruled. The words he had spoken became absurd little manikins of words, bowing at each other, striking idiotic postures before her. But he had done something and for some astounding reason wanted her to forgive him for what he had done. He was a fool. An impossible fool. He sat and looked like a fool. Not even a man.

Hazlitt raised her hand to his face. Tears fell

on it. Rachel felt them crawling warmly over her fingers. They were too intimate.

"You make me feel almost clean again. Your hand's like something clean and pure. If I come back . . ."

He stared at her in desperation. He seemed suddenly to have forgotten his intention to die in France. He recalled Pauline. Was he sorry? No. It was over. Not his fault. All this to Rachel was a ruse. Clever way to get her sympathy. Not quite. But he felt better.

He became incomprehensible to Rachel. The things he had said—his weeping, gulping—all part of an incomprehensible business. She nodded her head and looked serious. It was something that had to do with a far-away world.

"Good-bye. Remember, I love you. And I'll come through clean because of you. . . ."

She held out her hand and said, "Good-bye."

But he didn't go. Now he was completely a fool. Now there was something so completely foolish about him that she must laugh. The light in his face detained her laughter.

"You forgive me . . . for . . ."

She nodded her head again. It seemed to produce a magical effect—this nodding of her head up and down. His eyes brightened and he appeared to grow taller.

"Then if I die, I'll go to heaven."

She winced at this. An unbearable stupidity. But Hazlitt stood looking at her for an instant.

quite serious, as if he had said something noble. He saluted her, his hand to his cap, his heels together, and went away.

The memory lingered. Hazlitt had always been incomprehensible. His stupidity was easy enought to understand. But something under it was a mess. Now he was a fool. Stiff and idiotic and making her feel ashamed as if she were sorry for him. . . . Tesla came back and stood on a step dropping blood from his fingers. Brander came back and whispered with his ugly face. Hazlitt, Tesla, Brander—three men that jumped out at her from the superfluous streets. Like the three men in the park walking horribly across the white park in the night. . . . An idiot, a bleeding man, and an ugly face. But they had passed her and gone. They were things seen outside a window.

Her eyes looking at a clock said to her, "Two hours more. Oh, in two hours, in two hours!"

She sat motionless until the clock said, "One hour more, one more hour!"

Then she stood up and walked slowly out of the hotel. Things had changed since she had left the streets. The strange world full of Marys, Hazlitts, and Teslas had added further superfluities. A band of music. Soldiers marching. Buildings waving flags and crying, "Boom, boom! we have gone to war! . . ."

She came to her home. A red-brick house like other red-brick houses. But her home. What a fool she had been to leave it. It would have been easier waiting here. She walked into the two familiar rooms filled with the memory of Erik—two rooms that embraced her. Her hat fell on the bed. She would have to eat. Downstairs in the dining-room. Other boarders to look at. But Erik would have eaten when he came. He preferred eating alone.

Rachel took her place at one of the smaller tables and dabbled through a series of uninteresting dishes. An admiring waitress rebuked her . . . "Dearie, you ain't eating hardly anything."

She smiled at the waitress and watched her later bringing dishes to a purple-faced fat man at an adjoining table. The fat man was futilely endeavoring to tell secrets to the waitress by contorting his features and screwing up his eyes. He reminded Rachel of Brander, only Brander told secrets without trying. She finished and hurried out. She would be hungry later, but it didn't matter. Erik would be there then.

In the hallway Mrs. McGuire called, "Oh, Mrs. Dorn!"

Being called Mrs. Dorn always frightened her and made her dizzy. She paused. Some day Mrs. McGuire would look at her shrewdly and say, "You're not Mrs. Dorn. I called you Mrs. Dorn but I know better. Don't think you're fooling anybody. Mrs. Dorn, indeed!"

But Mrs. McGuire held out her hand.

"A letter for your husband. Do you want to sit in the parlor, Mrs. Dorn? You know I want all my boarders to make themselves entirely at home."

"Thank you," said Rachel. "You're so nice. But I have some work to do upstairs."

Escaping Mrs. McGuire was one of the difficult things of the day. A buxom, round-faced woman in black with friendly eyes, Mrs. McGuire had a son in the army and a sainted husband dead and buried, and a childish faith in the friendliness and interest of people. Rachel hurried up the stairs. In her room she looked at the letter. For Erik. Readdressed twice. From Chicago. She stood holding it. It said to her, "I am from Anna. I am from Anna. Words of Anna. I am the wife of Erik Dorn."

Anna was a reality. Long ago Anna had been a reality. A background against which the dream of Erik Dorn raised itself. She remembered sitting close to Anna and smiling at her the first time she had visited Erik's home. Why had she gone? If only she had never seen Anna! Her tired, sad eyes that smiled at Erik. Rachel's fingers tightened over the envelope. She laughed nervously and tore the letter. He was hers. Anna couldn't write to him.

A pain came into her heart as the paper separated itself into bits in her fingers. She felt herself tearing something that was alive. It was cruel to tear the letter. But it would save Erik pain.

. . . To read Anna's words, to hear her cries, see her sad tired eyes staring in anguish out of the writing—that would hurt Erik.

She dropped the bits into the waste-paper basket and stood wide-eyed over them. She had dared. As if he had belonged to her. What would he say? But he wouldn't know. Unless Mrs. McGuire said, "There was a letter for you, Mr. Dorn." Why hadn't she read the letter before tearing it up? Perhaps it was important, saying Anna had died. When Anna died Erik would marry her. She would have children and live in a house of her own. Mrs. Rachel Dorn, people would call her. This was a dream. . . . Mrs. Rachel Dorn. He would laugh if he knew; or worse, be angry. But . . . "Oh, God, I want him. Like that. Complete." Anna had had him like that. The other thing. Not respectability. But the possession of little things.

She would have to tell him about the letter. She couldn't lie to him, even silently. The clock on the dresser, ticking as it had always ticked, said, "In a half-hour . . . a half-hour more."

She sprang from the bed and stood listening.

Someone was coming down the hall. Strange hours fell from her. Now Erik was coming. Now life commenced. The empty circle of the day was over.

Her body grew wild as if she must leap out of herself. Her eyes hung devouringly upon the blank door—a door opening and Erik standing, smiling at her. It was still a dream. It would never become real. She would always feel frightened. Though he came home a hundred thousand times she would always wait like now for the door to open with a fear and a dream in her heart. But why did he knock?

She opened the door with a feverish jerk. Not Erik. A messenger-boy blinking surprised eyes.

"Mrs. Dorn?"

"Yes."

"Sign here, second line."

A blank door again. The message read:

"I'll be home late. Don't worry. ERIK."

Chapter Three

WARREN LOCKWOOD was a man who wrote novels. He had lived in the Middle West until he was thirty-five and begun his writing at his desk in a real-estate office of which he had been until then a somewhat bored half owner.

During the months Erik Dorn had been working on the staff of "the *New Opinion*—an Organ of Liberal Thought," he had encountered Lockwood frequently—a dark-haired, rugged-faced man with a drawling, high-pitched masculine voice. Dorn liked him. He talked in the manner of a man carefully focusing objects into range. Lockwood was aware he had gotten under the skin of things. He talked that way.

The change from the newspaper to the magazine continued, after several months, to irritate Dorn. The leisureliness of his new work aggravated. There was an intruding sterility about it. The *New Opinion* was a weekly. From week to week it offered a growing clientèle finalities. There were finalities on the war, finalities on the social unrest; finalities on art, life, religion, the past, present, and future. A cock-sure magazine, gently, tolerantly elbowing aside the mysteries of existence and holding up between carefully manicured thumb and forefinger the Gist of the Thing. The Irrefutable Truth. The Perfect Deduction.

There were a number of intelligent men engaged in the work of writing and editing the periodical. They seemed all to have graduated from an identical strata. Dorn, becoming acquainted with them, found them intolerable. They appealed to him as a group of carefully tailored Abstractions bombinating mellifluously in a void. The precision of logic was in them. The precision of even tempers. The precision of aloof eyes fastened upon finalities. Theoretical radicals. Theoretical conservatives. Theoretical philosophers. Any appellation preceded by the adjective theoretical fitted them snugly. Of contact with the hurdy-gurdy of existence which he as a journalist felt under the ideas of the day, there was none. Life in the minds of the intellectual staff of the *New Opinion* smoothed itself out into intellectual paragraphs. And from week to week these paragraphs made their bow to the public. Mannerly admonitions, courteous disapprovals. A style borrowed from the memory of the professor informing a backward class in economics what the exact date of the signing of the Magna Charta really was.

Lockwood was the exception. He wrote occasional fictional sketches for the magazine. Dorn had been attracted to him at first because of the curious intonations of his voice. He had not read the man's novels—there were four of them dealing with the Middle West—but in the repressed singsong of his voice Dorn had sensed an unusual character.

"He's a good writer, an artist," he thought, hearing him talking to Edwards, one of the editors. "He talks like a lover arguing patiently and gently with his own thoughts."

After that they had walked and eaten together. The idea of Warren Lockwood being a lover grew upon Dorn. Of little things, of things seemingly unimportant and impersonal, the novelist talked as he would have liked to talk to Rachel—with a slow simplicity that caressed his subjects and said, "These are little things but we must be careful in handling them, for they're a part of life." And life was important. People were tremendously existent. Dorn, listening to the novelist, would watch his eyes that seemed to be always adventuring among secrets.

Once he thought, "A sort of mother love is in him. He keeps trying to say something that's never in his words. His thoughts are like a lover's fingers stroking a girl's hair. That's because he's found himself. He feels strong and lets his strength come out in gentleness. He's found himself and is trying to shape secrets into words."

In comparing Lockwood with the others on the staff of the magazine he explained, "There's the difference between a man and an intellect. Warren's a man. The others are a group of schoolboys reducing life to lessons."

There grew up in Dorn a curious envy of the

novelist. He would think of him frequently when alone, "The fellow's content to write. I'm not. He's found his way of saying what's in him, getting rid of his energies and love. I haven't. He feels toward the world as I do toward Rachel. An overpowering reality and mystery are always before him; but it gives him a mental perspective. What does Rachel give me? Desires, ambitions— a sort of laughing madness that I can't translate into anything but kisses. I'm cleverer than I was before. I talk and write better. There's a certain wildness about things as if I were living in a storm. Yes, I have wings, but there's no place to fly with them. Except into her arms. There must be something else."

And he would rush through the day, outwardly a man of inexhaustible energies, stamping himself upon the consciousness of people as a brilliant, dominating personality. Edwards, with whom he discussed matter for editorials and articles, had grown to regard him with awe.

"I've never felt genius so keenly before," Edwards explained him to Lockwood. "The man seems burning up. Did you read his thing on Russia and Kerensky? Lord, it was absolutely prophetic."

Lockwood shook his head.

"Dorn's too damn clever," he drawled. "Things come too easily to him. He's got an eye but—I can't put my finger on it. You see a fella's got to have something inside him. The things

Erik says cleverly and prophetically don't mean anything much, because they don't mean anything to him. He makes 'em up as he goes along."

Edwards disagreed. He was a younger man than Lockwood, with an impressionable erudition. Like his co-workers he had been somewhat stampeded by Dorn's imitative faculties, faculties which enabled the former journalist to bombinate twice as loud in a void three times as great as any of his colleagues.

"Well, I've met a lot of writing men since I came East," he said. "And Dorn's the best of them. He's more than a man of promise. He's opened up. Look what he's done in the new number. Absolutely revolutionized the liberal thought of the country. You've got to admit that. He's a man incapable of fanaticism."

"That's just it," smiled Lockwood. "You've hit it. You've put your finger on it. He's the kind of man who knows too damn much and don't believe anything."

The friendship between Lockwood and Dorn matured quickly. The two men, profoundly dissimilar in their natures, found themselves launched upon a growing intimacy. To Lockwood, heavy spoken, delicate sensed, naïve despite the shrewdness of his forty-five years, Erik Dorn appealed as some exotic mechanical contrivance might for a day fascinate and bewilder the intelligence of a rustic. And the other, in the midst of magnificent bombinations that amazed his friend, thought,

"If I only had this man's simplicity. If on top of my ability to unravel mysteries into words I could feel these mysteries as he does, I might do something."

At other times, carried away by the strength of his own nature, he would find himself looking down upon Lockwood. "I'm alive. He's static. I live above him. There's nothing beyond me. I can't feel the things out of which he makes his novels, because I'm beyond them."

He would think then of Lockwood as an eagle of a rustic painstakingly hoeing a field. On such days the disquiet would vanish from Dorn's thought. He would feel himself propelled through the hours as if by some irresistible wind of which he had become a part. To live was enough. To live was to give expression to the clamoring forces in him. To sweep over Edwards, hurl himself through crowds, pulverize Warren, bang out astounding fictions on the typewriter, watch the faces of acquaintances light up with admiration as he spoke—this sufficed. The world galvanized itself about him. He could do anything. He could give vision to people, create new life around him. This consciousness sufficed. Then to rush home from a triumphant day, a glorious contempt for his fellows lingering like wine in his head—and find Rachel—an eagle waiting in a nest.

Joy, then, become a mania. Desires feeding upon themselves, devouring his body and his senses and hurling him into an exhausted sleep as if death alone could climax the madness of his spirit—these Dorn knew in the days of his strength.

But the days of disquiet came, confronting him like skeletons in the midst of his feastings upon life. The ecstasy he felt seemed suddenly to turn itself inward and demand of him new destinations. On such days he had fallen into the habit of going upon swift walks through the less crowded streets of the city. During his walking he would mutter, "What can I do? What? Nothing. Not a thing." As if secret voices were debating his destiny.

Restless, vicious spoken, venting his strainings in a sky-rocket burst of phrases upon the inanity and stupidity of his fellow creatures for which he seemed to possess an almost uncanny vision, he fled through these days like the victim of some spiritual satyriasis. No longer a wind at his heels riding him into easy heights, he found himself weighted down with his love, and strangely inanimate.

The direction in which he was moving loomed sterilely before him. His love itself seemed a feverishly sterile thing. His work upon the magazine, his incessant exchange of intolerant adjectives with admiring strangers—these became absurdly petty gestures, absurdly insufficient. There was something else to do. As he had longed for Rachel in the black days before their coming together, he longed now for this something else. Without name or outline, it haunted him. Another face of stars, but this time beyond his power to understand.

Yet it demanded him, as Rachel had demanded him, and towards it he turned in his days of disquiet, inanimate and bewildered.

"I must find something to do," he explained to himself, "that will give me direction. People must have a monomania as a track for their living, or else there is no living."

Then, as was his custom, he would begin an unraveling of the notion.

"Men with energies in them wed themselves quickly to some consuming project, even if it's nothing more than the developing of a fish market. Rachel isn't a destination. She's a force that fills me with violence and I have no direction in which to live to use this violence. I don't know what to do with myself. So I'm compelled to live in the violence itself. In a storm. A kind of Walkyrie on a broomstick. But, good God, what else is there? Sit and scribble words about fictitious characters. Bleat out rhapsodies. Art is something I can spit out in conversation. If I do anything it's got to be something too difficult for me to do. My damned cleverness puts me beyond artists who find a destination for their energies in the struggle to achieve the thing with which I begin. If not art, then what? War, politics, finance. All surfaces meaning nothing. If I did them all there'd still be something I hadn't done. I want something that's not in life. Life's too damned insufficient. I want something out of it."

Rachel had thought at first that his fits of brooding restlessness came from a memory of Anna. But phrases he had blurted out half-consciously had given her a sense of their causes. The thought of Anna had died in him. Neither consciousness of her suffering nor memory of the years they had lived together had yet awakened in him. He had been moving since the night he had walked out of his home and there had been no looking back.

Undergoing a seeming expansion of his powers, Erik Dorn had become a startling, fascinating figure in the new world he had entered. The flattery of men almost as clever as himself, the respect, appreciation of political, literary, and vaguely social circles, of stolid men and eccentric acquaintances, were continually visited upon him. He was a personality, a figure to enliven dinner parties, throw a glamour and a fever into the enervated routine of sets, cliques, and circles.

He had made occasional journeyings alone and sometimes with Rachel into the homes of chance acquaintances, and had put in fitful appearances at the various excitements pursued by the city's more radical intelligentsia—little-theater premiers, private assemblings of shrewd, bored men and women, precious concerts, electric discussions of political unrest. From all such adventurings he came away with a sense of distaste. Friendships, always foreign to his nature, had become now almost an impossibility. He felt himself a procession of adjectives exploding in the ears of strangers.

With Warren Lockwood alone he had been able

to achieve a contact. In the presence of the novelist there was a complement of himself both in the days of his disquiet and strength. Together they took to frequenting odd parts of the city, visiting lonely cafés and calling upon strangers known to the novelist. The man's virile gentleness soothed him. He was never tired of watching the turns of his naïveté, delighting as much in his friend's unsophisticated appreciation of the arts as in the vivid simplicity of his understanding of people and events.

He had finished a stormy conference with the directors of the magazine on the subject of a new editorial policy toward Russia—new editorial policies toward Russia had become almost the sole preoccupation of the *New Opinion*—when Lockwood arrived at the office, resplendent in the atrocities of a new green hat and lavender necktie.

"There's a fella over on the east side you ought to meet," Lockwood explained. "I was going over there and thought you'd like to come along."

He leaned over, seriously confidential.

"If you can lay off a while in this business of revolutionizing the liberal thought of the whole country, Erik, I'll tell you something. Between you and me, this man we're going to see is the greatest artist in America. I know."

Lockwood waved his hand casually as if dismissing once and for all an avalanche of contradictions. Dorn hesitated. It was one of his days of disquiet;

and he had left a note with Rachel saying he would be home at eight. It was now six.

"If you've got a date," went on Lockwood, "call it off. Lord, man, you can't afford missing the greatest artist in the world."

Dorn frowned. He might telephone. But that would mean explanations and the pleading sound of a voice saying, "Of course, Erik." He would send a message, and scribbled it on a telegraph blank:

"I'll be home late. Don't worry.

"Erik."

"We'll make a night of it," he laughed.

Lockwood looked at him, shrewdly affectionate.

"What you need," he spoke, "is a good drink and some fat street woman to shake you out of it. You look kind of tied up."

"I am," grinned Dorn. "Wound up and ready to bust."

Lockwood nodded his head slowly.

"Uh-huh," he said, as if turning the matter over carefully in his thought. "Why don't you buy a new hat like I do when I get feeling sort of upside down? Buying a new hat or tie straightens a man out. Come on!" He laughed suddenly. "This artist's name is Tony. He's an old man—seventy years old."

They entered the street, Lockwood watching his companion with dark, fixed eyes as if he were slowly arriving at some impersonal diagnosis.

"A lot of fools," he announced abruptly, waving

Erik Dorn 225

his hand at the crowds. "They don't know that something important's happening in Russia." He pronounced it Rooshia. Dorn saw his eyes kindle with a kindliness as he denounced the rabble about them.

"What do you figure is happening in Rooshia?" he inquired of the novelist.

"I don't figure," smiled Lockwood. "I feel it. Something important that these newspaper Neds around this town haven't got any conception of. It's what old Carl calls the rising of the proletaire." He chuckled. "Old Carl's sure gone daft on this proletaire thing." His face abruptly hardened, the rugged features becoming set, the swart eyes paying a far-away homage. "But old Carl's a great poet—the greatest in America. God, but that old boy can write!"

Dorn nodded. In the presence of the novelist the unrest that had held him by the throat through the day seemed to ebb. There was companionship in the figure beside him. They walked in silence for several blocks. The day was growing dark quickly and despite the crowds in the streets, there seemed an inactivity in the air—the wait of a storm.

Into a ramshackle building on the corner of a vivaciously ugly street Lockwood led his friend in quest of the greatest artist. An old man in a skull cap, woolen shirt, baggy trousers and carpet slippers appeared in a darkened doorway. With his long white beard he stood bent and rheumatic before them, making a question mark in the gloom of the hall.

"Hello, Tony," Lockwood greeted him. "I've brought a friend of mine along to look at your works."

The old man extended thin fingers and nodded his head. Dorn entered a large room that reminded him of a tombstone factory. Figures in clay, some broken and cracked, cluttered up its floor and walls. In a corner partly hidden behind topsy-turvy busts and more figures was a cot with a blanket over it. Dorn after several minutes of silence, looked inquiringly at his friend. The works of art, despite an obvious vigor of execution, were openly banal.

"He's got some more in the basement," announced Lockwood with an air of triumph. "And there's some stuck away with the family upstairs. The whole street here's full of his works."

The old man nodded.

"He doesn't talk much English," went on Lockwood. "But I'll tell you about him. I got the story from him. He's the greatest artist in the world."

As Dorn moved politely from figure to figure, the old man like a museum monitor at his heels, Lockwood went on explaining in a caressing singsong:

"This old boy came to New York when he was in his twenties. And he's been living here ever since and making statues. He's working right now on a statue of some general. Been working for fifty years without stopping, and there's nobody in this town ever heard of him or come near him. Get this picture of this old boy, Erik, buried in this hole for fifty years making statues. Working away day after day without anybody coming near him. I brought a sculptor friend of mine who kept squinting at some of the things the old boy did when he first came over and saying, 'By God, this fella was an artist at one time.' Get the picture of this smart-aleck sculptor friend of mine saying this old boy was an artist."

The eyes of Warren Lockwood grew hard and seemed to challenge. He extended his arm and waved his hand gently in a further challenge.

"The fools in this town let this old boy stay buried," he whispered, "but he fooled them. He kept right on making statues and giving them away to the folks that live around here and hiding them in the basement when there wasn't anybody to take them."

Lockwood grasped the arm of his friend excitedly and his voice became high-pitched.

"Don't you get this old man?" he argued. "Don't you get the figure of him as an artist? Lord, man, he's the greatest artist in the world, I tell you!"

Dorn nodded his head, amused and disturbed by the novelist's excitement. The old sculptor was standing in the shadow of the figures piled on top of each other against the wall. He wore the air of a man just awakened and struggling politely to grasp his surroundings.

"A sort of altruistic carpenter," thought Dorn. "That's what Warren calls an artist. Works diligently for nothing."

The respect and awe in the eyes of his friend halted him.

"Yes, I get him," he added aloud. "Living with a dream for fifty years."

Lockwood snorted and then with a quiet laugh answered: "No, that isn't it. You're not an artist yourself so you can't quite get the sense of it." He seemed petulent and defeated.

They left the old man's studio without further talk. It had started to rain. Large spaced drops plumbed a gleaming hypotenuse between the rooftops and the streets. They paused before a basement restaurant.

"It looks dirty," said Lockwood, "but let's go in."

Here they ordered dinner. During their eating the noise of thunder sounded and the splash of the storm drifted in through the dusty basement windows. A thick-wristed, red-fingered waitress slopped back and forth between their table and an odorous kitchen door. Lockwood kept his eyes fastened steadily upon the nervous features of his friend. He thought as the silence increased between them: "This man's got something the matter with him."

Gradually an uneasiness came over the novelist,

his sensitive nerves responding to the disquiet in the smiling eyes opposite.

"You're kind of crazy," he leaned forward and whispered as if confiding an ominous, impersonal secret. "You've got the eyes of a man kind of crazy, Erik."

He sat back in his chair, his hands holding the edge of the table, his chin tucked down, as if he were ruminating, narrow-eyed, upon some involved business proposition.

"I get you now," he added slowly. "I'll put you in a book—a crazy man who kept fooling himself by imitating sane people."

Dorn nodded.

"Insanity would be a relief," he answered. "Come on."

He stood up quickly and looked down at his friend.

"Let's keep going. I've got something in me I want to get rid of."

In the doorway the friends halted. The grave, melodious shout of the rain filled the night. The streets had become dark, attenuated pools. The rain falling illuminated the hidden faces of the buildings and silvered the air with whirling lines.

As they stood facing the downpour Dorn thought, "Rachel's waiting for me. Why don't I go to her? But I'd only make her sad. Better let it get out of me in the rain."

Holding his friend's arm he stood staring at the storm over the city. Through the sparkle and fume of the rain-colored night the lights of café signs burned like golden-lettered banners flung stiffly into the downpour. About the lights floated patches of yellow mist through which the rain swarmed in flurries of gleaming moths. There were lights of doors and windows beneath the burning signs. The remainder of the street was lost in a wilderness of rain that bubbled and raced over the pavements in an endless detonation.

He spoke with a sudden softness: "I didn't get your artist, Warren, but you don't get this storm. It's noise and water to you."

The novelist answered with a sagacious nod.

"There's something alive in a night like this," Dorn went on, "something that isn't a part of life."

He pulled his friend out of the doorway. They walked swiftly, their shoes spurting water and the rain dripping from their clothes. Dorn felt an untightening. His eyes hailed the scene as if in greeting of a friend. He became aware of its detail. He smiled, remembering the way in which he had been used to hide his longing for Rachel in the desperate consciousness of scenes about him. Now it was something else he was hiding. Beneath his feet he watched the silver-tipped pool of the pavement. Gleaming in its depths swam reflections of burning lamps, like the yellow script of another and wraith-like world staring up at him out of a nowhere. The rest was darkness and billowy stripes of water. People had vanished. Later a sound of thunder crawled out of the sky.

A vein of lightning opened the night. Against its blue pallor the street and its buildings etched themselves.

"Stiff, unreal, like a stage scene," murmured Dorn. "Another world."

The rain flung itself for an instant in great ghostly sheets out of the lighted spaces. He caught a glimpse in the distance of a hunched, moving figure like some tiny wanderer through tortuous fields. Then darkness resumed, seizing the street. A wind entered the night outlining itself in the wild undulations of the rain reaching for the pavements.

Dorn forgot his companion, as they pressed on. Disheveled rain ghosts crowded around him. The fever that had burned in him during the day seemed to have become a part of the storm. The leap and hollow blaze of the lightnings gave him a companionship. His eyes stared into the inanimate bursts of pale violet outlines in the dark. His breath drank in the spice of water-laden winds. The stumble of thunder, the lash and churn of rain were companions. The something else that haunted him was in the storm. He turned to Lockwood, who seemed to be lagging, and shouted in his ear:

"Great, eh? Altar fires and the racket of unknown gods."

Lockwood, his face filmed with water, grunted indignantly:

"Let's get out of this."

The night was growing wilder. Dorn's eyes bored into the vapors and steam of the rain.

"We're in a good street," he cried again. "A nigger street."

A blinding gust of light brought them to a halt. Thunder burst a horror of sound through its dead glare. Dorn stiffened and stared as in a dream at a face floating behind the glass of a door. A woman's face contorted into a stark grimace of rapture. Its teeth stood out white and skull-like against the red of an open mouth.

Silence and darkness seized the street. Rain poured. The sound of a laugh like some miniature echo of the tumult that had torn the night drifted to them. Lockwood had started for the door.

"Come on," he called, "this is crazy."

Dorn followed him. The streaming door opened as they approached and two figures darted out. They were gone in an instant and in pursuit of them rushed a rollicking lurch of sound. Dorn caught again the shrill staccato of the laugh, and the door closed behind them.

Dancing bodies were spinning among the tables. Shouting, swinging noises and a bray of music spurted unintelligibly against the ears of the newcomers. A chlorinated mist, acrid to the eye, and burning to the nose, crawled about the room. Dorn, followed by Lockwood, groped his way through the confusion toward a small vacant table against a wall. From here they watched in silence.

A can-can was in progress. The dancers, black

and white faces glued together, arms twined about each other's bodies, tumbled through the smoke. Waiters balancing black trays laden with colored glasses sifted through the scene. At the tables men and women with faces out of focus sat drinking and shouting. Niggers, prostitutes, louts. The slant of red mouths opened laughters. Hands and throats drifted in violent fragments through the mist. The reek of wine and steaming clothes, the sting of perspiring perfumes and the odors of women's bodies fumed over the tumble of heads. Against the scene a jazz band flung a whine and a stumble of tinny sounds. Nigger musicians with silver instruments glued to their lips sat on a platform at the far end of the room. They danced in their chairs as they played, swinging their instruments in crazy circles. A broken, lurching music came from them, a nasal melody that moaned among the laughters.

Dorn's fingers lay gripped about the arm of his friend. His senses caught the rhythm of the scene. His eyes stared at the dancing figures, blond heads riveted against black satin cheeks; bodies gesturing their lusts to the quick whine and stumble of the music; eyes opening like mouths.

"God, what an orgie!" he whispered. "Look at the thing. It's insane. A nigger hammering a scarlet phallus against a cymbal moon."

His words vanished in the din and Lockwood remained with eyes drawn in and hard. When he turned to his friend he found him excitedly pounding his fist on the table and bawling for a waiter. A man, seemingly asleep amid confusions, appeared and took his order.

"There's a woman in here I've got to find," Dorn shouted.

"You're crazy, man."

"I saw her," he persisted, talking close to his friend's ear. "I saw her face in the door. You wait here."

Lockwood seized his arm and tried to hold him, but he jerked away and was lost in a pattern of dancing bodies. Lockwood watching him disappear, frowned. He felt a sudden uncertainty toward his friend, a fear as if he had launched himself into a dark night with a murderer for a companion.

"He's crazy," he thought. "I ought to get him out of here before anything happens."

He sat fumbling nervously with the stem of a wine-glass. Outside, the rain chattered in the darkness and the alto of the wind came in long organ notes into the din of the café. He caught sight of Dorn pulling an unholy-looking woman through the pack of the room.

"Here she is—our lady of pain!"

Dorn thrust the creature viciously into a seat beside Lockwood. She dropped with a scream of laughter. The music of the nigger orchestra had stopped and an emptiness flooded the place. Dorn bellowed for another glass. Lockwood looked slowly at the creature beside him. She was watching Dorn. In the swarthy depths of her eyes moved threads of scarlet. Beneath their lashes her skin was darkened as if by bruises. An odd sultry light glowed over the discolorations. Her mouth had shut and her cheeks were without curves, following the triangular corpse-like lines of her skull. Her lips, like bits of vermilion paper, stared as from an idol's face. She was regarding Dorn with a smile.

He had grown erratic in his gestures. His eyes seemed incapable of focusing themselves. They darted about the room, running away from him. The woman's smile persisted and he turned his glance abruptly at her. The red flesh of her opened mouth and throat confronted him as another of her screaming laughs burst. The laugh ended and her gleaming eyes swimming in a gelatinous mist held him.

"A reptilean sorcery," he whispered to Lockwood, and smiled. "The face of a malignant Pierrette. A diabolic clown. Look at it. I saw it in the lightning outside. She wears a mask. Do you get her?" He paused mockingly. Lockwood shifted away from the woman. Erik was drunk. Or crazy. But the woman, thank God, had eyes only for him. She remained, as he talked, with her sulphurous eyes unwaveringly upon his face.

"She's not a woman," he went on in a purring voice. "She's a lust. No brain. No heart. A stark unhuman piece of flesh with a shark's hunger inside it."

He leaned forward and took one of her hands as Lockwood whispered,

"Christ, man, let's get out of here."

The woman's fingers, dry and quivering, scratched against Dorn's palm. He felt them as a hot breath in his blood.

"What's the matter, Warren?" he laughed, emptying a wine-glass. "I like this gal. She suits me. A devourer of men. Look at her!"

He laughed and glared at his friend. Lockwood closed his eyes nervously.

"I've got a headache in this damned place," he muttered.

"Wait a minute." Dorn seized his arm. "I want to talk. I feel gabby. My lady friend doesn't understand words." The sulphurous eyes glowed caresses over him. "You remember the thing in Rabelais about women—insatiable, devouring, hungering in their satieties. The prowling animal. Well, here it is. Alive. Not in print. She's alive with something deeper than life. Wheels of flesh grinding her blood into a hunger for ecstasies. She's a mate for me. Come on, little one."

He sprang from the table, pulling the woman after him.

"Wait here, Warren," he called, moving toward the door. It opened, letting in a shout and sweep of rain, and they were gone.

"A crazy man," muttered the novelist, and remained fumbling with the stem of his glass.

Outside Dorn held the body of the woman

against him as they hurried through the storm. Her flesh, like the touch of a third person, struck through his wet clothes.

"Where we going?" he yelled at her.

She thrust out an arm.

"Up here."

They came breathless up a flight of stairs into a reeking room lighted by a gas jet.

In the café, Lockwood waited till the music started again. Then he rose and, slapping his soggy hat on his head, walked out of the place. The rain, sweeping steadily against the earth, held him prisoner in the doorway. He stood muttering to himself of his friend and his craziness. Gone wild! Crazy wild with a mad woman in the rain. Long ago he might have done it himself. Yes, he knew the why of it. The rain fuming before him made him sleepy. He leaned against the place and waited. The storm faded slowly into a quiet patter. Starting for the pavement, Lockwood paused. A hatless figure had jumped out of a doorway across the street and was running toward him.

"It's Erik," he muttered, and hurried to meet him.

Dorn, laughing, his clothes torn and his face smeared with blood under his eye, drew near. He took his friend's arm and walked him swiftly away. At the corner Dorn stopped and regarded the novelist.

"I've had a look at hell," he whispered, and with a laugh hurried off alone. Lockwood watched him moving swiftly down the street, and yawned.

Chapter Four

IT was near midnight. Rachel's eyes, brightened with tears, watched her lover bathing his face.

"It seemed so long," she murmured, "till you came."

"That damned Warren Lockwood led me astray," he smiled. He dried his face and came toward her. She dropped to the floor beside him as he sat down and pressed her cheeks against his knees. His hands moved tenderly through her loosened hair.

"You told me to be careful about getting run over," she smiled sadly, "and you go out and get all cut up in a brawl. Oh, Erik, please—something might have happened."

"Nothing happened, dearest."

She asked no further questions but remained with her face against his knees. This was Rachel whose hair he was stroking. Dorn smiled at the thought. After a silence she resumed, her voice softened with emotion:

"Erik, I've been lying to you—about my love. It's different than I said it was. I've said always what you've wanted me to say. You've always wanted me to be something else than a woman—

something like a dream. But I can't. I love you as—as Anna loved you. Oh, I want to be with you forever and have children. I'm nothing else. You are. I can't be like you. For me there's only love for you and nothing beyond."

"Dear one," he answered, "there's nothing else for me."

"Now you're telling me lies," she wept. "There is something I can't give you; and that you must go looking for somewhere else."

"No, Rachel. I love you."

"As you loved Anna—once."

"Don't! I never loved Anna—or anyone. Or anything."

"I can't help it, Erik. Forgive me, please. I love you so. Don't you see how I love you. I keep trying to be something besides myself and to give other names to the things I feel. But they're only sentimental things. My dreams are only sentimental dreams—of your kissing me, holding me, being my husband. Oh, go way from me, Erik, before I make you hate me! You thought I was different. And I did too. I *was* different. But you've changed me. Women are all the same when they love. Differences go away."

She looked up at him with tear-running eyes.

"Different than other people! But now I'm the same. I love you as any other woman would. Only perhaps a little more. With my whole soul and life."

"Foolish to talk," he whispered back to her.

"Words only scratch at things. I love you as if I had never seen you or kissed you."

"But I'm not a dream, Erik. Oh, it sounds silly. But I want you."

He raised her and held her lithe body close to him. The feeling that he was unreal, that Rachel was unreal, rested in his thought. There was a mist about things that clung to them, that clung about the joyousness in his heart.

"There's nothing else," he whispered. "Love is enough. It burns up everything else and leaves a mist."

His arms tightened.

"Erik dear, I'm afraid."

His kiss brought a peace over her face. She had waited for it. She looked up and laughed.

"You love me? Yes, Erik loves me. Loves me. I know."

She watched his eyes as he spoke. The eyes of God. They remained open to her. She began to tremble and her naked arms moved blindly toward his shoulders.

"This is my world," she whispered. "I know, Erik. I know everything. You are too big for love to hold. The sun doesn't fill the whole world. There are always dark places. I know. Don't hide from me, lover."

She smiled and closed her eyes as her lips reached toward him.

The eyes of Erik Dorn remained open and staring out of the window. There was still rain in the night.

Chapter Five

ERIK DORN to Rachel, September, 1918:
"... and to-night I remember you are beautiful, and I desire you. My arms are empty and there is nothing for my eyes to look at. Are you still afraid. Look, more than a year has gone and nothing has changed. You are the far-away one, the dream figure, and my heart comes on wings to you. . . . I write with difficulty. What language is there to talk to you? How does one converse with a dream? Idiot phrases rant across the paper like little fat actors flourishing tin swords. I've come to distrust words. There are too many of them. Yet I keep fermenting with words. Interlopers. Busybody strangers. I can't think . . . because of them. . . . Alas! if I could keep my vocabulary out of our love we would both be better off. Foolish chatter. I thought when I sat down to write to you that the sadness of your absence would overcome me. Instead, I am amused. Vaguely joyous. And at the thought of you I have an impulse to laugh. You are like that. A day like a thousand years has passed. Dead-born hours that did not end. Chill, empty streets and the memory of you like a solitude in which I sat mumbling to phantoms. And now in the darkness

my heart sickens with desire for you and the night sharpens its claws upon my heart. Yet there is laughter. Words laugh in my head. The torment I feel is somehow a part of joyousness. The claws of the night bring somehow a caress. Even to weep for you is like some dark happiness whose lips are too fragile to smile. Dear one, the dream of you still lives—an old friend now, a familiar star that I watch endlessly. You see there are even no new words. For once before I told you that. It was night—snowing. We walked together. I remember you always as vanishing and leaving the light of your face burning before my eyes. I shall always love you. Why are you afraid? Why do you write vague doubts into your letters? I will be with you soon. You are a world, and the rest of life is a mist that surrounds you. . . . I have nothing to write. I discover this as I sit staring at the paper. I remember that a year has passed, that many years remain to pass. Dear one, I know only that I love you, and words are strangers between us."

Rachel to Erik, September end, 1918:
" . . . when I went away you were unhappy and restless. Now that I have gone you are again happy and calm. Oh, you're so cruel! Your love is so cruel to me. I sit here all day, a foolishly humble exile, waiting for you. I keep watching the sea and sometimes I try to feel pain. When your letter comes I spend the day reading it. . . .

I am beautiful and you desire me. Oh, to think me beautiful and to desire me, suffices. You do not come where I am. Nothing has changed, you write with a joyous cruelty. In your lonely nights your dream of me still brings you torments and I am a star that you watch endlessly. I laugh too, but out of bitterness. Because what you write is no longer true and we both have known it for long. I am no longer a dream or a star, but a woman who loves you. Yes, nothing has changed, except me. And you remedy that by sending me away. When you send me away I too become unchanged in your thought. I am again like I was on the night we parted in the white park and you can love me—a memory of me—that remains like a star. . . .

"But here I am in this lonely little sea village. There is no dream for me. I am empty without you and I lie at night and weep till my heart breaks, wondering when you will come. It were better if I were dead. I whisper to myself, 'you must not write him to come to you, because he is too busy loving you. He weeps before the ghost of you. He sits beside an old dream. You must not interrupt him. Oh, my lover, do you find me so much less than the dream of me, that you must send me away in order to love me? My doubts? Are they doubts? We have grown apart in the year. On the night it snowed and I went away from you you said, 'people bury their love behind lighted windows. . . .' Dearest, dearest, of what do I complain? Of your ecstasies and torments of which I am not a part, but a cause? Forgive me. I adore you. I am so lonely and such a nobody without you. And I want you to write to me that you long for me, to be with me, to caress me and talk to me. And instead you send phrases analyzing your joyousness. Oh, things have changed. I am no longer Rachel, but a woman. I feel so little and helpless when I think of you. Strangers can talk to you and look at you but I must sit here in exile while you entertain yourself with memories of me. You are cruel, dear one, and I have become too cowardly not to mind. This is because I have found happiness—all the happiness I desire—and hold it tremblingly. And you have not found happiness but are still in flight toward your faraway one, your dream figure. I cannot write more. I worship you and my heart is full of tears. I will sit humbly and look at the sea until you come."

Rachel to Frank Brander, September:
" . . . I answer your letter only because I am afraid you would misunderstand my silence. I send your letter back because I cannot throw it away. It would make the sea unclean. As you point out, I am the mistress of Erik Dorn and he may some day grow tired of me, at which time you are prepared to be my friend and protect me from the world. I will put your application on file, Mr. Brander, if there is a part of my mind filthy enough to remember it."

Rachel to Emil Tesla:

" . . . I was glad to hear from you. But please do not write any more. I am too happy to read your letters. I never want to draw pictures for *The Cry* again. I hope you will be freed soon. I can think of nothing to write to you."

Erik Dorn to Rachel, November, 1918:
"DEAREST ONE!

"Beneath my window the gentle Jabberwock has twined colored tissue-paper about his ears and gone mad. He shrieks, he whistles, he blows a horn. The war, beloved, appears to have ended this noon and the Jabberwock is endeavoring to disgorge four and a half years in a single shriek. 'The war,' says the Jabberwock, in his own way, 'is over. It was a rotten war, nasty and hateful, as all wars are rotten and hateful, and everything I've said and done hinting at the contrary has been a lie and I'm so full of lies I must shriek.'

"Anybody but a Jabberwock, dear one, would have died of apoplexy hours ago. But the Jabberwock is immortal. Alas! there is something of pathos in the spectacle. Our gentle friend with tissue-paper around his ears prostrates himself before another illusion—peace. Says the shriek of the Jabberwock beneath my window, 'The Hun is destroyed. The menace to humanity is laid low. The powers of darkness are dispelled by the breath of God and the machine-guns of our brave soldats. The war that is to end war is over. Hail, blessed peace!'

"Why do I write such arid absurdities to you? But I feel an impulse to scribble wordly words, to stand in a silk hat beside the statue of Liberty and gaze out upon the Atlantic with a Carlylian pensiveness. Idle political tears flow from my brain. For it is obvious that the war the Jabberwock has so nobly waged has been a waste of steel and powder. Standing now on his eight million graves with the tissue-paper of Victory twined about his ears, the Jabberwock is a somewhat ghastly, humorous figure. He has, alas! shot the wrong man. To-morrow there will be an inquest in Paris and the Jabberwock will rub his eyes and discover that the corpse, God forgive him, is that of a brother and friend and that the Powers of Darkness threatening humanity are advancing upon him . . . out of Moscow. I muse . . . yes, it was a good war. War is never pathetic, never wholly a waste. Maturity no less than childhood must have its circuses. But the Jabberwock . . . Ah! the Jabberwock . . . the soul of man celebrating the immortal triumph of righteousness . . . the good Don Quixote has valiantly slain another windmill and your Sancho Panza shakes his head in wistful amusement.

"I did not send you this letter yesterday and many things have happened since I wrote it. I will see you in a few days. It has been decided that I go to Germany for the magazine. Edwards insists. So do the directors, trusting gentlemen. I will stop at Washington and try to get two passports and then come on to you, and we will wait together until the passports are issued. Another week of imbecile political maneuverings in behalf of the passports and I will again be your lover,

"ERIK."

Chapter Six

"WE'VE been separated almost three months," he thought, looking out of the train window. "I'll see her soon."

There were four men in the smoking-compartment. They were discussing the end of the war. Dorn listened inattentively. He was remembering another ride to Rachel. Looking out of a train window as now. Whirling through space. A locomotive whistle wailing in the prairies at night like the sound of winds against his heart.

The memories of the ride drifted through his mind. He saw himself again with the tumult of another day sweeping toward Rachel. What had he felt then? Whatever it was, it was gone. For he felt nothing now but a sadness. He had telegraphed. She would be waiting, her face alight, her hands trembling. He had started from Washington elatedly enough. But now in the smoking-compartment where the men were discussing the end of the war he felt no elation. He was thinking, "It'll be difficult when we see each other." He became aware that he was actually shrinking from the meeting. The voices of the men about him began to annoy and he returned to his seat in the train.

Early evening. Another two hours and the train

would stop to let him off. Dear, dear Rachel! He had wept tormented by a loneliness for her. Now he was coming to her with sadness. There had been another ride when he had come to her in a halloo of storms. Things change.

The porter brushed him and removed his grips to the platform. The far lights of a village sprinkled themselves feebly in the darkness. This was where Rachel was waiting.

Dorn stepped from the train. It became another world, lighted and human. He looked about the dingy little station. Rachel was walking toward him.

"She looks strange and out of place," he thought.

They embraced. Her kisses covering his lips delighted him unexpectedly. He found himself walking close to her in the night and feeling happy. They entered a darkened wooden house and Rachel led the way up-stairs.

"I can't talk, Erik."

She held his hand against her cheek.

"No, don't kiss me. Let me look at you. Sit over here. I must look at you."

She laughed softly, but her eyes, unsmiling, stared at him. He remained silent. The sadness that had fallen upon him in the train returned now like a hurt in his heart. He had expected it to vanish at the sight of her. But her kisses had only hidden it. She came to his side after a pause and whispered gently,

"Perhaps it would have been better if you hadn't come, dearest. I've become almost used to being alone."

He embraced her and for the moment the sadness was hidden again. Rachel's hands crept avidly to his face, holding his cheeks with hot fingers.

"Erik, oh, Erik, do you love me? I'm not afraid to hear. Tell me."

"Yes, dear one. You are everything."

"What makes you cry?"

He kissed her lips.

"I don't know," he whispered. "Only it's been so long."

"Oh, you are so sad."

Her voice had grown thin. Her eyes, dry, burning, haunted the dark room. She removed herself from his arms and stood with her hand in her hair. She looked at the dark sea that mirrored the night outside the window. Turning to him after a pause she murmured:

"I had forgotten Erik Dorn was here."

A sudden stride, the gesture of another Rachel, and she had thrown herself on the bed.

"Oh, God!" she sobbed. "I knew, I knew!"

Dorn, kneeling on the floor, pulled her head toward him. He whispered her name. Why was he sad, frightened? A thought was murmuring in him, "You must love her."

"Rachel, I love you. Please. Your tears. Dearest, what has happened? Tell me."

"Don't ask that." Her tears came anew. "But you come to me sad, as if I were no longer Rachel to you."

The thought kept murmuring, "You must love her. . . ."

"Beautiful one," he said softly, "you're weeping because something has happened to you."

The thought murmured, "because something has happened to you, not her."

"No, no, Erik!"

"Then why? If you loved me you would be happy."

Absurd sentences. They would deceive no one.

A belated emotion overcame him. Now he was happy. His arms grew strong about her. He would say nothing, but lie beside her kissing her until the tears ended. This was happiness. He watched her lips begin to smile faintly. Her face touched him as if she had sighed. She whispered after a long silence, "Oh, I thought you had changed."

He laughed and pulled her to her feet. His head thrown back, his eyes amused and warm, he asked, "Do I seem changed now?"

He waited while she regarded him. Why was he nervous? Must he answer the question too?

"No," she said, "you are the same."

Her face shining before him. Her head quickly lifted.

"I was a fool. Look, Erik, I am happy — happier than anybody on earth."

She dropped to her knees, kissing his hand.

"I am so happy, I kneel. . . ."

They stood together in the window and laughed.

"There's a wonderful old woman here. We've talked a great deal, about everything, and you. You don't mind? To-morrow we'll lie all day on the shore. Oh, Erik. Erik!"

"We'll never be alone again, Rachel."

"Never!" she echoed.

Chapter Seven

A CALM had fallen upon Erik Dorn, an unconsciousness of self. He sprawled through the sunny days, staring at the sea with Rachel or walking alone to the fishing-boats at the other end of the village, or sitting with Mama Turpin, the old woman in whose cottage they lived. With Mama Turpin he held interminable talks that rambled on through the night at times. Religion was Mama Turpin's favored topic. Her round body in a rocking-chair, her seamed, vigorous face raised toward the sky, the old woman would fall into a dream and talk quietly of her God. She would begin, her voice coming out of the dark reminding Dorn of a girl.

"Yes, I have always known this here one thing. Everybody must have a religion. Because there's something in everybody that's way beyond their selves to understand. And there's nobody to give it to excepting God. Some God, anyways. . . ."

Rachel, sitting in the shadows, would listen with her eyes upon Erik. The fear that he had brought her was growing in her heart, making her thought heavy and her gestures slow. She would listen, almost asleep, to his words.

" . . . Yes, Mama Turpin, religion comes to

all people. But not for long. We all get a flame in us at some time and it burns until it burns itself out, and then we sit and forget to wonder about things. . . ."

Talk perhaps for her to understand. But why should he hint when words outright were easier? Rachel carried questions in her heart.

Among the fishermen Dorn listened sometimes to stories of great catches and storms. He was usually silent watching them empty their nets on the shore and remove the catch into basins and pails. The men accepted his interest in their work with a pleased indifference.

Rachel sometimes walked with him or stretched beside him on the sand. But he felt an uneasiness in her presence. Her eyes questioned him silently and seemed to answer their own questions.

Since the evening of his coming there had been no scenes. He was grateful for this. But the eyes of Rachel sometimes haunted him at night as she lay asleep beside him. What spoke in her eyes? He felt calm when alone, at peace with himself. But at night while she slept he would become sleepless and a sadness would enter him. Thoughts he did not seem to be thinking would move through his head. "Things pass. Years pass. The sea and the stars remain the same. But men and women change. Life eats into men and women— eats things away from them. . . ."

In his sadness there would come to him a memory of Anna. Thoughts of Anna and Rachel would mingle themselves. . . . Anna had once lain beside him like this. He remembered now. Her body was different from Rachel's—softer, warmer . . . a woman named Anna had lived with him. Now a woman named Rachel. And to-morrow, what? There were yesterdays. These were not sad. Things already dead were not so sad. But things that are to die. . . .

His heart would grow weak, seeming to dissolve. Something unspoken in the night. Tears in his heart. Calm in his thought. He would figure it out sometime. His words were alert little busybodies. They could follow things into difficult crevices. But was there anything to figure out? He was growing old and a to-morrow was haunting him. Some day he would close his eyes slowly and in the slow closing of his eyes the world would end. Erik Dorn would have ended. Was there such a thing as ending? Yes, things were always ending. Now he was different than the night he had lain beside Rachel and whispered, "You have given me wings." But how? He felt the same. Change came like that. Leaving one the same. He would write things from Europe that would startle. He could write. . . . But, something unspoken in the night. He must say it to himself. . . . "You must love her. . . ." Then that was it. He no longer loved her.

He lay listening to her breathing. An end to his love. Preposterous notion! How, since the thought of parting from her wrenched at his heart?

"If I went away from Rachel I would die." Unquestionably sincere. . . . "I'd die." Not, of course, die. But feel death. Yet, there was something changed. But a man doesn't remain an ecstatic lover. There comes a time. Well, he loved her like this—quietly, happily, and if he went away from her he would feel an end had come to his life. The other love had been words flying in his head. Nice to have felt as he had. But life—practical, material rush of hours. Words had flown in his head once. He smiled. "Wings, what are they?" He remembered having spoken and thought a great deal about wings. Now the idea seemed somewhat absurd. They were not a part of life. Inventions. An invention. A phrase to explain an unusual state of physical and mental excitement. . . . Sleep intruded and the sadness melted out of him. As he closed his eyes his hand reached dreamily for Rachel and lay upon her shoulder.

A week of silence followed. Dorn talked. Politics, economics, the coming peace treaty. Rachel listened and made replies. Yet their words seemed only the part of a silence between them. A letter from Washington interrupted them. A passport was being issued for Erik Dorn, but the bureau was not issuing passports for women and would have to deny Mrs. Rachel Dorn . . . "enclosed please find $1 deposit made for Mrs. Dorn at this office."

"Well, that ends it," he laughed. "Perhaps I

shouldn't have lied about your being Mrs. Dorn. God is a jealous God and punishes liars."

"You must go on," Rachel said. "Perhaps I'll get one later."

"No, we'll both wait. I couldn't go without you."

Rachel regarded him tenderly. They were sitting on Mama Turpin's porch.

"Yes, you will," she said.

He shook his head, pleased at the opportunity for sacrifice. He hoped as he smiled that Rachel would plead with him to go alone. In her pleading she would point out all the things he was giving up by not going. She might even say, "You must go, Erik. You can't sacrifice your career."

Then he could shrug his shoulders, remain silent for a moment as if weighing his career beside his love for her, and smile suddenly and say, gently, "No. It's ended. Please, it's ended and forgotten." A laugh, a bit too casual, would leave the thing on the proper plane. Later there would be times when he could grow thoughtful and abstract and Rachel, looking at him, would know that he had sacrificed—his career.

On Mama Turpin's porch Dorn's thoughts rambled in silence. Rachel had said nothing. He looked at her and grew confused before the straightness of her eyes, as if she knew the tawdry little plot moving through his mind. Then an irritation . . . why didn't she plead? Did she think it was nothing to give up his plans? Was it anything?

No. He endeavored to evade his own questioning, but his thoughts mocked him with answers. . . . "I'm playing a game with her. I want her to feel sorry and grateful for my not going and to feel that I've made a sacrifice for her. Because I could cherish it against her . . . later. Have something I could pretend to be sad about. It would give me an excuse to scold her. . . . Merely by looking at her I could remind her that she is indebted to me for a sacrifice. Make-believe sacrifice gives one the unconsciousness of virtue without any of its discomforts. I'm irritated because she refuses to play her part in the farce and so makes me seem cheap. She knows I'm lying but she can't figure out how or what about. So she looks at me and says to herself, 'Erik has changed. He's different.' She means that I've become an actor and able to offer her cheap things. But she doesn't know that in words."

As he sat thinking, an understanding of himself played beneath his thoughts. He was irritated with her. The passport business was something he could hang his irritation on. It offered an opportunity to make the petulant, indefinable aversion he sometimes felt toward her into a noble, self-laudatory emotion.

He stood up abruptly. Make amends by being truthful and putting an end to the theatrics. . . . "Listen, Rachel, it's foolish for us to take this seriously. I don't give a damn about going, and I never did. It would bore me. It means nothing to me, and it's no sacrifice or even inconvenience. Please, I mean it. Put it out of your head."

He leaned over and took her hands.

"I love you. . . ."

Despite himself there was a note of sacrifice. He frowned. His "I love you" had startled him. He had said it as one pats a woman reassuringly on the shoulder. More, as one turns the other cheek in a forgiving Christian spirit. He was not an actor. He had become naturally cheap.

Rachel smiled wanly at him and kissed his hands. He noticed that she looked thin about the face and that her eyes seemed ill with too much weeping. He wondered when it was she wept. When she was alone, of course. For a moment the thought of her flung across the bed and weeping stirred him sensually. Then . . . what made her cry so much? Good God, what did she want of him? He was giving up. . . . Again he frowned. "I've become a cad," he thought. "I can't think honestly any more. Thoughts act themselves in my head. I've gotten to thinking lies and thinking them naturally without trying to lie. . . ."

"I'm going for a walk," he announced, and went off toward the shore where the fishing-boats were drifting in becalmed.

Mama Turpin came out on the porch. Rachel smiled at the old woman.

"It's peaceful here, Mama Turpin."

"Yes, honey. My work's all done for the day now."

"Nothing ever changes here," Rachel murmured. "The sea is just the same as when I came. I think I'll be leaving soon, Mama Turpin. Mr. Dorn will stay on for a little while. I have some work I must get back to."

She paused and shaded her eyes from the setting sun.

"It's been wonderful down here. I'll never forget it. Perhaps some day I'll come back to visit again."

She arose and sighed.

"What's the matter, honey?" the old woman asked, watching her.

Rachel waited till her lips could smile again. Then she said:

"Oh, I hate to leave it here. But I have so much work to do."

She entered the house swiftly. In her room she lay on the bed, her face in the pillow as if she were waiting for tears. But none came. She lay in silence until it grew dark and she heard Erik outside asking Mama Turpin where she was.

Chapter Eight

IT was dawn when they awoke. Rachel opened her eyes first. A lassitude filled her. She remained quiet for moments and then sat up and stared at Erik. His face was flushed and he was sleeping lightly, his eyes almost open.

"Erik," she whispered. When he looked at her she leaned over and kissed him.

"Last night was wonderful," she murmured.

He smiled sleepily.

"I want to lie in your arms for just a minute. And then we'll get up, Erik."

Her head sank against his shoulder and she remained with her eyes closed. He murmured her name. Over Rachel's face a curious light spread itself. She sat up and turned her eyes to him.

"My dear one, my lover!"

Dorn regarded her with a sudden confusion. Her eyes and voice were confusing. Women were strange. Her eyes were large, burning, devouring . . . "I will be a shrine to you always. Let me look at you. I have never looked at you. . . ." Why was he remembering that? He felt himself grow frightened. Her eyes were saying something that must not be said. His arms reached out.

Crush her to him. Hold her tightly. Sing his love to her. . . .

She had slipped from the bed and was standing on the floor, shaking her head at him. Her face seemed blank. Dorn sat up and blinked ludicrously. She had jumped out of his arms. He laughed. Coquetting. But her eyes had been strange. . . .

"Listen, Erik, do you mind if I spend the morning alone? I have some letters to write and things. Then I'll meet you on the beach and we'll go swimming and lie on the sand together. Will you?"

He nodded cheerfully and swung himself out of bed. His calm had returned. The memories of the curiously abandoned, shameless Rachel of the night lingered for a moment questioningly and then left him.

They ate breakfast together and Dorn strode off alone. He felt surprised at himself. He had forgotten all about his trip to Europe.

"The sun and the rest here are doing me good," he thought. "I'm getting normal. But a little stupidity won't hurt."

The morning slipped away and he returned to the beach from a walk through the village. It was early afternoon and the sands were deserted. The sea lay like a great Easter egg under the hot sun, a vast and inanimate daub of glittering blue, green, and gold. He seated himself on the burning sand and stared at it. Years could pass this way and he could sit dreaming lifeless words, the sea like a painted beetle's back, the sea like a shell of water resting on a stenciled horizon. A wind was dying among the clouds. It had blown them into large shapeless virgins. Puffy white solitudes over his head. He looked down and saw Rachel coming toward him. She was carrying a woolen blanket over her arms.

She approached and appeared excited. Her face flushed.

"Shall we go in?"

He nodded. Her voice disturbed him. He would have preferred her calm, gentle. Particularly after last night. She unloosened her clothes quickly and hurried nude toward the water. Dorn, after an uneasy survey of the empty beach, watched her. In the glare of the sun and sand her body seemed insistently unfamiliar. He would have preferred her familiar. He joined her and they pushed into the water together. Her excited manner depressed him.

"Let's swim," he called.

A blue, singing moment under the water and they were up, swimming slowly into the unbroken sheet of the sea. Rachel came nearer to him, the water sparkling from her moving arms.

"Do you like it, Erik?"

He laughed in answer. Her head was turned toward him and he could see her dark eyes smiling against the water.

"Wouldn't it be nice," she said softly, "to swim

out together like lovers in a poem? Out and out! And never come back!"

Her voice, slipping across the water, became unfamiliar. They continued moving.

"Yes," he answered at length, smiling back at her. "It would be easy. And I'm willing."

They swam in silence. He began to wonder. Were they going out and out and never coming back? Perhaps they were doing that. One might become involved in a suicide like that. He closed his eyes and his head moved through the coldness of the water. What matter? What was there to come back to? All hours were the same. He might wait until a thousand more had dragged themselves to an ending. Or swim out and out. When he grew tired he would kiss her and say, "It is easier to make our own endings than to wait for them." The sun would be shining and her eyes would sing to him for an instant over the water.

"We'd better turn now, Erik."

"No," he smiled. "We're lovers in a poem."

She came nearer.

"Come, we must go back, Erik."

"No."

He answered firmly. It pleased him to say "no." He felt a superiority. He could say "no" and then she would plead with him and perhaps finally persuade him.

"Not now, Erik. Some other time, maybe. . . ."

"But it would be a proper ending," he argued. "What else is there? You are unhappy. And perhaps I am too. Come, it will be easy."

For a moment a fright came into him. She was not pleading. She was silent and looking at him as they drifted. What if she should remain silent? "I don't want to die," he thought, "but does it matter?" He wondered at himself. He had spoken of dying. Sincerely? No. But if she remained silent they would keep swimming until there was nothing left to do but die. Then he was sincere? No. He would drown as a sort of casual argument. Good God! Her silence was asking his life. What matter? He cared neither to live nor to die. He looked at her with an amused smile in his eyes. His heart had begun to beat violently.

A sudden relief. She had turned and was swimming toward the shore. He hesitated. Absurd to turn back too hurriedly. He waited till she looked behind her to see if he were coming. Her looking back was a vindication. She had believed then that he might go on, out and out. . . . He could follow her to the shore now. . . .

The swim had exhausted them. Rachel threw herself on the sand, Dorn covering her with the blanket. They lay together, the whiteness and the blaze of the sky tearing at their eyes. Her hair had spread itself like a black fan under her head.

The oven heat of the day dried the burn of the sun into a chalked and hammering glare—an unremitting roar of light that seemed to beat the world into a metallic sleep. The sea had stiffened itself into a dead flame. Molten, staring sweeps of color burst upon their eyes with a massive intimacy. The etched horizon, the stagnant gleaming arch of the water, and the acetylene burn of the sand gave the scene the appearance of a monstrous lithograph.

The figures of the lovers lay without life. Rachel had turned her head from the glare. Through veiling fingers Dorn remained staring at the veneer of isolation about them. Waves of heat crept like ghost fires across the nakedness of the scene. He thought of the sun as a pilgrim walking over the barren floor of an empty cathedral. Over him the motionless smoke-bellied clouds hung gleaming in the dead fanfare of the sky. He thought of them as swollen white blooms stamped upon a board. As the moments slipped, he became conscious that Rachel was talking. Her voice made a tiny noise in the grave torpitude of the day.

"It's like listening to singing, Erik. What are you thinking of?"

"Nothing. I like the way the heat tightens my skin and pinches."

"Do you remember," she asked softly, "once you said beauty is an external emotion?"

He answered drowsily, "Did I? I'm tired, dearest. Let's nap awhile."

"No. I want to hear you talk just a little."

He pressed his face into his arm, drawing his clothes carelessly over him for protection.

"I can't think of anything to say, Rachel, except that I'm content. The sun brings a luxurious pain into one's blood. . . ."

"Yes, a luxurious pain," she repeated quietly. "Please let's talk."

"Too damn hot."

"I always expect you to say things. As if you knew things I didn't, Erik. I've always thought of you as knowing everything."

"Ordinarily I do," he mumbled.

"Wonderful Erik. . . ."

Flattery was annoying. There were times for being wonderful and times for grunting at the sand.

"My vocabulary," he mumbled again, "has curled up its toes and gone to sleep."

His eyes grew heavy.

Drowsily, "I'm an old man and need my sleep."

He felt Rachel's hand reaching gently for his head.

A cool gloom squatted on the sand about him when he opened his eyes. The scene was a stranger. The sea and sand, dark strangers. His body felt stiffened and his skin hurt. He sat up and stared about with parched eyes.

The sun had gone down. A hollow light lingered in the sky, an echo of light. He turned toward the blanket beside him. Rachel was gone. She had left the blanket in a little heap, unfolded. Why hadn't she wakened him? She must be on the beach somewhere, waiting.

In the distance he saw the shapeless figures of

the fishermen moving from their grounded boats. Staring about at the deserted scene he felt unaccountably sad. It would have been pleasant to have wakened and found Rachel sitting beside him.

A sheet of paper was pinned on the blanket. He noticed it as he slipped painfully into his shirt. He continued to dress himself, his eyes regarding the bit of paper. His heart had grown heavy at the sight of it.

When he was dressed he folded the blanket carefully and removed the note. A pallor in his thought. Something had happened. He had fallen asleep under a glaring sun. Rachel stretched beside him. Now the glare of the sun was gone and the sea and the sand were vaguely unreal, dark, and unfriendly. The little blanket was empty.

He sat wondering why he didn't read the note. But he was reading it. He knew what it said. It said Rachel had gone and would never come back. A very tragic business. . . . "You do not love me any more as you did. You have changed. And if I stayed it would mean that in a little while longer you would forget all about me. Now perhaps you will remember."

Quite true. He had taught her such paradoxes. He would remember. That was logical . . . "to remember how you loved me makes it impossible to remain with you. Oh, I die when I look at you and see nothing in your eyes. It is too much pain. I am going away. . . . Dearest, I have known for a long time."

His eyes skipped part of the words. Unimportant words. Why read any further? The thing was over, ended. Rachel gone. More words on the other side of the paper. His eyes skimmed . . . "you have been God to me. I am not afraid. Oh, I am strong. Good-bye."

Still more words. A postscript. Women always wrote postscripts—the gesture of femininity immortalized by Lot's wife. Never mind the postscript. Tear the paper into bits. It offended his fingers. Walk over to the water's edge and scatter it on the sea.

He had lain too long in the sun. Probably burn like hell to-night. "Here goes Rachel into the sea." Soft music and a falling curtain.

He read from one of the scraps. . . . "Erik, you will be grateful later. . . ." Let the sea take that. And the "good-bye, my dear one. . . ." A patch of white on the darkened water, too tiny to follow. Would she be waiting when he came back to the room? No, the room would be empty. A comb and brush and tray of hairpins would be missing from the dressing-table.

A smile played over Dorn's face. His movements had grown abstract as if he were intensely preoccupied with his thoughts. Yet there were no thoughts. He walked for moments lazily along the water's edge kicking at the sand, his eyes following the last of the paper bits still afloat. They vanished and he sighed with relief. . . . "It's all a make-believe. The sea, Rachel, the war.

Things don't mean anything. Last night there was someone to kiss. To-night, no one. But where's the difference. Nothing . . . nothing. . . . Will I cave in or keep on smiling? Probably cave in. One must be polite to one's emotions. The sea says she's gone," his thought rambled, "dark empty waters say she's gone. Rachel's gone. Well, what of it? Like losing a hat. Does anything matter much? An ending. Leave the theater. Draw a new breath. Remember vaguely what the actors said or what they should have said. All the same. What was in the postscript? Not fair to throw it away without reading it. Should have read carefully. Took her hours to pick the right words. Night . . . night. It'll be night soon."

His words left him and he walked faster. He began to run. She would be waiting in their room. On the bed . . . crying . . . "I couldn't leave you, Erik. Oh, I couldn't." And later they would laugh about it.

Mama Turpin was on the porch. He slowed his run. To rush breathless past the old woman would make a bad impression, if nothing had happened.

"Good evening, Mr. Dorn."

Of course she was upstairs. Or would Mama Turpin say good-evening?

"Hello," he called back casually, and walked on, his legs jumping ahead of him.

The room was empty. More than empty, for the comb and brush and tray of hairpins were missing. His eyes had swept the dressing-table as he came in. They were gone.

There would be another note. Why didn't she leave it some place where he could find it at a glance, instead of making him hunt around? Hunt around. Under the bed. On the chairs. No note. Good God, she was insane! Going away—why should she go away? . . . "we'll have a long talk about it and straighten it out, of course, but . . ." The insanity of the thing remained. Gone!

He stopped and felt his head aching. The sun . . . "you won't find me if you look for me. Please don't try. One good-bye is easier and better than two. Erik, Erik, something has died for always. . . ."

Then he had read it. That had been in the postscript. He had given it a glance, not intending to follow the words. Unimportant words.

"Died for always," he mumbled suddenly.

. . . His head pressed against the pillow in the dark room, he began to weep. The odor of her hair was still in the pillow. Yes, the dream had died. And she had run from its corpse, leaving behind the faint odor of her hair on a pillow. How, died! Better to have her gone. . . . Tears burned in his eyes. He repeated aloud, "better. . . ."

An agony was twisting itself about his heart. His face moved as if he were in pain. With his fists he began to beat the bed. It had gone away. It had come and smiled at him for a moment, lifted him for a moment, and then gone away as if it had never been. But it would come back. He would weep and pound on the bed with his fists and bring it back. The face of stars, eyes burning, devouring, eyes kindling his soul into ecstasies.

"Rachel!" he cried aloud.

Silence. His tears had ended. He lay motionless on the bed, his body suddenly weak, his thought tired. Someone had shouted a name in his ears. A dead man had shouted the name of Rachel. It was the cry of an Erik Dorn who was dead. He'd heard it in the dark room. An old, already forgotten Erik Dorn who had laughed in a halloo of storms, heels up, head down. Madness and a dream. Wings and a face of stars. They had vanished with an old and almost forgotten Erik Dorn who had called their name out of a grave. So things whirled away.

He arose and stood looking out of the window. Night had come . . . "dark rendezvous of sorrows. Silent Madonna of the spaces. . . ." He whispered to see if there were still phrases in him. His lips smiled against the window. Phrases . . . words . . . and the rest was a make-believe once more. A pattern precise and meaningless. His little flight over. Now it was time to walk again.

Anna had stood one night staring at him. He remembered. Oh, yes, he'd run away quickly for fear he might hear her shriek. And then, Rachel. But these things were passed. It was time to walk. Did he still love her? Yes. It would have been easier to walk with her—calmly, placidly, their hands sometimes touching. Forgetting other days and other kisses together. But he would not lie to himself. An end to that now. Love made a liar of a man. At the beginning and at the end— lies. The ache now was one of memory, not of loss. The pain was one of death. Dead things hurt inside him. Afterward his heart would carry them about unknowingly. The dead things would end their hurt. But now, leaden heavy, they kept slipping deeper into him as if seeking graves that did not yet exist.

Standing before the window, Dorn's smile grew cold.

"A make-believe," he whispered, "but not quite the same as it was before. A loneliness and an emptiness. Ruins in which once there was feasting. And now, nothing . . . nothing. . . ."

PART FOUR

ADVENTURE

Chapter One

LONG days. Short days. Outside the window was an ant-hill street. And an ant-hill of days. In the stores they were already selling calendars for the next year. Outside the window was a flat roof. By looking at the flat roof you remembered that Mary James was married. Unexpectedly. You came out of the ant-hill street, climbed the stairs, and sat down and looked at the flat roof. Long days, short days turned themselves over on the flat roof, and turned themselves over in your heart.

Occasionally an event. Events were things that differed from putting on your shoes or buying butter in the grocery store. There was an event now. It challenged the importance of the flat roof. Hazlitt was sitting in the room and talking. Rachel listened.

An eloquent event. But words jumbled into sound. Loud sounds. Soft sounds. They made her sleepy, as rain pattering on a window made her sleepy, or snow sinking out of the sky. There were sleepy words in her mind that had nothing to do with the event. Then the event came and mingled itself, mixed itself into the words . . . "no sorrow. No remorse. The dead are dead.

Oh, most extremely dead! So I'll sit by my sad little window and listen to this unbearable creature make love. The idiot'll go 'way in an hour and I'll be able to draw. Funny, my thoughts keep moving on, despite everything. Like John Brown's soul, or something. Words get to be separate, like the snickers of dead people. You think as one adds figures. Thoughts add, and draw pictures the same way. A line here. A line there. And you have a face. Curve a line up and the face laughs. Curve it down and the face weeps. You lie dead. Always dead. You lie dead in the street. The day tears your heart out. The night tears your eyes out. And when somebody passes, even a banana peddler, your eyes jump back, your heart jumps back, and you look up and snicker and say, 'It's all right. I'm just lying here for fun. I'm dead for fun. . . . He still loves me. I must answer him.'"

She spoke aloud:

"No, George, I hear you. But I don't love you. I can't say it more plainly, can I?"

Her thoughts resumed. "Dear me. He talks almost as well as Erik. Lord, he thinks I'm a virgin. His pure and unfaltering star. Well, well! Why am I amused? Is life amusing, after all? Am I really happy? Alas! my heart is broken. I must not forget my heart is broken. You forget sometimes and begin snickering and somebody rings the bell and hands you a telegram reading, 'Your heart is broken.' Rachel of the broken heart! It was all very beautiful. This talk of his somehow brings it back . . . Oh, God. That was a line curved down. What eloquence! There, now, I must speak. I'll have to tell him again."

Aloud she went on, "You're mistaken in me, George."

A flurry of silent words halted her. . . . "Ye gods, what a speech; she is not all his fancy painted him. Indeed! Not mistaken. His heart tells him. Poor boy! Poor little clowns who pay attention to what their hearts say! I mustn't be rude."

She interrupted him, "If you'll listen to me, George . . ."

Then, "What'll I say? If only he inspired something by his eloquence—a phrase, at least. But my heart snickers at him. Ah! the dead are wonderfully dead. I'll tell him I'm not a virgin. That'll be surprising news. But how? Like a medical report? The woman was found not to be a virgin. The thing seems to hinge on that. Why in God's name does he keep virgining?"

"No, George," she answered aloud, "I'm sorry. I don't believe in love. . . ." Listen to her! "You see, I've been in love myself. Indeed I have. That's why you find me changed."

He protested and her words followed silently. "My laughing makes him angry. But I must laugh. Love is something to laugh over, isn't it? Oh, God, why doesn't he go 'way?" The flat roof vanished. There was a rising event in the room and the flat roof bowed good-bye and walked away.

"Yes, I was in love for quite a while with a man," she answered him. "And I'm in love with him yet—in a way. But we've parted. He had to go to Europe." Nevertheless he still thought she was a virgin. He'd started another virgining speech. There would have to be a medical report. "We lived together for over a year. We weren't married, of course, because he had a wife. You see, you're terribly mistaken." He must be impressed by her calm. "Because what I really am is a vampire. I lured a man from his wife, lived with him, and cast him aside."

The event jumped to its feet. No room to talk for a moment, so her thought resumed, "I'm lying. He thinks I'm lying. I should have confessed in tears. With a few 'Oh, Gods.' Amusing! Amusing! That was Erik's favorite word. I'm beginning to understand it now. But there's nothing to be amused about . . . in itself an amusing circumstance . . . but you look at the banana peddler and snicker. Will he hit me? Oh, very red-faced. Speechless. I'd better talk. If he hit me. . . . He'll start in a minute. . . ."

"Yes, you know him, George," she cried suddenly. "And if you doubt me you can ask a lot of people. Ask Tesla or Mary James or Brander or New York." She'd make him believe. God, what an idiot! She'd claw his eyes out with words. Throw roofs on him. But it was a good thing Erik was in Europe, or he'd be killed.

"Yes. I've told you in order to get rid of you.

I'd rather be rid of you than keep my good name in your estimation. So now, run along and do your yelling outside. I'm sick of you."

She paused on a high gesture. . . . "He's going to hit me. Strike a woman. War has brutalized him. Dear me!" But he asked a question ominously and she answered,

"Erik Dorn. Yes. Erik Dorn."

This made it worse. It was bad enough without a name. But a name made it realler. And very ominous. She moved toward a chair.

"I'll sit still and then he won't hit me. If I'm calm, serene like a nun facing the wrath of God. This is melodrama. He can squeeze my shoulders all he wants. What good will it do him? If I giggled now he'd kill me. Sorry? Oh, so I must be sorry. Because I've offended him. Dear God, what a mess!"

She twisted out of his grasp and cried.

"No, I'm not sorry. You fool! I'm glad I was his woman. I'll always be glad, as long as I live. Leave me alone. You're a fool. I've always thought of you as a fool. You make me want to laugh now. You're a clown. I'll give myself to men. But not to you. I gave myself to Erik Dorn because I love him. If he wants me again I'll come to him not as a lover, because he doesn't love me any more—but as a prostitute. Now do you know me? Well, I want you to. So you'll go way and never bother me again. . . ."

That was a good speech. She stood dramatically silent as hands seized her shoulder again. "He hurts me. Why this? Oh, my shoulder! Does he want to? Oh, God, this is me! He'll let me go in a minute if I don't move. Very still. Silent . . . I don't want him to cry. Can't he see it's amusing? If he'd only look at me and wink, I'd kiss him. No, he's a fool. I'll not say anything more. Let him cry! His life is ruined. Dear me, I have ruined his life. His love. I was his dream. Through the war . . . rose of no-man's land. Amusing, amusing! He looks different. Contempt. He has contempt for me. And horror. Oh, get out, get out, you fool! You sniveling nincompoop, get out! I want to draw pictures, and forget. Console him . . . for what? I don't know, I don't know. He's going. Thank God! Oh, I don't know anything. Poor man, he should know better than to have dreams. Dreams are for devils, not for men or women. Dreams . . . dreams . . . I don't know . . . I'll draw a picture. But I don't want to. He'll never come back. I'm sad again. The flat roof says something. Is it Erik? Dear Erik! Poor Erik! I love you. But I'll begin crying. Pretty tears, amusing tears. Erik mine, dead for always. But it's not as bad as it was. Another month, year, ten years. Oh, it chokes me. I can't help it. Your eyes are the beckoning hands of dream. Whose eyes? Mine . . . mine. . . . Mine . . . I know. I know. I must keep on dying, keep on dying. But I'm not afraid. Look,

I can laugh! Amusing that I can laugh . . . Oh, God . . . God . . . ."

Beside her window looking out on the ant-hill street Rachel covered her face with her hands. When she removed them she caught a glimpse of the figure of Hazlitt walking as if it were a blind man in zig-zags down the pavement.

Chapter Two

THE thing that had been buried in Emil Tesla and that used to rumble under his fawning words, had come to life one day with two men twisting his wrists and hammering at his uncovered face. He had laughed.

The two men came into his office to seize him. When he started to protest they walked up to him slowly as if to shake hands. Instead, they began beating him. For a moment he wondered why the two men hated him so violently. He stood looking into their faces and thinking, "They're like me."

The visitors, however, saw no resemblance. They twisted his arm till it broke. Then they kept on battering at him with their fists till he fell to the floor. While he lay on the floor they kicked him, and his muscles grew paralyzed.

He never remembered the walk downstairs. But in the open he saw a crowd of faces drifting excitedly beneath him. This was a scene he remembered later.

It was while looking at the faces that he had grown strong. He laughed because it occurred to him at the moment he was unconquerable. Later, in prison, he often thought, "I have only my life to lose. I'm not afraid of that. When they hit me they were hitting at an idea. But they could only hit me. They couldn't touch the idea. I'll remember when I come out—they can only hit me. If they end by shooting me they'll not touch the idea even then. That's something beyond their fists and guns. I'll remember I'm only a shadow."

A year passed and Tesla came out. He returned to the office of *The Cry*. His friends noticed a change. He had grown quiet. He no longer bubbled with words. His eyes looked straight at people who spoke to him. His manner whispered, "I'm nothing—a shadow thrown by an idea. I don't argue, and I'm not afraid. I'm part of masses of people all over the world and cannot be destroyed."

The new Tesla became a leader. Among the radicals whose intellects were groping noisily with the idea of a new justice he often inspired a fear. His smile disquieted them and their arguments. His smile said, "Here, what's the use of arguing? There is no argument. It isn't words we must give the revolution, but lives. I'm ready. Here's mine."

When he looked at men and women who vociferated in the councils of radical pamphleteers, workers, organizers, theorists, new party politicians, Tesla thought, "That one's afraid. He's only a logician. His mind has led him into revolution. If he changed his mind he would become a conservative. . . . There's one that isn't afraid. He's like me. His mind helps him. But no matter what his mind told him he would always be in the revolution. Something in him drives him. . . ."

For the rabble of artists and near-artists drifting by the scores into radical centers, Tesla held a respectful dislike.

"He's in revolt because he must find something different than other people," he thought of most of them. "The revolution to him means only himself. It's something he can use to make himself felt more by people. And also he's a revolutionist because of the contrariness in him that artists usually have. Especially artists who, when they can't create new things, make themselves think they're creating new things by destroying old things."

Of himself Tesla thought, "I'll fight and not mind if I'm killed. Because people will still be left alive, and so the idea of which I'm a part will continue to live."

In the days before his going to prison Tesla had felt the need of writing and talking his revolution. This was because of an impatience and intolerance toward the enemy. Now that was gone. The enemy had become a blatant, trivial thing. The things it said and did were unimportant. He read with amusement the rabid denunciations of the radicals in the press of the day. The grotesque hate hymns against the new Russia, the garbled shriekings and pompous anathemas that fell hourly upon the heads of all suspects, inspired no argument in him.

Tesla's days were busy with organization. He had almost ceased his activities as pamphleteer, although still editor of *The Cry*. With a group of men, silent as himself, he worked at the radicalization of the factories and labor unions. Each day men left Tesla to seek employment in shops throughout the country, in mines and mills. Their duties were simple. Tesla measured them carefully before sending them on. . . . This one could be relied upon to work intelligently, to talk to workingmen at their benches and during noon hours without antagonizing, or, worse, frightening them. Another was dubious. His eyes were too bright. He would be discovered and arrested by the company. But he might do some good. The arrest of a radical always did some good to the cause. Where would Christianity have been without the incompetent agitators who blundered into the clutches of the Roman law and the amphitheater?

Aloud he would say, "Work carefully. Remember that the revolution is for all; that the workers, no matter what they say to you, are comrades. Remember that strikes are better than fights. The time hasn't come yet for fighting. What we must do is put into the hearts of the workers the knowledge that there is nothing in common between them and their bosses. The workers are the producers. They work and make no money. The bosses are the exploiters. They don't work and make all the money. If you get the workers to thinking this they'll want more money themselves and declare strikes. By strikes we can paralyze industry and give the workers consciousness of their power. This is only a step; but the first and most important step. Make strikes. Make dissatisfaction. But don't argue about fighting and revolution."

Over and over Tesla repeated his instructions through the days. He spoke simply. Men listened to him and nodded without questioning. They saw that his eyes were unafraid and that if he was sending them upon dangerous missions, he would some day reserve a greater mission for himself. Tesla had become a leader since he had laughed on the step overlooking the pack of faces.

Chapter Three

AT his desk in *The Cry* office Tesla was preparing the April issue of the magazine for the printer. It was night. A garrulous political poet named Myers was revising proofs at a smaller desk. Brander and a tall, thin woman stood talking quietly to each other in a gloomy corner of the office. Rachel, who had returned to the place after a hurried supper with Tesla, waited listlessly. He had promised to finish up in a half-hour, but there was more work than he had figured.

"We're reprinting a part of the article on the White Terror in Germany that Erik Dorn has in the *New Opinion*," Tesla said. Rachel nodded her head. Later Tesla asked her, "This Dorn, what is he? His writing is amusing, sometimes violent, but always empty. He doesn't like life much, eh?"

"I don't know," said Rachel.

"Yes," Tesla smiled. "He hates us all—reds and whites, radicals and bourgeoisie. Yet he can write in a big way. But he isn't a big man. He has no faith. I remember him once in Chicago. He hasn't changed."

Rachel's eyes remained steadily upon the socialist as he cleared his desk. He stood up finally and came to where she was sitting.

"It's necessary to have something besides self," he said softly. "I was born in a room that smelled bad. Perhaps that's why the world smells bad to me now. I still live there. It's good to live where there are smells. Our radicals sit too much in hotel lobbies that other people keep clean for them."

Brander thrust his large figure between them, the tall, thin woman moving vaguely about the room.

"Sometimes I think you're a fake, Emil," he said. "You're too good to be true."

He grinned at Rachel.

"By the way," he went on, looking at her, "I brought something to show you." His hands dug a paper out of his coat pocket. "You see, I've preserved our correspondence."

He held out a letter. Rachel's eyes darkened.

"Oh, there's no hurry," Brander laughed. "So long as you keep the application on file, you know."

Tesla, listening blankly, interrupted:

"It's late. We should go home. I'll go home with you, Rachel, and talk."

The thin woman, watching Brander anxiously, approached and seized his arm.

"All right," the artist whispered. "We'll go now."

Rachel felt a relief as Brander passed out of the door with the woman.

"He disturbs you," Tesla commented. She

nodded her head. Words seemed to have abandoned her. There was almost a necessity for silence. They walked out, leaving Myers still at his desk.

In the deserted streets Rachel walked beside Tesla. She felt tired. "He's never tired," she thought, her eyes glancing at the stocky figure. He wasn't talking as he said he would.

The night felt sad and cold. A dead March night. If not for Emil, what? "Perhaps I'll kill myself. There's nothing now. I'm always alone. No to-morrows."

In the evenings she came to the office to meet Emil for supper because there was nothing else to do. Emil seemed like an old man, always preoccupied, his eyes always burning with preoccupations. After supper he usually walked home with her, talking to her of poor people. There seemed no hatred in him, no argument. Poor people in broken houses. Christ came and gave them a God. Now the revolution would come with flaming embittered eyes but wearing a gentle smile for the poor people in broken houses, and give them rest and happiness.

But to-night he was silent. When they had walked several blocks he began to talk without looking at her.

"Come with me," he asked. "I live alone in a little house We can be happy there. You have nobody."

Rachel repeated "Nobody."

She looked at him but his eyes avoided her.

"My mother died long ago," he went on. "She was an old woman. She used to live in this house where I live. We were always poor. I had brothers and sisters. They've all gone somewhere. Things happened to them. I have only my work now. Nobody else. But I'm alone too much. Since we have seen each other I have been thinking of you. Brander has told me something but that doesn't matter. I would like to marry you."

He paused and seemed to grow bewildered.

"Excuse me," he mumbled. Rachel took his hand and held it as they walked. Tears in her whispered "Nobody . . . nobody." The homely face of Tesla was looking at her and saying something with its silence: "I am not for you as Erik was. But that is gone. Dead for always. . . ."

He was kind. It would be easy to live with him. But not married. A chill drifted through her. It didn't matter what she did. Life had ended one afternoon months ago. She remembered the sun shining on the sand, the burning sea, and Erik asleep. The memory said "I am the last picture of life."

It would be easy with Tesla. He loved elsewhere . . . a wild gentle thing—people. Poor people in broken houses. He would give her only kindness and companionship. And if he would let her cry to-night and make believe she was a child crying. . . .

They had taken a different direction. This was

the neighborhood where Tesla lived. Rachel looked about her in fear. She remembered the district. Now she was coming to live here in these streets where people begin to give forth an odor.

As she walked beside Tesla his silence became dark like the scene itself. She had always thought of him as somewhat strange. Now she understood why he had seemed strange to her. Because he carried an underworld in his heart. In his nose there was always the odor of the streets from which he had sprung, and in his mind there was always the picture of them. Other things did not fool him.

"Is it far?" she asked.

He looked at her, smiling.

"No," he said. "Do you want to go?"

She pressed his hand. It would be better. But her heart hurt. That was foolish. Emil was somebody different. Not like a man, but an old man—or an old background. There would be things to think about—Revolution. Before, revolution was people arguing and being dragged to jail. Sometimes people fighting. But it was something else—a thing hidden and spreading—and here in the dark street about them where Emil lived.

Emil seemed to vanish into a background. She walked and thought of the streets in which Emil lived. Here in the daytime the rows of sagging little houses were like teeth in an old man's mouth. From them arose exhalations of stagnant wood, decaying stairways; of bodies from which the sweats of lust and work were never washed. Soft bubbling alleys under a stiff sun. The stench like a grime leadened the air. Something to think about in places like this. Revolution crawling up and down soft alleys . . . something in the mud waiting to be hatched.

In this street lived men and women whose hungers were not complicated by trifles. In this way they were, as they moved thick-faced and unsmiling, different from the people who lived in other streets and who had civilized their odors and made ethics of their hungers. The people who lived here walked as if they were being pushed in and out of the sagging houses. Shrieking children appeared during the daytime and sprawled about. They rolled over one another, their faces contorted with a miniature senility. They urinated in gutters, threw stones at one another in the soft alleys, ran after each other, cursing and gesturing with idiot violence. They brought an awkward fever into the street. Oblivious of them and the débris about them, barrel-shaped women strutted behind their protuberant bellies, great flapping shoes over the pavements. They moved as if unaccustomed to walking in streets.

When it grew dark the men coming home from the factories began to crowd the street. They walked in silence, a broken string of shuffling figures like letters against the red of the sky. Their knees bent, their jaws shoved forward, their heads wagged from side to side. They vanished into the sagging houses, and the night came . . . an unwavering gloom picked with little yellow glows from windows. The houses lay like bundles of carefully piled rags in the darkness. The shrieking of the children died, and with it the pale fever of the day passed out of the air. There were left only the odors.

There were odors now, coming to them as they walked. Invisible banners of decay floating upon the night. Stench of fat kitchens, of soft bubbling alleys, of gleaming refuse. Indefinable evaporations from the dark bundles of houses wherein people had packed themselves away. They came like a rust into her nose.

She was moving into a new world. Drunken men appeared and lurched into the darkness with cursings and mutterings. Sometimes they sang. The smoke of the factory chimneys was now invisible, but the chimneys, like rows of minarets, made darker streaks in the gloom. And in the distance blast furnaces gutted the night with pink and orange flares. Figures of girls not yet shaped like barrels came into the street and stood for long moments in the shadows. Rachel watched them as she passed. They moved away into the depths of the soft alleys and vanished. It was late night. The exhalations of alleys and houses increased as if some great disintegration was stewing in the night. A new world. . . .

Rachel's fingers reached for Tesla's hand. She felt surprised. There was no thought of Erik.

This about her was a world untouched by the shadow Erik had left behind. So she could live here easily. And Emil was not a man like Erik. Erik, who stood alone, stark, untouched by life. Emil was a background. It would be easy. Her fingers, tightly laced in his, grew cold. Erik would come back. "Come back," murmured her thought. "Oh, if he should come back! No, I mustn't fool myself. It's over. And I can either live or die. I'll live a little while. Why? Because I still love him. Erik mine!"

But it didn't sadden her to walk up the dark steps of Tesla's house. "Erik, good-bye!" Not even that mattered. Erik was gone. That was all something else. Not gone. Oh, God, no! Only Erik had died. She still lived with a dead name in her heart. But here were odors—strange people.

It was barely furnished but clean inside. Later Rachel sat, her head in Tesla's arms, and wept. She was not sad. Her thought faltered, reaching for words, but drifting away. This is what had become of her—nothing else but this.

Tesla looked quietly at her and kept murmuring, "Little girl, the world is big. There are other things than self. Must you cry? Cry, then. I know what sadness is."

His hands moved gently through her loosened hair and he smiled sorrowfully.

"Dear child," he whispered, "you can always cry in my arms and I will understand. It is the way the world sometimes cries in my heart. I understand. . . . Yes . . . yes. . . ."

Chapter Four

A KALEIDOSCOPE of cities. A new garrulity. Words like busy little brooms sweeping up after a war. A world of foreigners. Europe was running about with empty pockets and a cracked head. England had had a nose-bleed, France a temporary castration, and the president of the United States was walking around in Paris in an immaculate frock-coat and a high silk hat. The President was closeted in a peace conference mumbling valorously amid lifted eyebrows, amused shoulder shruggings, ironic sighings. A long-faced virgin trapped in a bawdy house and calling in valiant tones for a glass of lemonade.

Erik Dorn drifted through a haze of weeks. This was London. This, Paris. This, Rotterdam. And this, after a long, cold ride standing up in a windowless coach, Berlin. But all curiously alike. People in all of them who said, "We are strangers to you."

There was nothing to see. No impressions to receive. More cities, more people, more words and a detachment. The detachment was Europe. In his own country there was no detachment. He was a part of crowds, newspapers, buildings. Here he was outside. Familiar things looked strange. The eyes busied themselves trying to forget things before them, scurrying after details and worried by an unrelation in architecture, faces, gestures.

It was mid-December when he sat in a hotel room in Berlin one night and ate blue-colored fish, boiled potatoes, and black, soggy bread. He had been wandering for days through snow-covered streets. Now there was shooting in the streets.

"Germany is starving," said an acquaintance. "Our children are dying off by the thousands, thanks to the inhuman blockade."

But despite even the shooting in the streets Dorn noticed the Germans had lost interest in the war. The idea of the war had collapsed. In England and France the idea was still vaguely alive. People kept it alive by discussing it. But even there it had become something unnatural.

One thing there was in common. Only a few people seemed to have been killed. London was jammed. Even though the newspapers summed it up now and then with "a generation has been killed." Paris, too, was jammed. And Berlin now, jammed also. The war had been fought by people who were dead. And the people who were alive were living away its memory.

In Berlin a week, and he thought, "A circus has pulled down its tent, carted off its gaudy wagons, its naphtha lights, and its boxes of sawdust. And a new show is staking out the lot."

The new show was coming to Berlin. Fences and building walls were plastered with its lithographs . . . "The Spirit of Bolshevism Marches . . . Beware the Wrecker of Mankind. . . ." Posters of gorillas chewing on bloody knives, of fiends with stringy hair setting the torch to orphanages and other nobly drawn edifices labeled "Kultur, Civilization, Humanitat. . . ." The spielers were already on the job. Machine-guns barked in the snow-covered streets. A man named Noske was a *Bluthund*. A man named Liebknecht was a *Schweinhund*.

In his hotel room Dorn, eating blue-colored fish, spoke to an acquaintance—an erudite young German who wore a monocle, whose eyes twinkled with an odd humor, and who under the influence of a bottle of Sekt was vociferating passionately in behalf of a thing he called *Welt* Revolution.

"I don't understand it yet, von Stinnes," Dorn smiled. "I will later. So far I've managed to do nothing more than enjoy myself. Profundity is diverting in New York, but a bore in Berlin. There's too much of it. Good God, man, there are times when I feel that even the buildings of the city are wrapped in thought."

Von Stinnes gestured with an almost English awkwardness. His English contained a slight French accent. His words, amused, careless, carried decision. He spoke knowingly, notwithstanding the Sekt and the smile with which he seemed to be belying his remarks. Thus, the Majority Socialists were traitors. Scheidemann had sold the revolution for a kiss from Graf Rantzau. The masses. . . . "Ah, m'sieur, they are arming. There will be an overthrow." And then, Ludendorff had framed the revolution—actually manufactured it. All the old officers were back. Noske was allowing them to reorganize the military. The thing was a farce. Social Democracy had failed. The country was already in flames. There would be things happening. "You wait and see. Yes, the Spartikusten will do something. . ."

Dorn nodded appreciatively. He felt instinctively that he had stumbled upon a man of value and service. But he listened carelessly. As yet the scene was more absorbing than its details. The local politik boiling beneath the collapse of the empire had not yet struck his imagination. There were large lines to look at first, and absorb.

Snow in unfamiliar streets, night soldier patrols firing at shadows, eager-eyed women in the hotel lobbies, marines carousing in the Kaiser's Schloss —a nation in collapse. Teutonia on her rump, helmet tilted over an eye, hair down, comely and unmilitary legs thrust out, showing her drawers and laughing. Yes, the Germans were laughing. Where was there gayety like the Palais de Danse, the Fox Trot Klubs, Pauligs; gayety like the drunken soldiers patrolling Wilhelmstrasse where a paunchy harness-maker sat in Bismarck's chair?

Gayety with a rumble and a darkness underneath. But such things were only wilder accents to laughter. If the detachment would leave him, if he could familiarize himself, he could lay hands on something; dance away in a macabré mardi-gras.

Two bottles of Sekt had been emptied. A polite Ober responded with a third. Von Stinnes grew eloquent.

"Not before March, Mr. Dorn. It will come only then. This that you hear now, pouf! Hungry men looking for crumbs with hand-grenades. The revolution is only picking its teeth. But wait. It will overturn, when it comes. And even if it does not overturn, if it fails, it will not end, but pause. You hear it whispering now in the streets. Hungry men with hand-grenades. Ah, m'sieur, if you wish we will work together. I am a man of many acquaintances. I am von Stinnes, Baron von Stinnes of a very old, a very dissolute, a very worthless family. I am the last von Stinnes. The dear God Himself glows at the thought. I will work for you as secretary. How much do you offer for a scion of the nobility?"

"Three hundred marks."

"A month?"

"No, weekly," laughed Dorn, "and you buy half the liquor."

Von Stinnes bowed.

"An insult, Mr. Dorn. But I overlook it. One becomes adept in the matter of overlooking insults. You will need me. I am known everywhere. I was with Liebknecht in the Schloss when he slept in the Kaiser's bed. Ho! it was a symbol for you to see him crawl between the sheets. Alas! he slept but poorly, with the marines standing guard and frowning at the bed as if it were capable of something. For me, I would have preferred beds with more pleasant associations. And when Bode tried to be dictator in his father's chamber in the Reichstag—yes," von Stinnes closed his eyes and laughed softly, "he seized the Reichstag with a company of marines. And he sat for two days and two nights signing warrants, confiscation orders. Until a soldier brought him a document issued by Eichorn the mysterious policeman who was dictating from the Stadt House. And poor Bode signed it. He was sleepy. He could not read with sleep. It was his own death warrant. It was I who saved him by taking him to the house of Milly. He slept for days with Milly, in itself a feat."

Von Stinnes swallowed another glass of wine. His eyes seemed to belie his unsteady, careless voice. His eyes remained intent and mocking upon Dorn.

"You have come a few weeks too late. There were scenes, dear God, to make one laugh. In the Schloss. Yes, we bombarded the Schloss—but after we had captured it. The Liebknecht ordered. Everything was done in symbols. Therefore the symbol of the bombardment of the Schloss. So we rushed out one night and opened fire, and when we had knocked off the balcony and peeled the plaster from the walls, we rushed in again and sang the *Marseillaise*. What wine, m'sieur! Ho, you have come a few weeks too late. But there will be other comedies. And I will be of service. I belong to three officers' clubs. One of them is respectable. Women are admitted. The other two . . . women are barred. And look. . . ." He slapped a wallet on the table and extracted a red card, "'member of the Communist Partei—Karl Stinnes,'" he read. "Listen, there are 75,000 rifles in Alexander Platz, waiting for the day."

"Where did you learn your English, von Stinnes?"

"Oxford. Italian in Padua. French, m'sieur, in Paris. During the war." The baron laughed. "Ah, *pendant la guerre, m'sieur, en Paris*."

"And now," Dorn mused, "you are a Spartikust."

The baron was on his feet, a wine glass raised in his hand.

"*Es lebe die Welt Revolution,*" he cried, "*es lebe das Rate Republik!*"

"What did you do in Paris, von Stinnes?"

"Pigeons, my friend. I played with pigeons and with vital statistics and made love to little French girls whose sweethearts were dying in the trenches. And in London. But I talk too much. Yes, my tongue slips, you say. But I am lonely and talk is easy. . . . I drink your health . . . *hein!* it was a day when we met. . . ."

Dorn raised his glass.

"To the confusion of the seven deadly virtues!" he laughed.

"I drink," the baron cried. "We will make a tour. We will amuse ourselves. I see that you understand Germany. Because you understand there is something bigger than Germany; that the world is the head of a pin spinning round in a glass of wine. I have been with the other correspondents. Pigs and donkeys. The souls of shopkeepers under the vests."

The baron seated himself carefully and pretended an abrupt seriousness.

"I have made up my mind to die behind the red barricades. Perhaps in March. Perhaps later. Another glass, m'sieur. Thanks. I shall die fighting for the overthrow of the tyranny of the bourgeoisie . . . Noske and his *parvenu* Huns. Ho! Dorn, we will amuse ourselves in a crazy world, eh, what? The tyranny of the bourgeoisie!"

The baron laughed as he rolled over the phrase.

"There will be great deal to enjoy," Dorn smiled. The wine was making him silent.

"Yes, to enjoy. To laugh," the baron interrupted. "I cannot explain now. But you seem to understand. Or am I drunk? *Ein galgen gelachter, nicht wahr?* I will take quarters at the hotel. I know the management well. I saved the place from being looted in the November excitement. Have you seen the Kaiser Salle? His Majesty dined there once. A witless popinjay. Liebknecht is a man. Flames in his heart. But a poor orator. He will be killed. They must kill him. A little Jew, Haase, has brains. You will meet him. And the Dadaists—they know how to laugh. The cult of the absurd. Perhaps the next emperor of Germany will be a Dada. An Ober Dada—who knows? Once the world learns to laugh we may expect radical changes. And in München I know a dancer, Mizzi. Dear God, what legs! You must come there to see legs. Faces in the Rhineland. Ankles in Vienna. But legs, dear God, in München! It is the Spanish influence. Let us drink to Mizzi. . . ."

The wine was vanishing. The baron paused out of breath and sighed. His face that seemed to grow firmer and more ascetic as he drank, took on a far-away shrewdness as if new ideas had surprised it.

"I've felt many things," Dorn spoke, "but thought nothing yet. So far Europe has remained strange. I am in a theater watching a pantomime. I have entered in the middle of the second act and the plot is a bit hidden. But we will have to find some serious work to do. I must meet politicians, leaders; listen to laments and prophecies. . . ."

"All in time, all in time," the baron interrupted. "Am I not your secretary? Well, then, trust me. You will talk to-morrow with Ebert. We begin thus at the bottom. Of all men in Germany who know nothing, he knows least. Thursday, Scheidemann. Treachery requires some shrewdness. The man is not quite an imbecile. If your Roosevelt were a Socialist he would be a Scheidemann.

Daumig, Pasadowsky, Erzburger—rely upon me, m'sieur. And Ludendorff. Ah, there we have real work. If Ludendorff will talk now. He is supposed to be in Berlin. I will find him and arrange for you. And so on. You will meet all the great minds, all the big stomachs. I will take you to Radek who is hiding with a price on his head. And Dr. Talheimer on the Rote Fahne, if they do not arrest him too soon. Bernstorff is in the hotel. A man with too much brains. Yes, an intelligent bungler. He will die some day with a sad smile, forgiving his enemies. And if we need women, mention your choice. Mine runs to the married woman of title. A small title is to be preferred. It is a slight insurance against disease. Others prefer the gamins. There is not enough difference to quarrel about. Or do you want a little red in your amours? A *sans culotte* from Ehrfurst or Spandau? In Essen you will find Belgian women. They will love for nothing. For that matter, a bottle of wine and a bar of chocolate and you can have anyone. There is no virtue left, thank God. And yet, for variety, I sometimes think there should be a little. Ah, yes, yes! I miss the virgins of my youth. Another bottle, eh? Where's the button? What do you think of German plumbing? It is our Kultur. We are proud of our plumbing. It was the ideal for which we fought. To introduce our plumbing throughout Europe—make a German bathroom of the world."

A sound of heavier firing in the streets interrupted. The two sat listening, the baron's face alive with an odd humor.

"*Es lebe die Welt Revolution,*" he whispered. "Do you hear it? Only a murmur. But it starts all over Germany again. Workingmen with guns. You will see them later. I among them. Stay in Europe, my friend, and see the ghost of Marat rising from a German bathtub."

"Who are shooting?" Dorn asked.

"Shadows," the baron laughed. "The government wishes to impress the good burgher that there is danger. So the government orders the soldiers to shoot at midnight. The good burgher wakes and trembles. *Mein Gott, das Bolshevismus treibt! Gott sei dank für den Regierung.* . . . So the good burgher gives enthusiastic assent to the increase in the military budget. Dear God, did he not hear shooting at midnight? But they play with more than ghosts. Noske's politik will end in another color. To-night there are only shadows to shoot at. To-morrow . . . remember what I tell you. . . ."

The telephone rang and Dorn answered. A voice in English:

"The gentlemen will have to put out the lights. The Spartikusten are coming."

"Thank you. . . ."

"What did he say?"

"We must put out the lights."

The baron laughed.

"It is nonsense. Come, your hat. We will go have a look."

They hurried down to the lobby. An iron door had been drawn across the entrance of the hotel. In the lobby the shooting seemed a bombardment of the building. A group of American and English correspondents were lounging in the heavy divans, drinking gin and talking to a trio of elaborately gowned women. The talk was in French.

"Hello, Dorn," one of the Englishmen called. Dorn approached the table, von Stinnes following, and whispering, "I will request the porter to open the gate."

"Baron von Stinnes, Mr. Reading."

The Englishman shook hands and smiled.

"I know the baron, Dorn. Rather old friends, what? Have a drink, damn it!"

"Later, if you please," von Stinnes bowed stiffly. Reading beckoned Dorn aside with an air of secrecy. Walking him to another part of the lobby he began whispering:

"I'd let that blighter alone if I were you, Dorn. I'm just telling you because you're rather new to these bloody swine."

Dorn nodded.

"I see," he said, and walked back to von Stinnes. Reading resumed his place with the party.

"Perhaps it was a timely warning," the baron murmured as Dorn drew near him. The gate had been opened and the two emerged. "I make a guess at what Reading told you," the baron pursued.

"It is immaterial," Dorn answered. "I engage you not for your honesty and many virtues, but because you're amusing. . . ."

"Thus you relieve my conscience," von Stinnes sighed.

The wide avenue was deserted. Moonlight lay on the new-fallen snow. A line of soldiers wheeled suddenly out of the Brandenburger Tor and came marching quickly toward the walkers.

"*Weiter gehen, weiter gehen,*" a voice from the troop called. Two detached themselves from the ranks and approached rapidly.

"*Ausweise. . . .*"

Von Stinnes glared through his monocle and answered in German, "What is the matter with you? Are you crazy? I am Baron von Stinnes. My friend is a member of the American Commission."

Dorn extracted a bit of stamped paper—his special credentials from the German Foreign Office. The soldier glanced at it without troubling to read. . . .

"*Sehr gut, mein Herrschaften,*" he mumbled. Dorn caught a glimpse of his face. Its importance had vanished. The line of soldiers marched on. When they had turned a corner the sound of firing suddenly resumed.

"Shadows again," chuckled von Stinnes.

Snow-covered streets, moonlight, waiting buildings, cold and shadows—here was reality. The thing under the gay tumult of the cafés. Under the baron's laughter. They were passing a stretch of empty shop windows.

"It's cold," Dorn muttered. The baron looked at him with a smile.

"It is cold everywhere in Germany," he said quietly. "Men's hearts are cold with hunger and fear. Brains are confused. Stomachs empty. The top has been knocked off. The soldiers in the streets are the sad little remains of a dead Germany. The new Germany lies cold and hungry in a workingman's bed. Life will come out of the masses. And I am always on the side of life. Not so? The old is dead. We drink wine to the new."

The sound of dance music drifted out of a café.

"Shall we stop?" the baron hesitated.

Dorn shook his head.

"Enough cafés. The streets are better. Dark windows."

They walked in silence through the snow, the baron humming a Vienna waltz as the blurred echoes of machine-gun fire rose in the night around them.

. . . Hours later Dorn lay sleepless in his bed. The smoke of wine was slipping out of his thought.

"I'm alone," he murmured to himself. An emotionless regret came to him.

"There are still years to live." He wrapped himself closer in the silk-covered quilts. "But how? Does it matter? I have loved, and that is over. Rachel is ended. Haven't thought of her for weeks. And now, I am like I was, only older and alone; yet not sad. So people adjust themselves to decay. Senses that could have understood and wept at sorrow die, along with the things whose death causes sorrow. Ergo, there is no sorrow. Wings gone, tears gone, everything gone. Empty again, yet content. I want nothing. . . . No desires. . . ."

His brain was mumbling sleepily as the cold wind from the opened window swept pleasantly through the room.

"Women to divert me. Wine to make me glad. And a companion—the baron. Droll tragedian! And scenes for my eyes. Yes, yes. . . . They keep shooting outside. Still shooting after five years. Shooting each other. The world speaks a strange language. What imbecility! Yet life is in the masses. It'll come out, perhaps. From Russia. Russians—a pack of idealists . . . a pack of illiterate Wilsons with whiskers. I'm like the baron. I admire revolution. Why? Because it diverts."

He closed his eyes for moments. Still no sleep, and his thought resumed, "Rachel, I once loved you. I can say it now without hurt. Empty memories now—like drawings in outline. And some day even the outlines will leave me."

A curious ache came into his heart. "Ah, she still touches me—still a little. Poor dear one! What a farce! A glorious farce! The nights when she whispered. Her face, I remember, yes, a little.

Ghosts! Your eyes are the beckoning hands of dream. That was the best sentence. . . . The rest were good too—sometimes."

He smiled sleepily on his pillow . . . "still shooting. It will be amusing here. Some day when we're old, Rachel and I will see each other again. Old eyes questioning old eyes. Old eyes saying. 'So much has died. Only a little more remains to die.' Sleep . . . I must sleep now. To-morrow, work, work! And forget. But nothing to forget. It forgets itself. It says good-bye. A sun gone down. What is it old Carl wrote? . . . 'The past is a bucket of ashes, a sun gone down . . . to-morrow is another day. . . .'"

Erik Dorn

Chapter Five

THE detachment vanished. Streets familiarized themselves.

"*Ich steh auf den Standpunkt,*" said the politicians; and the racket of machine-guns offered an obligato.

The new garrulity that had seemed strange to Dorn lost its strangeness. It became the victrola phrases of a bewildered diplomacy. But the diplomacy was not confined to frock-coats. It buzzed, snarled up and down the factory districts, in and out of the boulevard cafés and the squat resident sectors.

The German waiting for the knife of Versailles to fall was vomiting a vocabulary of fear, hope, threat, despair. Under cover of a confused Social Democracy the German army was slowly reorganizing itself.

It was three months after his arrival in Berlin that Dorn wrote his curious sketch of the German situation. The three months had witnessed a change in him. He had become a workman—industrious, inquisitive, determined. Under the guidance of von Stinnes he had managed to penetrate the heart of German *politik*. Tours through the provinces, daily interviews with celebrities, statesmen, leaders of the scores of political factions; adventures under the surface of the victrola phrases pouring from the government buildings and the anti-government buildings, had occupied even his introspections. Seemingly the empire had turned itself into a debating society. Life had become a class in economics.

Three months of work. Unfocused talents drawn into simultaneous activity. And Dorn arose one morning to find himself an outstanding figure in the turmoil of comment and commentators about him. Von Stinnes had wheedled his history out of him for publication in Berlin. Its appearance was greeted with a journalistic shout in the capitol. Radicals and conservatives alike pounced upon it. Haase, leader of the Independent Socialists, declaimed it almost in full before the National Assembly in Weimar.

Dorn had put into it a passionate sense of the irony and futility of his day. Its clarity arrested the obfuscated intellect of a nation groping, whining, and blustering under the shadow of the knife of Versailles.

The writing of it had rid him for the time of Rachel, of Anna, of the years of befuddling emptiness that had marked his attitudes toward the surfaces of thought about him. The emotionless disillusion of his nature had finally produced an adventure for him—the adventure of mental fecundity.

He had gone to Weimar to write. Here the

new government of Germany had assembled. Delegates, celebrities, frock-coats, strange hair formations; messiah and magician had come to extricate the nation from its unhappy place on the European guillotine. The narrow streets stuttered with argument. . . . Von Stinnes and a girl named Mathilde Dohmann accompanied him to the town. The Baron, bored for the moment with his labors, had immersed his volatile self in a diligent pursuit of Mathilde. He had discovered her among communist councils in Berlin and naïvely attached her as a part of Dorn's secretarial retinue.

"She will be of service," he announced.

Dorn, preoccupied with the scheme of his history, paid little attention to her. Arrived in Weimar he became entirely active, viewing with amusement the Baron's sophisticated assault upon the ardent-voiced, red-haired political spitfire whom he called Matty. Alone in an old tavern room, he gave himself to the arrangements of words clamoring for utterance in his thought. Old words. Old ideas. Notions dormant since years ago. Phrases, ironies remembered out of conversations themselves forgotten. The book was finished towards the middle of March—a history of the post-war Germany; with a biography between the lines of Erik Dorn. Von Stinnes had forthwith produced two German scholars who, under his direction, accomplished the translation with astonishing speed. Excerpts from the thin red- and black-covered volume found their way overnight into the press of the nation. Periodicals seized upon the extended brochure as a *Dokument*. In pamphlet form the gist of it started upon the rounds of Europe. The garrulity of the day had been given for the moment a new direction.

. . . .

"We will go to Munich. There will be a revolution in Munich. I have news from secret sources."

Baron von Stinnes, lounging wearily in front of a chess-board, spoke and raised a cup of mocha to his lips. Dorn, picking his way through a German novel, looked up gloomily and nodded.

"Anywhere," he agreed. "Munich, Moscow, Peking."

In a corner of the room Mathilde was curled on the luxurious hotel divan watching through half-closed eyes the figures of the men. The Baron turned toward her and frowned. In return her face, almost asleep, became vivid with a sneer. The Baron's love-making had gone astray.

"Matty is going to try to carry a million marks into Munich for the Communists," he announced.

The girl stared von Stinnes into silence.

"How do you know that?" she asked slowly.

He lowered his cup and with a show of polite deliberation removed his monocle and wiped it with a silk handkerchief.

"I know many things," he smiled. "The

money comes from Dr. Kasnilov and will be brought to Dr. Max Levine in Munich, and the good Max will buy a garrison of Landwehr with it and establish the soviet republic of Bavaria."

"You know Levine?"

"Very well," smiled the Baron.

Mathilde sat up. Her voice acquired a vicious dullness.

"You will not interfere with me, von Stinnes."

"I, Matty?" The Baron laughed and resumed his mocha. "I am heart and soul with Levine. If Dorn cannot go I will have to go alone. It is necessary I be in Munich when the soviets are called out."

"You will not interfere with me, von Stinnes," the girl repeated, "or I will kill you."

"You have my permission, Fräulein. The logical time for my death is long past."

Mathilde's sharp young face had grown alive with excitement. She sat with her eyes unwaveringly upon the Baron as if her thought were groping desperately beneath the smiling weariness of the man.

"Mr. Dorn," she spoke, "von Stinnes is a traitor."

Dorn smiled.

"If one million marks will cause a revolution, I'll take them to Munich myself," he answered. "I'm sick of Berlin. I need a revolution to divert me."

"I fear I am in the way," von Stinnes interrupted. He arose with formality. "Mathilde would like to unburden herself to you, Dorn. I am, she will inform you, a secret agent of Colonel Nickolai, and Colonel Nickolai is the head of the anti-bolshevist pro-royalist propaganda in Prussia." He paused and smiled. "I will meet you in the lobby when you come down."

He walked toward the door, halting before the excited face of the girl.

"Ah, Matty, Matty," he murmured, "you will not in your zeal forget that I love you?"

He bowed whimsically and passed out. Dorn laid aside his book and approached the divan. In the week since their return from Weimar he had become interested in the moody, dynamic young creature. The fact that she had resisted the expert persuasions of the Baron—a subject on which the nobleman had discoursed piquantly on their ride to Berlin—had appealed to him.

"Karl is a good fellow," he said, seating himself next to her. "And if it happens he is employed by Noske and Nickolai it doesn't alter my opinion of him."

"He is a scoundrel," she answered quietly.

"That is impossible," Dorn smiled. "He is merely a man without convictions and therefore free to follow his impulses and his employers. I thank God for von Stinnes. He has made Europe possible. A revolution alone could rival him in my affections."

The girl remained silent, and Dorn watched

her face. He might embrace her and make love. It would perhaps flatter, please her. She fancied him a man of astounding genius. She had practically memorized his book. Thus, one had only to smile humorlessly, permit one's eyes to grow enigmatic, and think of a proper epigram. He recalled for an instant the two women who had succumbed to his technique since he had left America. They blurred in his memory and became offensive. Yet Matty had been of service and perhaps her moodiness was caused by a suppressed affection. As an amorous prospect she was not without interest. As a reality, however, she would obviously become a bore. In any case there was nothing to hinder polite investigation, mark time with kisses until von Stinnes brought on his promised revolution. He thought carefully. Pessimism was the proper note. Dramatize with an epigram the emptiness of life. His forte—emptiness. Not love but a hunger to live.

"Matty, I regret sadly that you are not a prostitute."

Startling!

"It would save me the trouble of having to fall in love with you, dear child."

She smiled, a sudden amusement in her eyes.

"You too, Mr. Dorn. I had thought different of you."

"As a creature beyond the petty agitations, eh?"

"As a man."

"It is possible for a Man, despite a capital M, to love."

"Yes, love. It is possible for him only to love. And you do not."

"Much worse. I am sad."

"Why?"

"Perhaps because it is the only emotion that comes without effort."

"So you would fall in love with me to forget that I bore you."

"A broader ambition than that. To forget that living bores me, Mathilde."

"There is someone else you love, Mr. Dorn."

"There was." He smiled humorlessly. "Do you mind if I talk of love? I need a conversational antidote."

"And if you talk of love you may be spared the trouble of having to make love," she laughed quietly. "But I would rather talk of von Stinnes. I am worried."

"You are young," Dorn interrupted, "and full of political error. I am beginning to believe von Stinnes. The most terrible result of the war has been the political mania it has given to women."

Mathilde settled back on the divan and stared with mocking pensiveness at her shoes. Dorn, speaking as if he desired to smile, continued:

"Do you know that when one has loved a woman one grows sad after it is ended, remembering not the woman, but one's self? The memory of her becomes a mirror that gives you back the image of something that has died—a shadow of youth and joy that still bears your name. It is the same with old songs, old perfumes. All mirrors. So I walk through life now smiling into mirrors that give back not myself, but someone else—another Dorn."

He arose and looked down at her.

"Does that interest you?"

"I understand you."

"There are many ways of making love. Sorrowful phrases are the most entertaining, perhaps."

"You make me think you have loved too much."

"Yes, it would be difficult to kiss you. I would become sad with memory of other kisses. Because you are young—as I was then."

"Was it long ago?"

"Things that end are always long ago."

"Then it was only yesterday."

"Yes, yesterday," he laughed, pleased with the ironic sound of his voice. "And what is longer ago than yesterday?"

She had risen and stood before him, an almost boyish figure with her fists clenched.

"I have something else I am in love with," she whispered. "I am in love with——"

"The wonderful revolution, I know."

"Yes."

"And some day in the future you, too, will look into a mirror and see not yourself but a glowing-faced girl that was in love with what was once called the revolution."

"But if things end it is only because we are too weak to hold them forever. So while we are strong we must hold them twice as eagerly."

"Sad. All most deplorably sad, Mathilde. Hands shuffle us into new combinations, when we would prefer the old. Thus you, too, will some day listen to the cry that rises from all endings."

"You are designing. You wish to make me sad, Mr. Dorn. And succeed."

"Only that I may contemplate the futility of your love and smile. As I cannot quite smile at my own. We do not smile easily at corpses."

His hands covered her fingers gently.

"I will give myself to you, if you wish," she whispered.

"And I prefer you like this," he smiled. "If you will come close to me and lay your head against me." He looked down at her as she obeyed. "There is an odor to your hair. And your cheek is soft. These things are similar things. You are almost like a phantom."

"Of her."

"No. She is forgotten. It's something else. A phantom of something that once lived in me, and died. It comes back and stares at me sometimes out of the eyes of strange women, out of the sounds of music. Now, out of your hair."

"And you do not want me, Erik?"

"I want you. But I prefer to amuse myself by fancying that you are unattainable."

"I've liked you, Erik. The rest does not matter

to me. I grew old during the war, and careless. My father and two brothers died. And another man."

"So we both need diversion."

"Yes."

"Diversion," he murmured, "the little drug. But what is there to drugs? No, come; we are lovers now."

"We will go to Munich together."

"Yes."

"And will you carry the money for Levine? They would never search you and they might recognize and search me. And besides, von Stinnes would not dare interfere if it was you, even if he is a spy, because he likes you too well."

Her voice had become eager and vibrant. Dorn smiled ruefully, the faint mist of a sigh in his thought. The girl had worked adroitly. Of course, he was someone to carry the money to the Munich radicals.

"It is just an ordinary-looking package. The station will be under a guard and all the roads coming in, too. They are expecting the revolution and . . ." She paused and grew red. Dorn's eyes were looking at her banteringly. "You are thinking I have tricked you," she cried, "and that it was only to use you as a . . . as a carrier that I . . . Well, perhaps it is true. I do not know myself. I told you you could have me. Yes, I give myself to you now . . . now . . . Do you hear?"

She laughed with bitterness.

"I have never given myself before. I would rather you smiled and were kind. But if you wish to laugh . . . and call it a bargain . . . it does not matter."

She had stepped away from him and stood with kindled eyes, waiting.

"One can be chivalrous in the absence of all other impulses, Mathilde. And all other impulses have expired in me. So I will take the package. We will start to-morrow early. And as for the rest . . . I will spare you the tedium of martyrdom."

He moved toward the door. "Come, we'll go downstairs. Von Stinnes will be getting impatient."

Mathilde came to him swiftly. He caught a glimpse of her face lighted, and her arms circled his neck. She was looking at him without words. A coldness dropped into his heart. There had been three of them before—he, Mathilde, and a phantom. Now there were only Mathilde and himself.

"She was not tricking," he thought, and felt pleased. "At least not consciously."

Her arms fell from him and she stared frightenedly.

"Forgive me, Erik. I thought you loved me. And I would have liked to make you happy. . . ."

He nodded and opened the door.

Chapter Six

THEY sat in the compartment of the train crawling into Munich. The Baron drooped with sleep. Dorn stared wearily out of the window. Springtime. A beginning of green in the fields and over the roll of hills. Formal sunlight upon factories with an empty holiday frown in their windows.

"I hear shooting," he smiled at Mathilde. "We're probably in time."

The girl nodded. Despite the sleepless night sitting upright in the compartment, her eyes were fresh and alive. The desultory crack of a rifle drifting out of the town as if to greet them brought an impatience into her manner. The train was moving slowly.

"Yes, we're in time," she murmured. "See, the white guards are still in possession."

A group of soldiers with white sleeve-bands over the gray-green of their uniforms passed in an empty street.

"There will be white guards at the station, too," she went on. "The attack will come to-night. It must."

She looked intently at von Stinnes who, opening his eyes suddenly, whispered, "Ah, Mathilde . . . there was once another München. . . ."

An uproar in the station. A scurry of guards and soldiers. White sleeve-bands. Machine-guns behind heaped bags of sand. A halloo of orders across the arc of the spacious shed. Passengers pouring out of the newly arrived train, smiling, weeping, staring indifferently.

The officer desired the passengers to line themselves up against the train. A suggestive order, and confusion. Whispers in the crowd. . . . "Personally, I prefer the guillotine. . . . No, no, madame. There is no danger. These are good boys. Soldiers of the government. You can tell by the sleeve-bands. White. Merely baggage inspection."

Dorn waited his turn. A group of soldiers approached slowly, delving into pockets for weapons, peering into opened pieces of baggage. Babble, expostulation, eager politeness of innocent travelers, and outside the long crack of rifles, an occasional rip of a machine-gun. The group of soldiers paused before him.

"I am an American," he spoke in English, "with the American commission."

The announcement produced its usual effect. Bows, salutes, smiles. He pulled out his passport and foreign-office credentials. An officer stepped forward and glanced at them.

"Very good," in courteous English, "you will

pardon for the delay. We are having a little trouble here."

He indicated the city with a nod of his head and smiled wryly. In German he continued sharply, "Gottlieb, Neuman, you will escort this gentleman and his friends to whatever place they wish to go. Take my car at post 10."

Two soldiers saluted. The officer bowed with a smile. The travelers moved off with their escort toward the street. Mathilde kept her eyes on von Stinnes as they entered a gray automobile.

"Von Stinnes and I will sit in the back," she whispered to Dorn.

The Baron nodded.

"Careful of your Leugger," he whispered, "the soldiers will see it. You can shoot me just as easily if you keep it hidden. I have frequently fired through my pocket."

In a hotel room a half-hour later, Mathilde, grown jubilant as a child, was clapping her hands and laughing.

"It was too simple!" she cried.

Dorn drew a small suitcase from under the bed and opened it.

"Here it is," he laughed. He removed an oblong package. His eyes sought von Stinnes, standing near the window leisurely smoking a cigarette.

"You will find Levine in the Gambrinus Keller," von Stinnes spoke without turning around. "I advise you to go at once, Matty, before the streets crowd up."

He wheeled and held an envelope toward the girl.

"Take this. It will make it easier for you to get in. They are very careful right now. It's a letter of credentials from Dr. Kasnilov."

Mathilde opened the envelope mechanically, her eyes seeking the thought under the Baron's smile.

"Thanks," she spoke in German. "I will go now. I will see you after. At dinner to-night. Here."

She walked quickly from the room, the oblong package under her arm.

Chapter Seven

THE thing hiding in the alleys and shops of the world—the dark, furtive hungers that Russia was thawing into life, emerged on a bright April day in the streets of Munich. Working men with guns. A sweep of spike-haired, deep-eyed troglodytes from the underworld of labor. Factories, shops, and alleys vomited them forth. Farm hovels and stinking bundles of houses sent them singing and roaring down the forbidden avenues, past the forbidden sanctuaries of satrap and burgher.

From behind curtained windows the upper world looked on with amazement and disgust. A topsy-turvy April morning. A Spring day gone mad. Here were the masses celebrated in pamphlet and soap-box oration. An ungodly spectacle, an overturning. Grinning earth faces, roaring earth voices come swaggering into the hallowed precincts of civilization. Workingmen with guns marching to take possession of the world. An old tableau decked with new phrases—the underfed barbarian at the gate of the grainary.

The singing and the roaring continued through the morning.

"*Es lebe die Welt Revolution! Es lebe das Rate*

Republik! Hoch! die soviet von Bayern . . . Hoch! Hoch!"

From the twisting, blackened streets, *"Hoch!"* Men and women squeezing aimlessly around corners. Closely packed drifts of bobbing heads. A crack of rifles dropping punctuations into the scene. *"Hoch! Hoch!"* from faces clustered darkly about the grimacing, inaudible orators in the squares.

Red flags, red placards like a swarm of confetti on the walls and in the air. A holiday war. . . . The morning hours marched away.

With noon, a silence gradually darkened the scene. A silence of shuffling feet and murmuring tongues. The revolution had sung its songs. An end of songs and cheerings. Drifting, silent masses. An ominous, enigmatic sweep of faces. Red placards under foot in cubist designs down the streets.

The afternoon waned, the hundred thousands closed in. Darkness was coming and the pack was welding itself together. Rifles were beginning. Machine-guns were beginning. Holiday was over. Quieter streets. The orators become audible. Still faces, raised and listening. The orators had news to give. . . . One of the garrisons had gone over to the soviets. Two garrisons had vanished. Treachery. A long murmur . . . treachery. The armies of General Hoffmann were marching upon Munich . . . twenty kilometers from Munich. They would arrive in the night.

. . .   "We will show them, comrades, whether the revolution has teeth to bite as well as a song to sing."

A growl was running through the twilight.
. . . . *Es lebe das Rate Republik!* A fierce whisper of voices. Workingmen looking to their guns, massing about the government buildings. A new war minister in the uniform of a marine, speaking from a balcony. Workingmen with guns, listening. Women drifting back to the hovels and stinking bundles of houses. In the cafés, satraps and burghers eating amid a suppressed clamor of whispers, plans. The foolishness was almost over. The armies of General Hoffmann were coming . . . Twenty kilometers out. . . . Arrive at night. The corps students themselves would saber the swine out of the city. . . .

Night. Darkened streets. Tattered patrols hurrying through mysteriously emptied highways, shouting, "Indoors! Inside, everybody!" Suddenly from a distance the bay of artillery. Workingmen with guns were storming the cannon of the artillery regiment outside the city. A haphazard cross-fire of rifles began to spit from darkened windows . . . an upper world showing its teeth behind parlor barricades.

In the shadows of the massive government buildings an army was forming. No ranks, no officers. Easy to drift through the sunny streets singing the *Marseillaise* and the International . . . to mooch along through the forbidden avenues dreaming in the daylight of a new world . . . with red flags proclaiming the new masters of earth. Hundred thousands, then. But now, how many? Too dark to see, to count. An army, perhaps. Perhaps a handful. . . .

Feverish salutes in the shadows. . . . *"Gruss Gott, genosse!"*

Was it alive? Did the revolution live? What was happening in the empty streets? Who was shooting? And the armies of Hoffmann? *Gruss Gott, genosse.* Under Rupprecht the armies had lain four years in the trenches. Great armies, swinging along like a single man, that had once battered their way almost into Paris against the English, against the French.

"Gruss Gott, genosse. Hoffmann kommt . . . Ja wohl, Gruss Gott!"

Now twenty kilometers away and coming down the highroad against Munich—against the drifting little clusters of lonely men whispering in the shadows—the great armies of the Kaiser, an iron monster clicking down the road toward Munich. Would there be artillery to meet them? *Gruss Gott, genosse, wer shusst dort?* No, they had only guns, old guns that might not shoot. Old knives at their belts. . . . Darkness and rifle-spattered silences. Where was the revolution? The shadows whispered, *"Gruss Gott. . . ."*

The shadows began to stir. A voice was talking in the night. High up from a window. Egelhofer, the communist. No, Levine. Who? A light in the window. . . . Egelhofer, thin-faced, tall, black-haired. Egelhofer, the new war minister. 'Shh! what was he saying? . . . *"Vorwaerts, der Banhoff. . . ."*

Yes, the armies of Hoffmann had come. The shadows stirred wildly. Forward . . . *es lebe die Welt Revolution!* This time a battle-cry, hoarse, shaking. Men were running. Workingmen with guns, guns that would shoot . . . *"Der Banhoff . . . der Banhoff. . . ."*

The shadows were emptying themselves. A pack was running. Two abreast, three abreast, in broken strings of men. Groups, solitary figures, hatless, bellowing. The revolution was moving. The empty streets filled. An army? A handful? Let God show in the morning. Workingmen with guns were running through the night. Munich was shaking. . . . *"Der Banhoff, genosse, vorwaerts!"*

The revolution was emptying itself into the great square fronting the station. Little lights twinkling outside the ancient weinstubes began to explode. There must be darkness. Pop! . . . pop! . . . a rattle of glass. A blaze of shooting. The railroad station was firing now.

"Es lebe das Rate Republik!" from the darkness in the streets. A sweep of figures across the open square. Arms twisting, leaping in sudden glares of flame. The revolution hurled itself with a long cry upon the barricades of thundering lead.

In the single lighted window of the government

buildings a face still spoke . . . *"Ich bin Egelhofer, ihr Krieg's minister . . . Ich komm. . . ."*

Waving a rifle over his head, the war minister rushed from the building. A marine from Kiel. A new pack loosened itself from the shadows. A war minister was leading.

Moving swiftly through the streets, Dorn hurried to the seat of the new government—the Wittelbacher Palais. Von Stinnes was waiting there. He had been delayed in joining the Baron by the sudden upheaval about the hotel.

The wave had passed. Almost safe now to skirt the scene of battle and make a try for the Palais. As he darted out of the darkened hotel entrance, the thing seemed for a moment under his nose. An oppressive intimacy of tumult.

"They're at the station," he thought. "I'll have to hurry in case they fall back."

He ran quickly in an opposite direction followed by the leap of firing. Several blocks, and he paused. Here was safety. The revolution a good half-mile off. He walked slowly, recovering breath. The street was lighted. Shop windows blinked out upon the pavements. A few stragglers walked like himself, intent upon destinations made serious by the near sound of firing. An interesting evening, thus far. A stout, red-faced man with a heavily ornamented vest followed the figure of a woman. Dorn smiled. Biology versus politics. . . . "Excuse me, pretty one, you look lonely. . . ." A charwoman. Black, sagging clothes. Dorn passed and heard her exclaim, "Who, me? You ask me to go with you? Dear God, he asks me! I am an honest workingwoman. Run along with you!" The woman, walking swiftly, drew alongside. She was chuckling and muttering to herself, a curious pride in her voice, "He asked me, dear God—me!"

The abrupt sound of rifle-fire around the corner startled her. Dorn halted. The woman turned toward him, puzzled.

"They are shooting a whole lot to-night," she spoke in German.

"Quite a lot," he answered.

She looked back at the red-faced man who had remained where she had left him.

"What do you think of that dunce?" she whispered, and hurried on.

Dorn followed leisurely in the direction of the Palais.

Chapter Eight

A RABBLE of dictators, ministerial fledglings, freshly sprouted governors, organizers, departmental heads, scurried through the dimly lighted corridors of the old Palais. Dorn, with the aid of a handful of communist credentials that seemed to flow endlessly from the pockets of the Baron, passed the Palais guard—a hundred silent men squatting behind a hastily erected barricade of sandbags.

Within he stumbled upon von Stinnes. The Baron drew him into a large empty chamber.

"We must be careful," he whispered. His voice buzzed with an elation. "Already two ministries have fallen. There is talk now of Levine. He's of the extreme left. I thought you would like to see it. It has its amusing side." He laughed softly. "I was with the men in the streets for a while. There was something there, Dorn. Life, yes . . . yes . . . It was amazing. But here it is different. What is it the correspondents say? 'All is confusion, there is nothing to report.' . . . Yes, confusion. There are at present three poets, one lunatic, an epileptic, four workingmen and a scientist from Vienna, and two school teachers. They are the Council of Ten. Look, there is Muhsam, the one with the red vandyke. A poet. He used to recite rhymes in the Café Stephanie."

The red vandyke peered into the room. "Stinnes, you are wanted," he called. "I have my portfolio. I am the new minister to Russia. I leave for Moscow to-morrow."

"Congratulations!" the Baron answered.

A tall, contemplative man with a scraggly gray beard—an angular Christ-like figure—appeared. He spoke. "What are you doing here, Muhsam? There is work inside."

"And you!" angrily.

"I must think. We must grow calm." He passed on, thinking.

"Landerdauer," smiled the Baron, "the Whitman translator."

"Yes," the vandyke answered, "we have appointed him minister of education. What news from the station, Stinnes?"

"It is taken."

Dorn followed the Baron about the corridors, his ears bewildered by the screechings from unexpected chambers of debate. He listened, amused, to the volatile von Stinnes.

"They are trying for a coalition. Nikish is at the top. A former schoolmaster. The communists under Levine won't come in. The workingmen are out overthrowing the world, and the great thinkers sit in conference hitting one another over the head with slapsticks. Life, Dorn, is a droll business, and revolution a charming comedy, *nicht wahr?* But it will grow serious soon. Munich will be cut off. Food will vanish. Aha! wait a minute. . . ."

He darted after a swaggering figure. Dorn watched. The baron appeared to be commanding and entreating. The figure finally, with a surly shake of his head, hurried off. The Baron returned.

"That was Levine," he said. "He won't come in unless Egelhofer is ratified as war minister. Egelhofer is a communist. Wait a minute. I will tell them to make Egelhofer minister. I will make a speech. We must have the Egelhofer."

He vanished again. Dorn, standing against a window, watched frantic men scurry down the corridor bellowing commands at one another. . . .

"Yesterday they were garrulous little fools buzzing around café tables," he thought. "To-night they boom. Rodinesque. And yet comic. Yes, comedians. But no more than the troupe of white-collared comedians in Wilhelmstrasse or Washington. The workers were different. There was something in the streets. Men in flame. But here are little matches."

He caught sight of Mathilde and called her name. She came and stood beside him. Her body was trembling.

"Did you spend the money?" he asked softly.

"Yes, but they will buy the garrisons back again. They have more funds than we. Oh, we need more."

"Who will buy them back?"

"The bourgeoise. They have more money than we. And without the garrisons we are lost."

She wrung her hands. Dorn struggled to become properly serious.

"There, it may come out very fine," he murmured. "Anyway, von Stinnes is making a speech. It should help."

"Stinnes. . . ."

"Yes, trying to bring Egelhofer in as war minister. He talked with Levine. . . ."

"I don't understand," she answered. "He is doing something I don't understand, because he is a traitor."

She became silent and moved closer to Dorn.

"Oh, Erik," she sighed, "I must cry. I am tired."

He embraced her as she began to weep. Von Stinnes emerged, red-faced and elated.

"It is settled," he announced. "Hello! what's wrong with Matty?"

"Tired," Dorn answered.

"We will go to the hotel."

They started down the corridor. A group of soldiers emerged from a chamber, blocking their way.

"Baron von Stinnes," one of them called. The Baron saluted.

"You are under arrest by order of the Council of Ten."

Von Stinnes bowed.

"Go to the hotel with Matty, Dorn. I will be on soon."

To the soldiers he added, "Very well, comrades. Take me to comrade Levine."

"We have orders. . . ."

"To Levine, I tell you," he interrupted angrily. "Are you fools?"

He removed a document quickly from his coat pocket and thrust it under the soldiers' eyes.

"From Lenine," he whispered fiercely. "Now where is Levine?"

The soldiers led the way toward the interior of the Palais.

Outside, Dorn supported the drooping figure of the girl. Runners passed them crying out, "It is over! We have taken the station!"

They arrived at the hotel. The lobby was thronged with people. A chocolate salesman from Switzerland was orating: "They have erected a guillotine in Marien Platz. They are shooting down and beheading everybody who wears a white collar."

The hotel proprietor quieted the crowd.

"Nonsense!" he cried. "Ridiculous nonsense! We are safe. They are all good Bavarians and will hurt nobody."

Dorn led Mathilde to his room. She threw herself on the bed.

"So tired!" she whispered.

"But happy," he added. "Your beloved masses have triumphed."

"Don't. I'm sick of talking. . . ."

"Too much excitement," he smiled.

They became silent. Dorn, watching her carelessly in the dimly lighted room, began to think. . . . "Disillusionment already. The dream has died in her. A child's brain overstuffed with slogans, it begins now to ache and grow confused. Tyranny, injustice, seem far away and vague. The revolution in the streets has blown the revolution out of her heart. There will be many like that tomorrow. The over-idealized idealists will empty first. The revolution was a dream. The reality of it will eat up the dream. Justice to the dreamer is a vision of new stars. To the workingman— another loaf of bread."

"Of what are you thinking, Erik?"

"Of nothing . . . and its many variants," he answered.

"We've won," she sighed. "Oh, what a day!"

He noted the listlessness in her voice.

"Yes," he said, "another sham has had heroic birth. Out of workingmen with guns there will rise some day a new society which will be different than the old, only as to-morrow is different than to-day. The rivers, Mathilde, flow to the sea and life flows to death. And there is nothing else of consequence for intelligence to record."

"You talk like a German of the last century," she smiled. "Oh, you're a strange man!"

This pleased him. He thought of words, a ramble of words—but a knock at the door. Von Stinnes entered. He was carrying a basket.

"Food," he announced cheerfully. "With food in our stomachs the world will seem more coherent for a while."

He busied himself arranging plates of sandwiches on a small table.

"Mathilde asleep?"

He walked to the bed and leaned over her. The girl's eyes were closed.

"Poor child, poor child!" the Baron whispered. He caressed her head gently. "We will not wake her up. But eat and leave her food. Do you mind if we go out for a while? It is still early and it will be hard to sleep to-night. I know a café where we can sit quietly and drink wine, perhaps with cookies."

Their eating finished, Dorn accompanied his friend into the street.

"It seems as if nothing had happened," he said, as they walked through the spring night. "People are asleep as usual, and there is an odor of summer in the dark."

Von Stinnes silently directed their way. After a half-hour's walk he paused in front of an ancient-looking building.

"We are in Schwabbing now," he said, "the rendezvous of the Welt Anschauers. I think this place is still open."

He led the way through a narrow court and entered a large, dimly-lighted room. Blank white walls stared at them. Von Stinnes picked out a table in a corner and orderd two flasks of wine from a stout woman with a large wooden ring of keys at her black waist.

They drank in silence. Dorn observed an unusual air about his friend. He thought of Mathilde's suspicions, and smiled. Yet there was something inexplicable about von Stinnes. There had been from the first.

"Inexplicable because he is . . . nothing," Dorn thought. "A chevalier of excitements, a Don Quixote of disillusion. . . ."

"You are thinking of me," the baron smiled over his wine-glass, "as I am thinking of you. Here's to our unimportant healths, Erik."

Dorn swallowed more wine. To be called Erik by his friend pleased him. He looked inquiringly at the humorous eyes of the man, and spoke:

"You are cut after my pattern."

The Baron nodded.

"Only I have had more opportunities to exercise the pattern," he replied. "For the pattern, dear friend, is scoundrelism. And I, God bless me . . ." He paused and gestured as if in a hopelessness of words.

"There is quality as well as quantity in scoundrelism," Dorn suggested. He was thinking without emotion of Anna.

"I have decided to remain in Munich," von

Stinnes spoke, "and that means that I will die here."

"The day's melodrama has gone to your head," Dorn laughed.

"No. There are people in Munich who know me quite well—too well. And among their virtues they number a desire for my death. In Berlin it is otherwise. Then too, this business of to-day can't last. It is already topheavy with thinkers, and will eventually evaporate in a dozen executions. It may come back, though. I cannot forget the workingmen who stormed the Banhoff."

He paused and drank.

"Yes, I have decided to stay and play awhile. There will be a few weeks more. One will find extravagant diversions in Munich during the next few weeks. I am already Egelhofer's right-hand man. I will organize the Soviet army, assist in the conduct of the government, try to buy coal from Rathenau in Berlin, make speeches, compose earth-shaking proclamations, and end up smoking a cigarette in front of a Noske firing-squad. . . . Do not interrupt. I feel it is a program I owe to humanity. And in addition, I am growing weary of myself."

Dorn shook his head.

"Romantics, friend. I do not argue against them."

"I wonder," von Stinnes continued, "if you realize I am a scoundrel. I have thought at times that you did, because of the way you smile when I talk."

"Scoundrels are creatures I do not like. And I like you. Ergo, you are not a scoundrel, von Stinnes."

The Baron laughed.

"A convenient philosophy, Erik. Well, I was in the German intelligence and worked in Paris during the second year of the war. Prepare yourself for a confession. My secrets bore me. And a little cocotte of a countess betrayed me. It is a virtue French women have. They are not to be trusted, and love to them is something which may be improved by the execution of a lover. But there was no execution. To save my skin I entered the French intelligence—without, of course, resigning from the German. Thus I was of excellent service to the largest number. To the French I was invaluable. German positions, plans, maneuvers, at my finger tips. . . . And to the Germans, unaware of my new and lucrative connection, I was also invaluable. Again positions, plans, maneuvers. I was transferred to Italy by the French and . . . But it's a complicated narrative. I haven't it straight in my own mind yet. Do you know, I wake up at night sometimes with the rather naïve idea that I, von Stinnes, who prefer Turkish cigarettes to women, even brunettes . . . But I stammer. It is difficult to be amusing, always. I think sometimes at night that I was personally responsible for at least half the casualties of the war."

"Megalomania," said Dorn without changing his smile.

"Yes, obviously. You hit it. A distorted conscience image. Ah, the bombardments I have perfected. The hills of men I have blown up. Frenchmen, Germans, Italians. Yes, a word from me . . . I pointed the cannon straighter. . . . But disregarding the boast . . . you will admit my superiority as a scoundrel."

"It is immaterial," Dorn answered. "If you betrayed the French, you made amends by betraying the Germans, and vice versa. As for the Italians . . . I have never been in Italy."

Von Stinnes laughed.

"You do not believe me, eh?"

"You are lying only in what you do not say," Dorn laughed.

"Yes, exactly. I will go on, if it amuses you."

"It is better conversation than ususal."

"I am now with the English," von Stinnes continued. "They play a curious game outside Versailles, the English. They have entrusted me with a most delicate mission." He paused and drained his glass. "It is quite dramatic. I tell it to you because I am drunk and weary of secrets. Five years of secrets . . . until I am almost timorous of thinking even to myself . . . for fear I will betray something to myself. But—it is droll. The million marks you so gallantly carried in for Matty, they were mine, Erik." He laughed. "I gave them to Dr. Kasnilov, and a very mysterious Englishman gave them to me. . . ."

"Gifts of a million are somewhat phenomenal," Dorn murmured.

"I stole only a hundred thousand," von Stinnes went on, "which, of course, everyone expected."

"But why the English, Karl?"

"A little plan to separate Bavaria from Prussia, and help break up Middle Europe. You know feeling between the two provinces is intense. There was almost a mutiny in the second war year. And anything to help it along. To-morrow, Franz Lipp the new foreign minister of the Soviets will telegraph to Berlin recalling the Bavarian ambassador; there *is* one, you know—a figurehead. And the good Franz will announce to the world that Bavaria has declared its independence of Prussia. This will be a politic move for the Soviets as well as England. For the bourgeoisie in Bavaria dislike Prussia as much as the communists dislike her. But I bore you with intrigue. We have had our little revolution for which you must allow me to accept an honest share of credit. . . . Let us have another flask."

"An interesting story," Dorn agreed.

"You still smile, Erik?"

"More than ever."

"Ah, then truly, we are of the same pattern."

Von Stinnes stared at him sadly.

"You are my first companion in five years," he added.

"As you are mine," Dorn answered. "Here . . . to the success of all your villainies and our friendship."

"Which is not one of them," the Baron murmured. "You believe me?"

"Of course."

"Ah! it is almost a sensation to be believed . . . for speaking the truth. I feel as if I have committed some exotic sin. Yes, confession is good for the soul."

"Shall we go back to the hotel?"

The Baron leaned forward and grasped Dorn's hand feverishly.

"I do not wish to joke any more," he whispered. "I have told you the truth. And you still smile at me. You are a curious man. I have for long sat like an exile surrounded by my villainies and smiling alone at the world. But it is impossible to live alone, to become someone whom nobody knows, whom trusting people mistake for someone else. I have wanted to be known as I am . . . but have been afraid. Ah! I am very drunk . . . for you seem still amused."

Dorn squeezed his hand.

"Yes, you are my first friend," he said. The Baron followed him to his feet. They were silent on the way to the hotel. Von Stinnes walked with his arm linked in Dorn's. Before the latter's room he halted.

"Good night, sweet prince," he mumbled drowsily, "and may angels guard thy sleep."

Alone, he moved unsteadily down the hall.

Mathilde was gone. Moving about the room, Dorn found a note left for him. He read:

"A man was here asking for you. An American officer. I met him in the lobby and mentioned there was an American here and he asked your name. When I told him he seemed to be excited. He said his name is Captain Hazlitt and he is in the courier service on his way from Paris to Vienna. I do not like him. Please be careful.

"MATHILDE DOHMANN."

Chapter Nine

IN the days that followed Dorn sought to interest himself in the details of the situation. The thing buzzed and gyrated about him, tiring his thought with its innumerable surfaces. Revolution. A new state. New flags and new slogans.

"I can't admire it," he explained to Mathilde at the end of the first week, "because its grotesqueries makes me laugh. And I cannot laugh at it because its intensity saddens me. To observe the business sanely is to come to as many conclusions as there are words."

Mathilde had recovered some of her enthusiasm. But the mania that had illuminated her thought was gone. She spoke and worked eagerly through the days, moving from department to department, helping to establish some of the innumerable stenographic archives the endless stream of soviet pronouncements and orders were beginning to require. But at night her listlessness returned.

"There is doubt in you too," Dorn smiled at her. "I am sorry for that. It has been the same with so many others. They have, alas! become reasonable. And to become reasonable . . . Well, revolution does not thrive on reason. It needs something more active. You, Mathilde, were a revolutionist in Berlin. Now you are a stenographer. Alas! one collapses under a load of dream and finds one's self in an uninteresting Utopia, if that means anything. Epigrams lie around the street corners of Munich waiting new text-books."

They were walking idly toward the café von Stinnes had appointed as a rendezvous. It was late and the dark streets were deserted. The shops had been closed all week. The Revolution was struggling in poorly ventilated council-rooms with problems of economics. Beyond the persistent rumors that the city, cut off from the fields, would starve in another two days and that the legendary armies of Hoffmann were within a stone's throw of the Hofbrau House, there was little excitement. "My employers," von Stinnes had explained on the fourth day, "are waiting to see if the Soviet can stand against the Noske armies from Prussia. The armies will arrive in a few weeks. If the Soviet can defeat them and thus establish its authentic independence, my employers in Versailles will then finance the Bavarian bourgeoisie and assist in the overthrow of the Communists. On the one condition, of course, that the bourgeoisie maintain Bavaria as an independent nation. And this the bourgeoisie are not at all averse to doing. It sounds preposterous, doesn't it? You smile. But all intrigue is preposterous, even when most successful."

"I quite believe," Dorn had answered. "I've long been convinced that intrigue is nothing more than the fantastic imbecilities unimaginative men palm off on one another for cleverness."

Now, walking with Mathilde, Dorn felt an inclination to rid himself of the week's political preoccupation. Mathilde was beginning to have a sentimental influence upon him.

"Perhaps if she loved me something would come back," he thought. "Anyway it would be nice to feel a woman in love with me again."

An innocuous sadness sat comfortably in his heart. Later he would embrace her. Kiss . . . watch her undress. Things that would mean nothing. . . . But they might help waste time, and perhaps give him another glimpse of . . . He paused in his thought and felt a dizziness enter his silence. Words spun. "The face of stars," he murmured under his breath, and laughed as Mathilde looked inquiringly up at him.

The café was deserted. Von Stinnes, alone in a booth, called "Hello" to them as they entered.

"We have the place almost to ourselves," he said. "There are some people in the other room."

He looked affectionately at the two as they sat down, and added, "How goes the courtship?"

"Gravely and with cautious cynicism," Dorn answered. "We find it difficult to overcome our sanities."

He smiled at the girl and covered her hand with his. Her eyes regarded him luminously. They sat eating their late meal, von Stinnes chatting of the latest developments. . . . A mob of communist workingmen had attacked the poet Muhsam while he was unburdening himself of proletarian oratory in the Schiller Square.

"They chased him for two blocks into the Palais," the Baron smiled, "and he lost his hat. And perhaps his portfolio. They are beginning to distrust the poets. They want something besides revolutionary Iambics now. Muhsam, however, is content. He received a postal card this afternoon with a skull and cross-bones drawn on it informing him he would be assassinated Friday at 3 P.M. It was signed by 'The Society for the Abolition of Monstrosities.' He is having it done into an expressionist placard and it will undoubtedly restore his standing with the Council of Ten. Franz Lipp, the foreign minister, you know, has ordered all the telephones taken out of the foreign office building. It's an old failing of his—a phobia against telephones. They send him into fits when they ring. He has incidentally offered to sign a separate peace with the Entente. A crafty move, but premature. And the burghers have been ordered under pain of death to surrender all firearms within twenty-four hours."

The talk ran on. Mathilde, feigning sleep, placed her head on Dorn's shoulder.

"You play with the little one," whispered von Stinnes. "She is in love."

Dorn placed his arm around her and smiled at her half-opened eyes.

A man, walking unsteadily across the empty café, stopped in front of the booth.

"I've been looking for you," he said. "You don't remember me, eh?"

Dorn looked up. An American uniform. An excited face.

"My name's Hazlitt. Come out here."

Von Stinnes leveled his monocle witheringly upon the interloper and murmured an aside, "He's drunk. . . ."

Dorn stood up.

"Yes, I remember you now," he said. The man's tone had oppressed him. "What do you want?"

He detached himself from Mathilde and stepped into the room. Hazlitt stared at him.

"I owe you something," he spoke slowly. "Come out here."

Watching the man as he approached, Dorn became aware of a rage in himself. His muscles had tightened and a nervousness was shaking in his words. The man was a stranger, yet there was an uncomfortable intimacy in his eyes.

Hazlitt stood breathing heavily. This was Erik Dorn—the man who had had Rachel. Wine swept a flame through his thought. God! this was the man. She was gone, but this was the man. Shoot him down like a dog! Shoot him down! Kill the grin of him. He'd pay. He'd killed something. Shoot him down! There was a gun under his coat—army revolver. Better than shooting Germans. This was the man.

"You're going to pay for it," he spoke. "Go on, say something."

Dorn's rage hesitated. A mistake. What the devil was up?

"Oh, you've forgotten her," Hazlitt whispered. Shoot him! Voices inside demanded wildly that he shoot. Not talk, but kill.

"Rachel," he cried suddenly. His eyes stopped seeing.

Dorn jumped for the gun that had appeared and caught his arm in time. Rachel—then this was something about Rachel? Hazlitt . . . Rachel. What? A fight over Rachel? Rachel gone, dead for always. Get the gun away, though. . . .

They were stumbling across the room, twisting and locked together. He saw von Stinnes rise, stand undecided. Mathilde's face, like something shooting by outside a car window. And a strong man trying to kill him . . . for Rachel. A Galahad for Rachel.

His thought faded into a rage. A curse as the man grabbed at his throat. The gun was still in the air. His wrist was beginning to ache from struggling with the thing. This was part of the idiocy of things. But he must look out. Perhaps only a moment more to live. The man was weeping. Mumbling . . . "you made a fool out of her . . . You dirty. . . ."

As they continued their stumbling and clutching, a fury entered Dorn. He became aware of eyes blazing against him—drunken, furious eyes that were weeping. With a violent lunge he twisted the gun out of the man's hand. There was an instant of silence and the man came hurling against him.

Dorn fired. Down . . . "my head . . ." He lay still. The body of Hazlitt sprawled over him. For a moment the two men remained embraced on the floor. Then the body of Hazlitt rolled slowly from on top. It fell on its back—a dead face covered with blood staring emptily at the ceiling.

Dorn, with the edge of an iron table foot embedded in his head, lay breathing unevenly, his eyes closed.

Chapter Ten

THE blinds were drawn. Cheering drifted in through the open window. Mathilde sat in a chair. She was watching him.

"Hello!" he murmured. "What's up?"

"Erik . . ."

She fell to her knees beside the bed and began to weep. He lay quietly listening to her. Bandages around his head. A lunatic with a gun. Yes. Rachel. The man had been in love with Rachel. Pains like noises in his ears.

"You mustn't talk. . . ."

"I'm all right. Where's von Stinnes?"

"'Shh. . . ."

He smiled feebly. She was holding his hand, still weeping. A memory returned vividly. A man with blazing eyes. He had lost his temper. But there had been something more than that. Two imbeciles fighting over a thing that had died for both of them. Clowns at each other's throat. A background unfolded itself. Against it he lay watching the two men. Here was something like a quaint old print with a title, "Fate. . . ."

"Bumped my head," he murmured. But another thought persisted. It moved through the pain in his skull, unable to straighten itself into lines of words. It was something about fighting for Rachel. He would ask questions.

"What happened, Mathilde? Where'd he go?"

"You mean the man? 'Shh. . . . Don't talk now."

"Come, don't be silly."

The thinness of his voice surprised him.

"What became of the fool?"

"He's dead."

"Dead?"

"Yes, you shot him. Now be quiet."

"Good God, so I did. I remember. When he jumped at me."

A sinking feeling almost drifted him away. He felt as if he had become hungry. The man was dead. . . . "I killed him. Well . . . what of it?"

He opened his eyes and looked at the room. It was day—afternoon, perhaps.

"The doctor says you'll be all right in a few days. But you must be quiet. . . ."

"Von Stinnes," he murmured. "There'll be trouble. Call him, will you?"

Mathilde turned away. Now the pain was less. He could hear cheering outside. A demonstration. Workingmen marching under new flags.

"Von Stinnes is under arrest, Erik."

"What for? A new government?" What a crazy business.

"No. Don't talk, please. Later. . . ."

He was too weak to sit up.

"Things will have to be straightened out," he muttered. "The fool was an American officer. There'll be trouble."

"No, don't worry. Von Stinnes has fixed things."

His eyes grew heavy and closed. Sleep . . . and let things, fixed or unfixed, go to the devil.

When he awoke again the room was lighted. Mathilde, standing by the window, turned as he stirred.

"Are you awake?"

"Yes, and hungry."

She brought a tray to his bed. He raised himself carefully, his head unbearably heavy. Mathilde watched him with wide eyes as he sipped some broth.

"What did they arrest the Baron for?" he asked.

She waited till he had finished, and cleared the bed, sitting down on the edge. Her face lowered toward him till her lips touched and kissed him.

"For murder," she whispered. Another kiss. "Now you must be quiet and I'll tell you. He gave himself up when the police came. We carried you out first. And then I left him."

"But," Dorn looked bewilderedly into the eyes of the girl.

"It was easier for him than for you. They would take you away for trial to America. But he will be tried here. And he will come out all right. Don't worry. We thought your skull was fractured, but the doctor says it was only a hard blow."

She lowered her head beside him on the pillow and whispered, "I love you! Poor Erik! He is defenseless—with a broken head."

"You are kind," he answered; "von Stinnes, too. But we must set matters right. . . ."

"No, no, be still!"

He grew silent. It was night again. In the morning he would be strong enough to get up. A misty calm, the pain almost gone, veins throbbing and a little split in his thought . . . but no more.

"I will sleep by you," Mathilde spoke. She stood up and removed her waist and shoes. He watched her with interest. Another woman curiously like Anna, like Rachel—like the two creatures in Paris. Shoulders suddenly bare. Possessive, unashamed gestures. . . . She lay down beside him with a sigh.

"Poor Erik! I take advantage of a broken head."

"No," he smiled.

They lay motionless, her head touching his shoulder timidly.

"I could live with you forever and be happy," she whispered.

"We will see about forever—when it comes."

"Do you like me—perhaps—now?"

He would have preferred her silent. Silence at least was an effortless lie. To make love was preposterous. How many times had he said, "I love you?" Too many. But she was young and it would sound pretty in her ears.

"Mathilde, dear one."

Her arm trembled across his body.

It was difficult, but he would say it. . . . "Yes, in an odd sort of way, Mathilde, I love you. . . ."

"Ah! you are only being polite—because I have fed you broth."

"No. As much as I can love anything. . . ."

"Later, Erik. 'Shh! Sleep if you can. Oh, I am shameless."

She had moved against him. He thought with a smile, "What an original way of nursing a broken head!"

Later, tired with a renewed effort to straighten out words about the fool and Rachel and himself, he closed his eys. Mathilde was still awake.

"I'll see von Stinnes in the morning," he murmured drowsily. "Von Stinnes . . . a gallant friend. . . ."

. . . Someone knocking on the door aroused him. Dawn was in the room.

"Matty," he called. She slept. He found himself able to rise and his legs carried him unsteadily to the door. A tall marine, outside.

"Herr Erik Dorn?"

Dorn nodded dizzily.

The man went on in German. "I come from Stinnes. I have a letter for you."

He took the letter from his hand and moved hurriedly to a chair.

"Thanks," vaguely. The marine saluted and walked off. Mathilde had awakened.

"What are you doing?"

She slipped out of bed and hurried to him.

"A letter," he answered. He allowed her to help him back to his pillow. Reclining again, his dizziness grew less.

"I'll read it for you," she said.

"No. Von Stinnes. . . ."

"It may be important."

"I'll be able to read in a moment."

She shook her head and slipped the envelope from his weakening fingers.

"I know about von Stinnes. Don't be afraid. May I?"

He nodded and she began to read:

"Dear Erik Dorn:

"I write this at night, and to-morrow I will be ended. You must not misunderstand what I do. It is a business long delayed. But I have made a full confesssion in writing for the Entente commission—ten closely written pages. A masterpiece, if I have to boast myself. And in order to avoid the anti-climax which your sense of honor would undoubtedly precipitate, I will put a period to it in an hour. A trigger pulled, and the nobility of my sad country loses another of its shining lights. I am overawed by the quaint justice of life. I end a career of villainy with a final lie. It would really be impossible for me to die telling a truth. The devil himself would appear and protest. But with a lie on my lips, it is easy. Indeed, somehow, natural. But I pose—a male Magdalene in tears. Do not misunderstand—too much. You are my friend, and I would like to live a while longer that we might amuse ourselves together. You have been an education. I find myself even now on this auspicious midnight writing with your words. But I mistrust you, friend. You would deny me this delicate martyrdom if I lived. For you are at bottom lamentably honorable. So now, as you read this, I am dead (a sentence out of Marie Corelli) and the situation is beyond adjustment. Please accept my service as gracefully as it is rendered. The confession, as I said, is a masterpiece. It would please my vanity if sometime you could read it. For in this, my last lie, I have extended myself. Dear friend, there is a certain awe which I cannot overcome—for the drama, or comedy, finishes too perfectly. You once called me a Don Quixote of disillusion. And now, perhaps, I will inspire a few new phrases. Let them be poignant, but above all graceful. I would have for my epitaph your smile and the whimsical irony of your comment. Better this than the hand-rubbing grunt of the firing-squad returning to barracks after its labors. Alas! that I will not be near you to hear it. But perhaps there will come to me as I submit myself to the opening tortures of

hell, an echo of your words. And this will bring
me a smile with which to cheat the devil. I bequeathe to you my silver cigarette-case. You are
my brother and I say good-bye to you.
"KARL VON STINNES."

"No postscript?" Dorn asked softly.

Mathilde shook her head. There was silence.

"Will you find out about him, please?" he whispered.

The girl dressed herself quickly and left the room without speaking. Alone, Dorn lay with the letter in his hand.

He spoke aloud after minutes, as if addressing someone invisible.

"I have no phrases, dear friend. Let my tears be an epigram."

PART FIVE

SILENCE

Chapter One

THE sea swarmed under the night. A moon road floated on the long dark swells. From the deck of the throbbing ship Dorn looked steadily toward the circle of moving water. In the salon, the ship's orchestra was playing. A rollicking sound of music drifted away into the dark monotone of the sea.

A romantic mood. A chair on an upper deck. Stars and a moon road over the sea. Better to sit mumbling to himself than join in the chatter of the cabin. The gayly lighted salon alive with laughter, music, and voices touched his ears—a tiny music-box tinkling valiantly through the dark sweep of endless yesterdays, endless to-morrows that sighed out of the hidden water. The night was an old yesterday, the sea an old to-morrow.

A sadness in his heart that kept him from smiling, a strange comedy of words in his thought, a harlequin with the night sitting on his lap. There were things to remember. There were memories. Unnecessary to think. Words formed themselves into phrases. Phrases made dim pictures as if the past was struggling fitfully to remain somehow alive. . . . His good-bye to Mathilde. And long, stupid weeks in Berlin. The girl had been absurd. Absurd, an impulsive little shrew. With demands. Four months of Mathilde. Unsuspected variants of boredom. Clothed in her unrelenting love like an Indian in full war dress. Yet to part with her had made him sad.

The sea rolled mystically away from his eyes.

"An old pattern," his thought murmured, "holding eternities. And the little music keeps tinkling downstairs. A butterfly of sound in the night. Like a miniature of all living. Ah, I'm growing sentimental. Sitting holding hands with the sea. She was sad when I left her. What of it? Von Stinnes. Dear friend! No sadness there. He was right. New phrases, graceful emotions. What an artist! But Warren couldn't write the story. It has to be played by a hurdy-gurdy on a guillotine."

He let his words wander gropingly over the water until a silence entered him. Thus life wandered away. The sea beat time to the passing of ships, changing ships. But always the same beat. It was the constancy of the stars that saddened him. September stars. The stars were yesterdays. Yes, unchanging spaces, unchanging yesterdays, and a ship's orchestra dropping little valses into the dark sea. He opened a silver cigarette-case—an heirloom with a crest on it. Von Stinnes again. Curious how he remembered him—a memory neither sad nor merry—but final like the sea. A phantom of word and incident that bowed with an enchanting irony out of an

April day. The other, the fool with the gun. . . .
Good God, he was a murderer! He smiled. Von
Stinnes, a melancholy Pierrot doffing his hat with
a gallant snicker to the moon. Hazlitt, a pantaloon. Yet tragic. Yes, there was something in
the café that night—two men hurling themselves
drunkenly against the taunting emptiness of life.
The rage had come because he had remembered
Rachel. A sudden mysterious remembering. A
remembering that she was gone. It had torn for
a moment at his heart, shouted in his ears and
driven him mad.

Something had taken Rachel out of him. Time
had eaten her image out of him. He had remembered this in the café. But why had he fired at
the stranger? Because the man's eyes blazed.
Because he had become for an instant an intolerable comrade.

"We fought each other for what someone else
had done to us," Dorn murmured. "Not Rachel
but someone that couldn't be touched. Absurd!"
Hazlitt slipped like a shadow out of his mind—
an unanswered question.

The throbbing ship with its tinkling orchestra,
its laughing, chattering faces, was carrying him
home over a dark sea. At night he sat alone
watching the circle of water. Four vanished
nights. Four more nights. He sighed. The
sadness that lay in his heart desired to talk to him.
He struggled to change his thinking. Ideas that
were new to him arose at night on the ship.

"Not now," he whispered. He was postponing something. But the night and the rolling sea were swallowing his resistance. Words that would tell him the pain in his heart waited for him. . . . "Anna. Dear God, Anna! It's that. But why Anna now? It was easy before."

Words of Anna waited for him. He stared into the dark.

"I want her. I must go back to her. Anna, forgive me!"

A murmur that the darkness might understand. The long rolling sea listened automatically. Weak fool! Yet he felt better. He could think now without hiding from words that waited.

His heart wept in silence. The unbidden ones came. . . . Anna—standing looking at him. A despair, a death in her face. Something tearing itself out of her. What pain! But no sound. An agony deeper than sound in her eyes. He trembled at the memory. The crucified happy one. . . .

Dear God, would he always have to remember now? Other pictures were gone. They had drifted away leaving little phrases dragging in his thought. Now Anna had found him. Not a phantom, but the thing as he had left it, without a detail gone. The gesture of her agony intact. His thought shifted vainly away. He knew she was standing as he had left her—horribly inanimate—and he must go back. He would hold her in his arms, kiss her lips, kneel before her weeping for forgiveness. Ah! he would be kind. At night he would sit holding her head in his arms, stroking her hair; whispering, "Forget . . . forget! A year or two of madness—gone forever. But years now waitng for us. New years. Everything is gone but us. That brought me back. Mists blew away. Dear Anna, I love you."

He was making love to Anna, his wife. A droll finale. Tears came in his eyes. There lay happiness. She would move again. The rigid figure that he had left behind and that was waiting rigidly, would smile again. He plunged desperately into the dream of words to be. The music from the salon had ended. Better, silence. Nothing to remind one of the fugitive tinkle of life. A dark, interminable sea, a moon road, a sigh of rolling water and a ship throbbing in the night.

"Dear Anna, I love you." And she would smile, her white face and eyes that were constant as the stars. Constant, eternal. Love that was no mystery but a caress of sea nights. Forgive him. And her sorrow would heal under his fingers. It would end all right. The two years— the halloo of strange sterile things—buried under the smile of her eyes . . . deep, sorrowful, beautiful. Words to be. "Anna we will grow old together, holding to each other and smiling; lovers whom the years make always younger." Words that were to heal the strange sadness that had come to him and start a dead figure into life.

He stood up and walked to the rail, staring into the churn of water underneath.

"It's slow," he murmured. "Four more days."

Anna's love would hide the world from him. But a fear loosened his heart. The smell of sea whirled in his veins.

"Perhaps," he thought dreamily, "perhaps there will be nothing. She will say no."

He hesitated, straightened with a sigh.

"A wife deserter, a seducer, a murderer. I mustn't expect too much, eh, von Stinnes?"

He smiled at the night. The sound of the Baron's name seemed to bring a strength into him. He walked toward his berth, his head unnecessarily high, smoking at his cigarette and humming a tune remembered from the Munich cafés.

Chapter Two

THERE were people in New York who came to Erik Dorn and said: "Tell us about Europe. And Germany. Is it really true that . . ." As if there were some inner revelation—a few precious phrases of undistilled truth that the correspondent of the *New Opinion* had seen fit to withhold from his communications.

The skyscrapers were intact. Windows shot into the air. Streets bubbled with people. A useless sky clung tenaciously to its position above the roof-gardens. The scene was amiable. Dorn spent a day congratulating himself upon the genius of his homeland. He felt a pride in the unbearable confusion of architecture and traffic.

But in the nine months of his absence there had been a change; or at least a change seemed to have occurred. Perhaps he had brought the change with him. It was evident that the Niagara of news pouring out of Europe into the press and periodicals of the day had inundated the provincialism of his countrymen. People were floundering about in a daze of facts—groping ludicrously through labyrinths of information.

It had been easy during the war. Democracy-Autocracy; a tableau to look at. Thought had been unnecessary. In fact, the popular intelligence had legislated against it. The tableau was enough—a sublimated symbol of the little papier-maché rigmarole of their daily lives, the immemorial spectacle of Good and Evil at death grips, limelighted for a moment by the cannon in France. The unreason and imbecility of the mob crowned themselves. Thought became *lèse majesté*.

Dorn returned to find the tableau had suffered an explosion. It had for some mysterious reason glibly identified as reaction burst into fragments and vanished in a skyrocket chaos. Shantung, Poland, little nations, pogroms, plebiscites, Ireland, steel strikes, red armies, Fourteen Points, The Truth About This, The Real Story of That, the League of Nations, the riots in Berlin, in Dublin, Milan, Paris, London, Chicago; secret treaties, pacts, betrayals, Kolchak—an incomprehensible muddle of newspaper headlines shrieked from morning to morning and said nothing. The distracted mob become privy for the moment to the vast biological disorder eternally existent under its nose, snorted, yelped, and shook indignant sawdust out of its ears.

In vain the editorial Jabberwocks came galloping daily down the slopes of Sinai bearing new tablets written in fire. The original and only genuine tableau was gone. The starry heavens which concealed the Deity Himself had become a junkpile full of its fragments.

"In the temporary collapse of the banalities

that conceal the world from their eyes," thought Dorn, "they're trying to figure out what's really what around them—and making a rather humorous mess of it."

He went about for several days dining with friends, conferring with Edwards and the directors of the *New Opinion*, and slowly shaping his "experiences abroad" into phonograph records that played themselves automatically under the needles of questions.

At night, he amused himself with reading the radical and conservative periodicals, his own magazine among them.

"The thing isn't confined to the bloated capitalists alone," he laughed one afternoon while sitting with Warren Lockwood in the latter's rooms. "The radicals are up a tree and the conservatives down a cellar. What do you make of it, Warren?"

"I haven't paid much attention to it," the novelist smiled. "I've been busy on a book. What's all this stuff about Germany, anyway? I read some things of yours but I can't figure it out."

Dorn exploded with another laugh.

"You're all a pack of simpletons and bounders, still moist behind the ears, Warren. The whole lot of you. I've been in New York three days and I've begun to feel that there isn't a remotely intelligent human animal in the place. I'm going to retreat inland. In Chicago, at least, people know enough to keep their mouths shut. I'll tell you what the trouble is in a nutshell. People want things straight again. They want black and white so's they can all mass on the white side and make faces at the evil-doers who prefer the black. They don't want facts, diagnosis, theories, interpretations, reports. They want somebody to stand up and announce in a loud, clear voice, 'Tweedledum is wrong. Tweedledee is right, everything else to the contrary is Poppycock.' Thus they'd be able to put an end to their own thinking and bury themselves in their own little alleys and be happy again. You know as well as I, it makes them miserable to think. Restless, irritable, indignant. It's like having bites—the more they're scratched the worse they itch. It's the war, of course. The war has been a failure. The race has caught itself red-handed in a lie. Now everybody is running around trying to confess to everybody else that what he said in the past was a lie and that the real truth is as follows. And there's where the trouble begins. There ain't no such animal."

"I see," said Lockwood, smiling.

"Yes, you do," Dorn grinned. "You don't see anything. The trouble is . . . oh, well, the trouble is as I said that the human race is out in the open where it can get a good look at itself. The war raised a curtain. . . ."

"What about the radicals, though? They seem to be saying something definite?"

"Yes, shooting one another down by the thousands in Berlin—as they will some day in New

York. Yes, the radicals are definite enough. . . . The revolution rumbling away in Germany isn't a standup fight between Capital and Labor. It's Radical *versus* Radical. Just as the war was Imperialist *versus* Imperialist. One of the outstanding lessons of the last decade is the fact that the world's natural enemies haven't yet had a chance at each other, being too busy murdering among themselves. It's coming, though. Another tableau. All this hysteria and uncertainty will gradually simmer down into another right-and-wrong issue—with life boiling away as always under a black and white surface."

"Do you think we're going to go red here?" Lockwood asked pensively.

"It'll take a little time," Dorn went on. He had become used to reciting his answers in the manner of a schoolmaster. "But it's bound to happen. Bolshevism is a logical evolution of democracy—another step downward in the descent of the individual. Until the arrival of Lenine and Trotzky on the field, there's no question but what American Democracy was the most atrocious insult leveled at the intelligence of the race by its inferiors. Bolshevism goes us one better, however. And just as soon as our lowest types, meaning the majority of our politicians, thinkers, and writers, get to realizing that bolshevism isn't a Red Terror with a bomb in one hand and a dagger in the other, but a state of society surpassing even their own in points of weakness and abnormal silliness, they'll start arresting everybody who isn't a bolshevist. Capital will put up a fight, but capital is already doomed in this country. It isn't respected for its strength, vision, and creative powers. It is tolerated to-day for no other reason than that it has cornered the platitude market. I'm telling you, Warren, that when we get it drummed into our heads that bolshevism isn't strong and powerful, but weaker, more prohibitive, more sentimental, more politically inefficient, and generally worse than our own government, we'll have a dictator of the proletaire in Washington within a week."

Lockwood sighed unhappily and lighted a pipe.

"If you were talking about men and women maybe I could join you," he answered. "But I got a hunch you're just another one of those newspaper Neds. The woods are full of smart alecks like you and they make me kind of tired, because I never can figure out what they're talking about. And I'll be damned if they know themselves. They think in big hunks and keep a lot of words floating in the air. . . . What old Carl calls 'Blaa . . . blaa. . . .'"

The two friends sat regarding each other critically. Dorn nodded after a pause.

"You're right," he smiled. "I'm part of the blaa-blaa. I heard them blaa-blaa with guns in Munich one night. And up in the Baltic. You're right. Anything one says about absurdity becomes absurd itself. And talking about the human race in chunks is necessarily talking absurdly. Tell me about that fellow Tesla."

"They deported him to Rooshia," Lockwood answered. "There was quite a romance about the girl. That was your girl, wasn't it?"

"Yes, Rachel. She wouldn't tag along, eh?"

"No. I suppose they wouldn't let her. I don't know. There was a lot of stuff in the newspapers."

The novelist seemed to hesitate on the brink of further information. His friend smiled understandingly.

"It doesn't matter, Warren. Go ahead. Shoot."

"Cured, eh?"

"No—dead."

Lockwood nodded sagely, his mouth half open as if his words were staring at Dorn.

"Well, there isn't much I know. I met a little girl the other day—Mary James; know her?"

"Yes."

"She was quite excited. She told me something about an artist that used to hang around Tesla. It seems that he kidnapped her and carted her to Chicago. This James girl was all upset."

An interruption in the person of Edwards the editor occurred. The talk lapsed once more into world problems with Lockwood listening, skeptically open-mouthed.

Late in the evening Edwards suddenly declared, "You're making a big mistake leaving New York,

Erik. You've got a market now. Your stuff went big."

"I'm through," Dorn answered. He arose and took his hat. "I'm leaving for Chicago to-morrow."

He paused, smiling at Lockwood.

"I'm going home."

The novelist nodded sagely and murmured, "Uh-huh. Well, good-night."

Making his way slowly through the night crowds and electrophobia of lower Manhattan, Dorn felt peacefully out of place. His thought had become: "I want to get back to where I was." In the midst of the mechanical carnival of Broadway he caught a memory of himself walking to work with a stream of faces—of a sardonic Erik Dorn to whom the street was a pattern; to whom the mysteries tugging at heels that scratched the pavements were the amusing variants of nothing.

Chapter Three

"EDDY."
"Yes, dear."
"I have some news for you."
The round, smiling face of Eddy Meredith that refused to change with age, beamed at Anna.
"Erik's back."
The beam hesitated.
"He wrote. He's coming to see me."
"Anna. . . ."
"Yes, dear, I know. It sort of frightens me, too. But," she laughed quietly, "there is nothing to be frightened about. He didn't give any address or I would have written him telling him."
"He must know you're divorced," Meredith spoke nervously.
"I don't know if he does, Eddy."
She reached her hand out and placed it over his, her eyes glancing at the figure of Isaac Dorn. He was asleep in a chair.
"Please, dearest, don't worry," she whispered.
"It'll be hard for you."
Meredith's face acquired an abnormal expression.
"Maybe you'll feel different." He sighed, and Anna shook her head. "When's he coming?"

"To-morrow night."

"Did he say anything in the letter?"

She stood up and went to a desk.

"Here it is." A smile touched her lips. "He always wrote curious letters. Words and words when there was nothing to say. And a single phrase when there was something." She read from a sheet of paper— "'Dear Anna, I am coming home. Erik.'"

In the corner Isaac Dorn opened his watery eyes and stared at the ceiling.

"Are you awake, father?"

"Yes, Anna."

"Did I tell you I'd heard from Erik?"

The old man mumbled in his beard.

"He'll be out to-morrow night," she said, smiling at him. He nodded his head, stared at her, and seemed to doze off again.

"Father is failing," Anna whispered. Meredith had arisen. His face had grown blank. He walked toward the hall, saying, "I'll go now."

Anna came quickly to him. Her hands reached his shoulders and she stood regarding him intently.

"There's nothing any more, dear. It all ended long ago. Perhaps I'll be sad when I see him. But sad only for him."

Meredith smiled and spoke with an effort at lightness.

"Remember, I don't hold you to anything. I want you only to be happy. In your own way. Not in my way. And if it will mean happiness

for you to . . . for you to go back, why . . ."
He shrugged his shoulders and continued to smile with hurt eyes.

"Eddy. . . ." Her face came close to his. He hesitated until her arms closed tightly around him. He felt her warm lips cling and open.

"You've never kissed like that before, Anna." There was almost a fear in his voice.

"Because I never knew I wanted you," she whispered, "till now—till this minute; till you said about my going back."

Her face was alive with emotion. A laugh, and she was in his arms again. They stood embraced, murmuring tenderly to each other.

Later in her bedroom Anna undressed slowly. Her thoughts seemed to be quarreling with her emotions, her emotions with her thoughts. This was Erik's room—ancient torture chamber. Something still clinging to its walls and furniture. Ah, nights of agony still in the air she breathed. Her words formed themselves quietly. They came to peer into her heart—polite visitors standing on tiptoe before a closed cell that hid something.

"Is there anything?" she murmured. "No. I'm different."

She thought of the day she had come out of a grave and resumed living. It had seemed as if she must learn to walk again, to breathe, to discover anew the meanings of words. At first—listless, uncertain. Then new steps, new meanings. Her mind moved back through the year. She had wept only once—on the night of the divorce. But that was as one weeps at an old grave, even a stranger's grave. The rest had been Eddy.

"I've changed. And I've been happier in many ways."

She was talking to herself. Why? "I'm a different Anna." But why think of it? It was settled.

She lay in the bed and her eyes opened at the darkness. Here was where she had lain when she had died. Each night, new deaths. Here the lonely darkness that had once choked her, torn at her eyes and made her scream aloud with pain. Things on the other side of a grave. Memories become alien. Things of long ago, when the whisper of the dark came like an insanity into her brain. "Erik gone! Erik gone! Gone!" A word that beat at her until she died—to awake in the morning and stumble once more through a day.

Now she regarded the dark quietly. Black. It had no shape. It lay everywhere about her. But it did not burn nor choke. A peaceful, harmless dark that could only whisper as if it were asking something. What was it asking? Long arms of night reaching out for something. But there was nothing to give, even if she wanted to. Not even tears. Nothing to give, even though it whispered for alms. Whispered, "Erik . . . Erik!" But there was no little memory. No big memory. Dead. Torn out of her. So the dark whispered to a dead thing in her that did not stir. A smile like a tired little gesture passed over her. "Poor Erik, poor Erik!" she murmured. "He must be thinking things that are no more."

She grew chill for an instant. . . . The memory of agonies, of the screams her love had uttered as it died.

"Poor Erik!"

She buried her cool cheek restlessly in the pillow.

Chapter Four

EVERYTHING the same as it had been. As if he had stepped out of the office for a walk around the block and come back. But a sameness that had lost its familiarity. Old furniture, old faces, intensely a part of his consciousness, yet grown strange. It was like forgetting suddenly the name of a life-long friend.

His entrance created a stir of excitement. He had spent the preceding two days arranging with the chief for his return. Barring the Nietzschean who had functioned in his absence, none had expected him.

He pushed open the swinging door with an old gesture, and walked to his desk. Here he sat fumbling casually with proofs and the contents of pigeonholes. An old routine saying, "Pick me up." Familiar trifles rebuked him. The staff sauntered up one by one to greet him. Crowley, Mortinson, Sweeney.

"Well, glad to see you back. We've sure missed you around here."

Handshakes, smiles, embarrassed questions. A few strange faces to be resented and ignored. A strange locker arrangement in a corner to be frowned at. But the rest of it familiar, poignant—

a world where he belonged, but that somehow did not seem to fit as snugly as once. Handshakes in the hall. A faint cheer in the composing-room as he sauntered for the first time to the stone. Slaps on the back. Busy men pausing to look at him with suddenly lighted faces. "Well, Mr. Dorn, greetings! How are ye? You're looking fine. . . ."

His world. It was the same, only now he was conscious of it. Before he had sat in its midst unaware of more than a detail here, a gesture there. Now he seemed to be looking down from an airplane—a strange bird's-eye view of things unstrange.

He returned to his desk. The scene again reached out to embrace him. Familiar colored walls, familiar chatter and flurry of the afternoon edition going to press. He felt its embrace and yet remained outside it. There were things in him now that could never be a part of the unchanging old shop.

During a lull in the forenoon he leaned back in his chair and stared into the pigeonholes. Memories like the unfocused images of a dream one remembers in the morning jumbled in his thought. The scene around him made things he recalled seem unreal. And the things he recalled made the scene around him seem unreal. He tried to divert himself by remembering definitely. . . . "We lay in a moon-lighted room and I whispered to her: 'You have given me wings.' I held a gun and pulled the trigger as he jumped at me. . . . Then

Erik Dorn 391

von Stinnes took the blame. . . . There's a restaurant in Kurfursten Damm where Mathilde and I . . . What a night in Munich! . . . at the Banhoff. What do I remember most? Let me see. . . . Yes . . . there was a note pinned on the blanket saying she was gone and I . . . But there's something else. What? Let me see. . . ."

He tried to evoke clearer pictures. But the sentences that passed through his mind seemed sterile, impotent. The past, set in motion by his effort, evaded him. Its details blurred like the spokes of a swiftly turning wheel. He smiled.

"A sinner's darkest punishment is forgetting his sins," he murmured to himself. He thought of the evening before him. "Better not think of that. Read proofs." He had deferred his meeting with Anna until he should be able to come to her from his desk in the office.

As the day passed an impatience seized him. The unfinished event brought a fear with it. . . . "I must put it out of my mind until to-night." But it remained and grew.

In the afternoon he sat for an hour talking to Crowley and Mortinson. He listened to them chuckle at his anecdotes. Their faces beaming with affectionate interest seemed nevertheless to say, "All this is interesting, but not very important. Not as important as sitting in the office here and sending the paper to press day after day."

The words he was uttering bored him. He had heard them too often. Yet he kept on talking, trying to bury his impatience and fear in the sound of his voice. His anecdotes were no longer memories. They seemed to have become complete in themselves, related to nothing that had ever happened. He wondered as he talked if he were lying. These things he was saying were somehow improvisations—committed to memory. He kept on talking, eagerly, amusingly.

The afternoon passed. A walk through familiar streets and it was time for dinner.

"I'm not hungry. I'll eat, though."

Yes, the evening ahead was important—very important. That accounted for the tedium of the day. But it would be dark soon. There would be a to-morrow. There had been other important evenings. It was not necessary to get too nervous. He had writhed before in the embrace of interminable hours, hours that seemed never to arrive. Then suddenly they came, looming, swelling into existence like oncoming locomotives that opened with a sudden rush from little discs into great roaring shapes. And once arrived they had seemed to be present forever. But suddenly the roaring shapes were little discs again. Hours died as people died—with an abrupt obliteration. Yet each new moment, like each new face, became again interminable. Time was an endlessness whose vanishing left its illusion unchanged.

But now it was night.

"At the end of this block is a house. Two doors more. I have no key. Ring the bell. God, but I'm an idiot. She'll answer the door herself. What'll I say? That's her step. Hello? No. Walk in. Naturally."

He stopped breathing. The door opened. His legs were made of whalebone. But there was a new odor in the hallway. . . . And something new here in her face. He stood looking at the woman with whom he had lived for seven years and when he said her name it sounded like that of a stranger. His features had a habit of smiling. An old habit of narrowing one of his eyes and turning up the right corner of his lips. He stood unconscious of his expression, his smile a mask that had slapped itself automatically over his face.

But they must talk. No, she had him at a disadvantage. Her silence could say everything for her. His silence could say nothing. He reached forward and took her hands.

"Anna. . . ."

She was different. A rigidness gone. When he had left her she was standing, stiffened. Now her hands were limp. Her face too, limp. Her eyes that looked at him seemed blind.

"I've come back, as you see."

That was banal. One did not talk like that to a crucified one. Her hands slipped away and she preceded him into the room. He looked to see his father, but forgot to ask a question about him. Anna was standing straight, looking straight at him. Not as if he were there, but as if she were alone with something.

"You must let me talk first, Erik."

Willingly. It was difficult to breathe and talk at the same time. He sat down as she moved into a chair opposite.

Something was happening but he couldn't tell yet. She was changed. Older or younger, hard to tell. But changed. It was confusing to look at someone and look at a different image of her. The different image was in his mind. When she talked he could tell.

"Did you know that I had gotten a divorce, Erik?"

That was it, then. She wasn't his wife any more. A sort of hocus-pocus . . . now you are my wife, now you aren't my wife.

"No, Anna."

"Four months ago."

"I was in Germany. . . ." Mathilde, von Stinnes, *es lebe die Welt Revolution*, made a circle in his head.

"Yes, I know. I'm sorry you didn't find out."

It was impossible. Something impossible was happening. Of course, he had known it would happen. But he had fooled himself. A clever thing to do. He was talking like a little boy reciting a piece from a platform.

"I've come back to you because everything but you has died. I begin with the end of what I have to say. I came back from Europe . . . because I wanted you. . . ."

She interrupted. "I wrote you a letter when I found out about her. I sent it to New York."

"I never got it."

"I'm sorry."

Quite a formal procedure thus far. A letter had miscarried. One could blame the mails for that. And a divorce. Yes, that was formal too . . . "whereas the complainant further alleges . . ." He felt that his legs were trembling. If he spoke again his voice would be unsteady. He did not want that. But someone had to speak. Not she. She could be silent.

"Anna"—let his voice shake. Perhaps it would help matters. "You've changed. . . ."

"Yes, Erik. . . ."

"I haven't much right to ask for anything else. . . ."

Why in God's name could he think clearly and yet only talk like a blithering fool? He would pause and gather his wits. But then he would start making a speech . . . four-score and seven years ago our forefathers . . .

"I'm sorry you came, Erik. . . ."

This couldn't be Anna. He closed his mouth and stared. A dream full of noises, voices, Anna saying:

"We mustn't waste time regretting or worrying each other about things. . . . It's much too late now."

He wanted to say. "It is impossible that you do not love me because you once loved me, because we once lay in each other's arms . . . seven years." But there was no Anna to say that to. Instead, a stranger-woman. An impulse carried him away. He was kneeling beside her, burying his face in her lap. It didn't matter. There was no one to see. Perhaps her hand would move gently over his hair. No, she was sitting straight. Still alone with something. She was saying:

"I'm sorry. Please, Erik, don't."

"I love you."

"No. No! Please, let's talk. . . ."

He raised his face. It was easier now that he was crying. He wouldn't have to be grammatical . . . or finish sentences.

"I understand, Erik. I was afraid of this. For you. But you mustn't. 'Shh! it's all over."

"No, Anna. It can't be. You are still Anna."

"Yes. But different."

He stood up.

"Really, Erik," she was shaking her head and smiling without expression, "everything is over. I would rather have written it to you. I could have made it plain. But I didn't know where to reach you."

He let her talk on and stood staring. Her face was limp. There was nothing there. He was looking at a corpse. Not of her, but somehow of himself. There in her eyes he lay dead—an obliteration. He had come back to a part of him that had died. It was buried where one couldn't see, somewhere behind her eyes.

"I have nothing more to say, Erik. But you must understand what I have said. Because it means everything."

He listened, staring now at the room, remembering. They had lived together once in this room. There was something beautiful about the room. A face that held itself like a lighted lamp to his eyes. "Erik, Erik, I love you. Oh, I love you so. I would die without you. Erik, my own!" The walls and books and chairs murmured with echoes. The familiar slanting books on their shelves. The large leather chairs under the light. He must weep. The little things that were familiar—mirrors in which he saw images and words . . . a white body with copper hair fallen across its ivory; white arms clinging passionately to him; a voice, rapturous, pleading. He must weep because he had come back to a world that had died, that looked at him whispering with dead lips, "Erik, my beloved. Oh, I'm so happy . . . so happy when you kiss me . . . my dearest. . . ."

He closed his eyes as tears burned out of them. Anna in a blur. Still talking quietly. Embarrassed by his weeping. He was offering her his silence and his tears. He had never stood like this before a woman. But it was something other than a woman—an ending. As if one came upon a figure dead in a room and looked at it and said without surprise, "It is I."

"So you see, Erik, it's all over. I can't tell you how. It took a long time, but it seemed sudden. I don't know what to say to you, but it will be better to leave nothing unsaid. I'm trying to think of everything. I'm going to be married next month. Remember, I'm not the Anna you knew. She isn't getting married again. I'm somebody totally different. I feel different. Even when I walk. You never knew me. I can remember our years together clearly. But it seems like a story that was once told me. Do you understand, Erik? I am not bitter or sad, and I have no blame for you. You are more than forgiven. . . ."

No words occurred to him. Somewhere behind the smooth face of her he fancied lived a woman whose arms were about his neck and whose lips were hungering for him.

"It's all very clear to me, Erik. I've thought of it often. You made me a part of yourself and when you deserted me, you took that with you, and left me as I am; as I was born. . . ."

"Will you play something on the piano for me, Anna?"

"No, Erik."

He seated himself slowly and remained with his head down. There was nothing to think.

"I'll go in a few minutes," he muttered.

Anna, standing straight, watched him as if she were curious. He felt her eyes trying to acquaint themselves with him, and failing. He was growing angry. Better leave before he spoke again. Anger was in him. It was she who had been the unfaithful one. He could smile at that. He stood up then, and smiled. This was a part of life, to be felt and appreciated. A handshake, a smile that von Stinnes would have applauded, and he would have lived another hour.

"On the boat I made love to you," he said softly, "and I am not unhappy. It is only—my turn to weep a bit."

He regarded her calmly. Yes, if he wanted to . . . there was something waiting. . . . Even though she thought it dead. If he wanted to, there was a grave to open, slowly, with tears and old phrases.

She let him approach her. He felt her body grow rigid as he placed his arms around her. His lips touched her cold cheek.

"It was to make sure that you were dead," he whispered.

She nodded.

. . . Another hour ended. He had returned. Now he was going away again and the hour was a disc whirling away, already lost among other discs.

The street was chilly. He walked swiftly. His thoughts were assembling themselves. Words that had lain under the tears in the room thawed out.

"She will marry Meredith and the old man will come to live with me. I should have gone upstairs and said hello. But he was probably asleep. I'll take my books and furniture. She won't need them with Meredith. Get an apartment somewhere. How old am I? About forty. Not quite. Changed completely. Curious, I didn't want her after she'd talked about it. I suppose because I didn't really come for her—for somebody else. Conrad in quest of his youth. Lost youth. How'd that damn book end? Well, what of it, what of it? Things die without saddening one. Yet one becomes sad. A make-believe. That's right. No matter what happens you keep right on thinking and breathing as if it were all outside. Yes, that's it—outside; a poignant comedy outside that talks to one. Death is the only thing that has reality. We must not take the rest too seriously. If I get too bored I can remember that I killed a man and develop a stricken conscience. Poppycock! . . . The old man'll be a nuisance. But he's quiet, thank God! Well, well . . . I'm too civilized. I suppose I made an ass of myself. No. . . . A few tears more or less. . . ."

His thought paused. He walked, looking at things—curbings, houses, street trees, lights in windows. He resumed, after blocks:

"Good God, what a thing happened to her! To change like that. An awfulness about it. Death in life. Have I changed? No. I'm the same. But that's a lie. I was in love once . . . a face like a mirror of stars. The phrase grows humorous with repetition. It doesn't mean anything. What did it mean? Like trying to remember a toothache . . . which tooth ached. But it only lasted

. . . let's see. Rachel, Rachel. . . . Nothing. It was gone a week after I came to her. The rest was—a restlessness . . . wanting something. Not having it. Well, it doesn't matter now."

In his hotel room he undressed without turning on the lights. He felt nervous, vaguely afraid of himself.

"I might commit suicide. Rather stupid, though. I'll die soon enough. Maybe a few more things left to see and feel and forget. Who knows? I'll have to look up some of the ladies."

He crawled into bed and grew promptly sleepless.

"If I'm honest I'll be able to amuse myself. If not . . . oh, Lord, what a mess! No. Why is it? Life runs away like that—hits you in the eye and runs away."

He closed his eyes and sighed. Like himself, the world was full of people who lived on. Things ended for them and nobody could tell the difference, not even themselves. Being happy—what the devil was that? Happiness—unhappiness—you slept as soundly and ate as heartily.

"I'm a little tired to-night." An excuse for something. He was afraid. He reached over to the small table near the bed and secured a cigarette. Lighting it, he lay on his back, blowing smoke carefully into the dark and watching the tobacco glow under his nose.

"Damn good thing I'm not an author. End up as a cross between Maeterlinck and Laura Jean.

One could write a volume on a cigarette glowing in the dark."

He puffed until the tobacco was almost ended. He placed the still-kindled stub on the table and sighed:

"Yes, that's me. Life has had its lips to me blowing smoke and fire out of me. And now a table top on which to glow reminiscently for a moment. And cool into ashes. Apologies to Laura Jean, Marie Corelli—and God."

Chapter Five

RACHEL, removing her heavy coat, walked briskly to the grate fire burning in the rear of the studio. She stood looking into the flames and rubbing the cold out of her hands.

"Well, I kept the appointment, Frank."

Brander, the artist, sprawled on a cushion-littered couch, sat up slowly. His heavy eyes regarded her.

"We had quite a talk. You know his wife has remarried."

"That so?" Rachel laughed.

"Mr. Dorn sends you his regards."

"That'll be enough."

"I must say he's much cleverer than you, Frank."

"What did you talk about? Soul stuff, eh?"

"Oh, not entirely."

She came over to the couch and patted his cheeks.

"My hands—feel how cold they are."

"Never mind your hands. What did our good friend have to say for himself?"

"Oh, talk." Her dark eyes glanced enigmatically from his stare.

Brander swore. "I want to know, d'you hear?"

"Dear me! Soulmate bares all." She laughed and walked with a sensual swing down the long room.

Brander, without stirring, repeated, "Yes, everything."

Rachel's face sobered

"Why, there's nothing Frank—of interest."

"Hell, I've caught you crying over him."

"Well, what of that? A woman's tears, you know, a woman's tears, don't mean anything."

"They don't, eh?"

"No." The sight of him hunched amid the cushions seemed to appeal to her humor. A large, strong monkey face against blue, green, and yellow pillow faces. She laughed.

"Well, I'll tell you something. There's going to be no soul stuff in this. You're mine. And if you start any flapdoodle hand-holding with our good friend, I'll knock your heads together into a pulp."

He raised his large shoulders and glowered majestically. Rachel, paused beside a canvas, regarded him with half-closed eyes and smiling lips.

"He sent his kindest wishes to you."

Brander left his seat and strode toward her.

"That's enough."

"And asked us to call. And if we couldn't come together, I might call alone," she spoke quickly. Her eyes were mocking. An oath from Brander seemed to amuse her.

"You're in love with him," he muttered, his

fingers tightening about her wrist. "Come, out with it! I want to know."

"Yes." Rachel's eyes grew taunting. "He is the knight in shining armor, fairy prince, and the man in the moon."

"Never mind laughing. I want to know."

"Well, listen then." Her voice grew vibrant as if a laugh were talking. "His eyes are the beckoning hands of dream. Poor Frank doesn't know what that means."

Brander swung her toward the couch. She fell amid the cushions with a laugh. He stood looking at her and then walked slowly.

"Don't touch me. Don't you dare!"

A grin crossed the artist's face.

"I know you and your kind," he answered, "mooney girls. Mooney-headed girls. I've had 'em before."

"Keep away. . . ."

Her face as he bent over her glowed with a sudden terror.

"Mooney girls," repeated Brander.

His hands reached her shoulders and held her carelessly as she squirmed.

"You're hurting me."

"I'll hurt you more. Talk out now. Are you in love with that loon?"

"Yes."

"More than me?"

"Yes."

Brander's face reddened. His hand struck

her chin. Rachel shut her eyes to hold back tears.

"Are you still?"

"Yes. Always." Her teeth clenched. "Go on, hit me, if you want to. I love him. Love him always. Every minute. As I did. Do you hear? I love him."

She opened her eyes and shivered. He was going to kill her. He tore at her clothes, beating her with his fists until her head rattled on her neck.

"I'll fix your love for him," Brander whispered. The pain of his blows and shakings were making her dizzy.

"Frank . . . dear, please. . . ."

"Do you love him?"

"Yes."

She tried to bury her head in her arms, but he untwisted her gesture. His hands, striking and clawing at her, made her scream. A mist—he had seized her.

"Frank! Frank!"

"Do you love him now?"

She opened her eyes and stared wildly into Brander's face. It grinned at her. Her arms clutched his body.

"No, no!" she cried, her mouth gasping. "Don't talk. Don't ask questions. Love . . ." she laughed aloud eagerly, brazenly. Her thin arms tightened fiercely about him. "I love this."

Chapter Six

ISAAC DORN was sitting in a chair beside the gas-log fire in his son's apartment. His thin fingers lay motionless on his knees. His head had fallen forward.

It was early evening when his son entered the room. Dorn paused and looked at the silent figure in the chair. The old man raised his head as if he had been spoken to and muttered. "Eh?"

He saw his son and smiled. He would like to talk to him. It was lonely all day in the house. And things were beginning to fade from his eyes. It was hard even to see if Erik was smiling. Yes, his face was happy. That was good. People should look as Erik did—amused. Wait . . . wait long enough and it all blurred and faded gently away.

"What made you so late, Erik?" he asked. Now his son was laughing. That was a good sign.

"A lot of work at the office. The Russians are at it again. And I met an old friend this afternoon. A dear old friend. Old friends make one sentimental and garrulous. So we talked."

He noticed the old man's eyes close but continued addressing him.

"We discussed problems in mathematics. How

many yesterdays make a to-morrow. That gas-log smells to high heaven."

He leaned over and turned out the odorous flames. He noticed now that the old man had dozed off again. But his talk went on. It had become a habit to keep on talking to his father who dozed under his words. "She's going to drop around and visit us. And we will perform a gentle autopsy. Stir a little cloud of dust out of the bucket of ashes, eh? And perhaps we will come to life for a moment. Who knows? At least, we shall weep. And that is something. To be able to weep. To know enough to weep. Her name is Rachel."

He paused and walked toward the window.

"Rachel," he repeated, his eyes no longer on the old man. "Her name is unchanged. . . ."

He opened von Stinnes's silver case and removed a cigarette. He stood gazing at the snow on roofs, on window ledges, on pavements. Crystalline geometries. Houses that made little puzzle pictures against the stagnant curve of the darkening sky. A zig-zag of leaden-eyed windows, and windows ringed with yellow light peering like cat eyes into the winter dusk. The darkness slowly ended the scene. Night covered the snow. The city opened its tiny yellow eyes.

A street of houses before him. A cigarette under his nose. An old man asleep. Outside the window the snow-covered buildings stood in the dark like a skeleton world, like patterns in black and white.

DATE DUE			
APR 10 '74			